Praise for *Coming Full Circle*

Coming Full Circle is a powerful story that takes the reader from humble beginnings in Atlanta, Georgia, to the scary jungles of Southeast Asia, through a life of self-destruction through alcohol and back to a triumphant renewal where it all began. For the first time in my life I understood what the Vietnam War was all about.

It is a journey of an individual told with brutal honesty as each episode unfolds in the life of Morocco Coleman. As a disciplined soldier, he believed and followed instructions to the letter, even at times when he faced harsh consequences he never shied away from speaking the truth. Above all, Morocco never allowed other people to trample on his rights or the rights of others; he fought against all forms of racism and oppression; his mission was to see justice accomplished. Even today he continues to be a shining example of a selfless passionate hero on behalf of the Vietnam veterans.

Congratulations my friend!

Welcome Msomi,
South African Acclaimed Playwright and Director

Jan 31, 2014

Coming Full Circle

To: Barbara Murrin—
Thanks for your interest
in my book. I hope you
enjoy my story and thanks
for your service!

Peace,
Morocco Coleman

Hebrews 11:1

Coming Full Circle

Morocco Coleman

ISBN: 978-0-692-00843-0

Library of Congress Control Number: 2012943809

Publishing support provided by:
BOOKLOGIX˙
Alpharetta, Georgia

Printed in the United States of America

∞This paper meets the requirements of ANSI/NISO Z39.48-1992 (Permanence of Paper)

Cover design by Keith Saunders, Marion Designs

The views and opinions expressed in this text are those of the author who has tried to recreate events, locations, and conversations from his memories of them.

All scripture quotations are taken from the King James Version of the Holy Bible.

Affectionately Dedicated

To my darling wife, Paula, whose love, support, and understanding are a daily inspiration to me.

My precious daughter, Azure Michele, my son, Jeffrey, and my father, T.R. "Bootee" Coleman

My brother, Mike, sister-in-law, Pat, and nephew, Michael

My uncle and aunt, Reverend Robert and Ernestine Johnson, cousin, Ed Coleman, and the greatest in-laws ever, Dr. Thomas (Dr. "J") and Annabelle (Moms) Jarrett

In Loving Memory of
My mother, Lelia N. Coleman, who showed me the way and my cousin, Brenda Judge Coleman, who knew what time it was

To every person I've ever met

A special thanks to Imam Jamil Al-Amin for showing me how it's done, and to each and every one of my true, real deal FRIENDS.

Table of Contents

Foreword   xi

Chapter One: Stepping into the Fire   1

Chapter Two: Settling In   9

Chapter Three: First Patrol   23

Chapter Four: Winning and Losing   37

Chapter Five: Sergeant Walker; an Enigma   57

Chapter Six: Illegally Legal   71

Chapter Seven: Was He the Son of God   89

Chapter Eight: The Pentagon Sends a Wire   101

Chapter Nine: How Did Talley Know?   105

Chapter Ten: They Were Killers, but Not from...   135

Chapter Eleven: Fire and Ice   129

Chapter Twelve: The Grim Reaper Goes on Patrol   143

Chapter Thirteen: Is That You, God?   165

Chapter Fourteen: I Saw the Tether Line   177

Chapter Fifteen: I Killed the Water Heater   195

Chapter Sixteen: Spiritual Happenings   207

Chapter Seventeen: Heads or Tails, Life or Death   223

Chapter Eighteen: Lord, Give Me the Words to Speak   237

Chapter Nineteen: Finding Paula and My Life's Mission   249

Foreword

The Vietnam War spawned some memorable films—*Platoon, Apocalypse Now*—and many riveting books. I am privileged to foreword one of those books here.

Morocco Coleman's story is the story of a consummate survivor. It is a story of the Vietnam War. It is a painfully vivid story of the aftermath of war and its impact on the veteran's civilian life. We have seen, but perhaps not understood, this picture many times over in the lives of our veteran friends and family members.

While in the 'Nam, Morocco survived the expected rigors of jungle warfare with the foreign enemy, "Charlie." He also survived the unexpected trauma of the enemy within his own ranks—Jim Crow, fellow soldiers, ugly Americans.

The author describes how his survival instincts saved his life and his career. His story reveals a keen intellect, one that thwarted an attempt to disgrace him in a kangaroo court-martial by detecting a flaw in the court documents.

Returning from the 'Nam to "the world," "Rock" experienced the demons of post traumatic stress disorder (PTSD), a condition which plagues many Vietnam veterans. Propelled through a series of personal crises, he finally hooked back up to the tether line. *Coming Full Circle* is a powerful book of understanding, discernment, and deliverance. It could just as well be entitled "Survival of the Fittest," and "Rock" is a fitting nickname for this man whose state mission in life is service to his fellow man.

Charles W. Dryden, Sr.

Author of *A Train: Memoirs of a Tuskegee Airman*

Lieutenant Colonel, U.S. Air Force

Retired Tuskegee Airman

CHAPTER ONE

Stepping into the Fire

"We are approaching Bien Hoa Air Base and will touch down in approximately ten minutes," announced the pilot over the intercom system of the big commercial jet as we streaked over the Republic of South Vietnam.

What the hell have I gotten myself into? I wondered aloud.

Less than forty-eight hours ago, I had been in Greenwich Village in New York City partying from one coffeehouse to another with three other GIs who were also on this flight with me. One of these guys was Harvey "Punchy" Jackson, a strapping six foot three, two hundred and ten-pound wild and crazy guy that I had grown up with in Atlanta, Georgia. Our families were friends and Punchy and I had been buddies since we were about six years old.

I had reported to Fort Dix, New Jersey on January 26, 1967 as ordered by the US Army to await a flight to Vietnam in three days. The first night at Ft. Dix, I went to the Enlisted Men's Club to have some beers and drown my troubles. While sitting at the bar, I noticed someone who looked familiar enter the doorway. That someone turned out to be Punchy. I couldn't believe my eyes! I hadn't seen him since 1964 when I had gone away to college for three years. He and his two friends joined me and we reminisced and downed quite a few pitchers of beer. One of the guys with Punchy was named Dino Barnes, a slick little hustler from Detroit and Cedric Harris, a tall, slim pleasant kind of guy who wore thick glasses which gave him a rather bookish look.

After a couple of hours, around eleven o'clock p.m., we all decided to slip off of the Post and catch a bus over to New York City, and go to Greenwich Village. When we got off of the Greyhound Bus at the Port Authority in New York and entered the terminal, the Military Police stationed there immediately

1

surrounded us. They had readily identified us as being AWOL (absent without leave) from Ft. Dix because all of us were wearing the light weight jungle fatigues that had been issued upon our arrival. Also, the temperature was twenty-two bone chilling degrees and six inches of snow was on the ground.

After the MPs checked our IDs and realized we were scheduled to go to Vietnam in a couple of days, they put us on a Greyhound Bus to be transported back to Ft. Dix. When the bus had traveled a few blocks I told the driver to let us get off, which he did. I had made up my mind that I was going to go to The Village 'cause it just might be the last opportunity I would ever have. We then grabbed a cab and continued our trek to The Village. When we got to the Village we walked around and peered into the numerous coffeehouses lining the streets. Finally we agreed on one in particular to enter, so we went in and sat at a table and ordered drinks. There were two beautiful women on stage singing; one was black and one was white. They were singing a song that had been recorded by the group Peter, Paul and Mary entitled "If I Had a Hammer." Needless to say, we could feel and see the curious stares of-the other patrons present. Here we were dressed in combat jungle fatigues, AWOL, about to go to Vietnam and sitting calmly sipping drinks in a room full of "hippies" and "peaceniks."

When the women had finished singing they came over to our table and introduced themselves. The black girl was named Nzinga and her friend was Linda. They had been singing at the coffeehouse for a few months and worked as secretaries during the day to supplement their incomes. The singers joined us and we ordered another round of drinks. During the ensuing conversation I found out that Nzinga was a political science graduate from UCLA and grew up in Berkeley, California. Linda was a graduate of Kent State and was from some small town in Michigan. At two o'clock in the morning the girls had finished their last set. They invited all of us to go with them to their apartment, which we did. When we got to the apartment Linda served up some food, wine and reefer while we all laid around on the floor with throw pillows grooving on Jimmie Hendricks singing "All Along The Watchtower."

A while later, we were all engaged in this deep conversation concerning the moral issues surrounding the war in Vietnam. The girls were saying it was an unjust war and how the fat cats in Washington were making millions of dollars off of the war while they sent young men to die. The dialogue was getting heavier when Nzinga said,

"Why don't you guys go to Canada or Sweden to avoid Vietnam and possibly dying for nothing?"

"Are you crazy?" I asked her. "We don't have any way of getting to Sweden." That's when she hit me with a bombshell! She said, "Linda and I are involved in the underground movement, which helps GIs who don't want to go to Vietnam escape to neutral countries that will harbor them." My mouth fell open in amazement when I realized that they were serious! I started examining the pros and cons of the opportunity these ladies were laying out. After thinking about it for a while, I decided to call my Dad in Atlanta and discuss the situation with him. My dad and I had always been able to dialogue pretty well and I respected his opinion on a lot of issues. After telling him the whole story he said,

"Well son, it's your decision, but you do realize that you may never be able to return to the United States? You will be considered a deserter and you'll be relinquishing your citizenship."

He went on to say, "You've always been a survivor and you've had all kinds of military training to prepare you for what lies ahead in Vietnam, so I would advise that you go on to Vietnam do your time, get it over with and come on back home."

After hanging up, I told the ladies that I was going to have to pass on the free trip they were offering and that I had decided to take the other free trip my "Uncle Sam" was providing for me. Punchy, Dino, and Cedric all agreed with me, so the issue was settled: we were all going to Vietnam to kick butt, end the war and get the hell on back home!

By the time our plane touched down we had been flying for almost twenty-four hours. We'd flown through many different time zones and had burst right through the International Date Line. The time was one o'clock in the afternoon and the date was January 30, 1968. When I got off of the plane and reached the tarmac the first thing I noticed was the stifling heat. It must have been about 125 degrees in the shade. Then I noticed the lush green jungle foliage and tall mountainous terrain that surrounded the airfield in all directions. The scenery was as breathtaking as the oppressive heat and I wondered to myself, *How can such a beautiful looking country be so hazardous to your health?* The next thing I noticed was a strange smell in the air which I later discovered was the smell of death, destruction, and burning diesel fuel used in open trenches to burn the human feces collected from the out houses which were used by the GIs within the military compounds.

For the next three hours, Punchy, Dino, Cedric, and I were herded around with hundreds of other GIs like sheep from one processing station to another. After being fed and drawing our clothing allowances, the four of us started comparing the orders we had been issued which would tell us where we were going to be stationed. The names on the orders looked like hieroglyphics. Dino was going to a place called Dong Ha; Cedric to Ban Me Thuot, Punchy to Sharange Valley and my orders were for a city named Qui Nhon in the Central Highlands. We said our sad good-byes to one another promising to hook-up once we got back to the "World" and to finish the party we had started in Greenwich Village. As I was boarding the C-130 troop carrier plane which would take me to the Central Highlands, I looked back over my shoulder at the guys as they waved their farewells to me and I experienced a feeling of foreboding. I would never see either Cedric or Dino again.

I arrived in Qui Nhon at nine o'clock p.m. and the airfield was about two miles from the compound where I was to report. We were loaded onto buses which had metal grill work covering the windows which I thought strange until the guy next to me, who was returning to 'Nam for a second tour of duty explained,

"It keeps the 'Gooks' from throwing hand grenades into the open windows."

"Whew!"

As I peered out of the window the surrounding darkness gave way to light filtering through the open doorways of little shacks made out of surplus plywood. There were Vietnamese people squatting down in the doorways talking to one another in a strange syncopated, singsong language and observing our procession as we meandered down the otherwise dark road. Five minutes later I noticed that the road had become wider and we seemed to be entering a small city which I surmised was Qui Nhon. Both sides of the street were lined with shops and businesses with colorful neon lights proclaiming whatever wares were available inside. To my surprise, right in the middle of this small well-lighted area was an American sign to my left announcing the entrance to the Headquarters of the First Logistical Command. The compound looked to be about a mile and a half in circumference and completely surrounded by a ten-foot tall cyclone fence, topped off with miles and miles of coiled barbed wire interspersed with razor sharp blades called concertina wire. Every fifty yards or so around this wire perimeter was a thirty-foot guard tower manned by a GI. Each tower was equipped with an M-79 grenade launcher (called a "blooper"), a sixty-caliber machine gun (called a "pig"). Each GI had his standard issue weapon that was either an M-14 rifle or the newest issued weapon the Colt M-16 rifle.

Our buses stopped in front of a group of barracks across the road from an impressive looking building I discovered was the 67th Medical Evacuation Hospital. It was herding time again, so we were herded off of the buses and given the order to fall into formation. Once the formation had been achieved we were marched single file into the billeting area to collect our bedding gear, bunk assignments and general information on the do's and don'ts of the compound. We were then marched to the chow hall for a late meal. At ten thirty p.m., I stretched out across my bunk. My last thoughts before drifting off to sleep were, *Man, what the hell am I doing in this screwed-up place 14,000 miles from home?*

At two a.m. I awoke to a heart stopping, colossal, ear-splitting explosion. The concussion from the explosion catapulted me across the room, where I hit the floor rolling. Outside I heard screaming and yelling, orders being barked out, the wail of a siren, machine gun and small arms incessant firing along with mortar rounds walking in from only God knew where!

THINK, THINK!! What the hell should I do?

In an instant, I sprinted for the door and ran about thirty yards to the door of the arms room which I seen earlier when I had first entered the compound. Since my arrival I had not been issued a weapon. The arms room was locked and the bodies of two American soldiers were sprawled at the base of the door and they looked wasted. I reached down and grabbed the bandoleer of bullets and the M-16 off of one of the bodies and sprinted to one of the sandbagged bunkers near the Med Evac Hospital. When I slid and half fell into the bunker opening, I found six other GIs who had the same idea as I had. We took up firing positions utilizing the portals made available in the structure. When my bunker mates and I assessed the situation, we realized that the perimeter had been breached. Dead Viet Cong bodies were dangling from the concertina wire where they had tried to gain access to the compound. They looked like abandoned marionettes doing a dance of death after the puppet master has cut their strings. Fires were burning all around, the sounds of mortar rounds exploding were coming from the direction of the airfield, the smell of cordite permeated the air and I was scared damn near to death. My newfound team in the bunker took turns rotating to the portals to lay down a barrage of defensive fire. "Charlie" was not only in the wire but, was running around and indiscriminately firing his own weapons and setting off "satchel" charges (packages of explosives). After what seemed like a couple of hours, Huey helicopter gunships entered the fray from overhead with their mini guns spitting out pure unadulterated death and destruction. The thought occurred to me, "If Beethoven were here writing a symphony about the illumination cast by the fires and the flares on the back drop of the black night sky, the sounds of bullets and explosions in their pristine clarity, and the screams of agony and death, he could title it CHAOS!"

As early morning darkness began to give way to gray morning light, the enemy began to break contact and pull back. At day break my new partners and I crawled out of the bunker to survey the carnage. We only sustained one casualty in the bunker group; a guy whose nametag read Skadowski sustained a rather serious injury of his left eyeball from ricocheting debris caused by a bullet, which passed too close. Everyone in the compound was sort of walking around with a dazed look on their faces. Upon examination, it seemed that no quadrant of the compound had gone unscathed. This attack had been executed for the optimum effect of annihilation. All strategic points of the compounds perimeter had been attacked simultaneously. The compound was littered with the dead bodies of black pajama clad VC (Viet Cong or "Victor Charlie") and a less significant number of dead GIs. There were casualties at the 67th Med Evac. Two nurses had been killed when a Viet Cong "sapper" had gained access to the building and dispatched his deadly payload. Late in the afternoon, everybody stood down after removing bodies and assisting the wounded and "policing up" the area. The company's senior NCO called for a formation briefing to take place at six o'clock p.m. Everyone assembled at the appointed time for the briefing. The Company Commander, a full bird Colonel named Schlosinger, stepped forward. He was about 6'1," 210 lbs. Built like General Patton, he wore a shaved head and looked like he could kick ass and take names. He fixed the assembled group with a steely gray eyed stare and proceeded,

"People, at two o'clock a.m., 30 January 1968, the Viet Cong Guerrillas and the North Vietnamese Army marked the beginning of their Lunar New Year, known as Tet, by attacking every major city, town and American military base in South Vietnam."

The Colonel stated further, "We have accounted for 22 American dead and 107 wounded...210 enemy dead and 3 live captures." It seemed that before the Tet Offensive took place, American officials had been confidently predicting that the war was being won. American troops were riding high coming off of the Xmas and New Year's holidays and had missed the warning signs, which had been evident that something like the Tet Offensive was brewing. Very much like Pearl Harbor, we got caught with our pants down. Evidence later showed that for months the enemy had been digging underground tunnels, which led right up to the perimeters of some of the more remote outposts and bases.

We, like all American military bases were put on a 48-hour Red Alert which meant "be ready for anything and if it moves kill it."

For the next two nights we drew sporadic sniper fire and there were a couple of soft probes by "sappers" at some of the unilluminated listening posts along the perimeter. My first experience in a combat situation had been terrifying, but my instincts and training had taken over and I was able to remember the things that I had been taught to do. My initial introduction to Vietnam was a "baptism by fire"!"

CHAPTER TWO

Settling In

For the next two and a half weeks my primary job was pulling guard duty. This was a responsibility I detested with a passion. Every evening at 5:30 I had to report to the guard barracks in full gear. My full gear was an M-14 rifle and web gear (thick, olive drab canvas suspenders attached to a thick canvas pistol belt), on the web gear I carried a flashlight with a red lens for night vision; on the pistol belt were attached two canvas ammo pouches which held two ammunition clips each. Each clip held twenty rounds (bullets). On my head I wore the traditional Army helmet known as a steel pot and it was constructed of steel. To top things off, I wore a thick bulky vest known as a flak jacket. The flak jacket was to offer protection from exploding metal fragments such as hand grenades. Most "newbies" (new guys) mistakenly thought it was a bulletproof jacket and usually found out differently when it was too late! Needless to say, all of this gear was bulky, cumbersome and heavy in the humidity and heat of Southeast Asia. But, it could mean the difference between life and death.

At 5:45 p.m., twelve of us guards were loaded into a 3/4-ton truck and driven around the perimeter of the compound and deposited one at a time to one of the twelve guard towers. When I would arrive at my tower I'd climb the thirty-foot ladder up to the platform, which was covered by a roof, and check to make sure that the 60-caliber machine gun was operable and fully loaded. Next I would check the grenade launcher and my own weapon. Most of the towers had a field telephone in them in case you needed to call for help. But in my two weeks of rotating to the other 12 towers, I had never found one that worked. One night the truck hadn't come at ten o'clock p.m. to bring my relief and to take me back and I was pissed. At ten thirty p.m., I aimed the 60caliber machine gun out into the night vastness and pulled the trigger as if

I were Audie Murphy starring in the movie "To Hell and Back." Needless to say, the truck along with my replacement appeared shortly thereafter. It was a no-no to fire your weapons and unnecessarily upset everybody.

When the Sergeant driver asked, "What the hell were you firing at?!" I merely stated, "I thought I saw something moving."

They were never late picking me up again.

When your four-hour tour was over, you were taken back to the guard barracks to sleep for four hours and at two a.m. you were awakened to pull four more hours of duty in another tower until six a.m.

In all honesty, I don't know which was worse the loneliness in those towers or the fear. Ten of the towers were in dark isolated areas where you just peered out into the night towards the jungle and foliage and looked and listened for anything unusual. Even though I hated this type of duty, I did take it seriously. Early on I realized that I was stuck out on the perimeter as a sacrificial lamb. If my position came under attack, it was very possible that I wouldn't be able to hold out long enough for reinforcements to bring me help before my position was over-run and I was annihilated. The military logic was that the sound of my butt getting kicked would warn the others that "Victor Charlie" was coming.

Sometimes fatigue would take its toll on me and I would have to fight with all of my will not to succumb to the drowsiness or sleep that would stealthily try to envelop me. At other times I would try to quiet the cold eerie fear that would creep into my soul when I'd hear a rustle of noise that seemed to have no source, or when my eyes, tired from the strain of peering into the darkness for hours, would detect a momentary flicker of something in the dark that had no rhyme or reason. Months later, while visiting another compound, I viewed the bodies of two dead white GIs whose throats had been cut from ear to ear by "VC" who had caught them sleeping on guard duty up in their tower.

There were two guard towers near the entrance to our compound, which were well lighted and were directly across the road from a business street in the heart of the city of Qui Nhon. There were usually people and regular activities going on in this area until about midnight. Whenever I was assigned to one of those towers, it was interesting to observe the Vietnamese people and their culture. The children would come up to the fence and beg for money or whatever they could talk the GIs into giving them. Many of them were young con artists and were called "cowboys." They were known for being able to deftly pick your pocket or just as gingerly drop a live hand-grenade into your pocket. Quite a large number of Vietnamese children were taught the rudiments of war fare early and by the age of fourteen were seasoned jungle fighters and killers. I maintained my distance from them because I didn't trust them and I definitely didn't ever want to have to hurt one of them. During the first week of March, my platoon Sergeant told me to pack up all of my gear because I was going to be shipped out to my permanent unit

I asked, "Where is my new unit going to be?"

Sarge replied, "You're going to Long My Valley."

"Where is Long My Valley?" I inquired.

"Long My Valley is about thirty 'klicks' (kilometers or miles) from here and it's the location where the ammo dump was blown up the morning that we got hit when the Tet Offensive started." This latest revelation wasn't very encouraging.

I joined four other GIs I didn't know in the 3/4-ton truck. They were also going to Long My. I rode in silence watching the strange looking countryside pass by. We traveled on a blacktop road, which had been built by the military's Corps of Engineers. The road ran almost straight for thirty klicks flanked on both sides and the front by tall jungle covered mountains, which looked to be about ten miles away. The flat land extending from the road to the distant mountains was of lush green vegetation, interspersed with large square rice paddies, shored up by small dikes to hold the water in. This breath taking view was dotted here and there with little colorful pagodas in the distance. Every now and then I would see women and young girls out in the rice paddies planting or harvesting the rice plants and an old Papa-San plowing through the water with a water buffalo pulling the plow. There wasn't any modern John Deere equipment for the poor farmers to use in planting and harvesting their rice crops. A thought occurred to me: "Vietnam is a dichotomy; so much of what I have seen here is culturally modern and yet so much that I see is so culturally antiquated; two completely different worlds where one exists by the old ways and the other by embracing the new ways brought by the Americans."

Eventually, we made a left turn coming down off of a mountain pass into the entrance of another Valley and in the distance I could see a large desolate looking military compound nestled against a jungle covered mountain. Looking hundreds of yards down into a gorge on my right something caught my eye. When I looked more closely, I realized that I was looking at the twisted, wreckage of an Air Force fighter jet which looked as if it had crashed there months before. When I looked up I saw a sign announcing, "You are now entering the 1st Logistical Command Support Compound." The compound looked to be about three miles in circumference, surrounded by a large fence and concertina wire just like the compound in Qui Nhon. The terrain was brown, sandy dirt and there were roads winding all around inside the compound which were made by trucks that sprayed oil on the ground and it dried to simulate a blacktop. There were rows and rows of semi large warehouses. There was a small motor pool, which housed trucks, and jeeps and I also observed six, two story, wooden barracks with no windows in them. Where windows should have been there were open areas covered by mesh screens. Next, I saw three small, one-story buildings. One was the orderly room (Headquarters), the other was a Mess Hall and the third was called "The Beer Hall." All of these structures looked as if they had been built from some child's tinker toy set. Near an isolated area of the compound was a very large canvas tent, which housed the GIs that had been chosen for guard duty for the night. Twenty-five Guard towers like the ones in Qui Nhon protected the perimeter. In the Company area there were about twenty bunkers, some above ground and some not and to top this off, there was a six seater, deluxe model, outdoor privy.

I was processed into the unit by the Quartermaster Sergeant and assigned a bunk and a new Colt M-16 rifle. My bunk was on the top floor of one of the barracks. As I was stowing my gear, I met the brother who had the bunk next to mine. His name was Ron Owens, but he told me I could call him "Silky." He was from Harlem, New York and he only had nineteen days before he was going home. Silky looked and acted a lot like Dino. He was dark complexioned, had a slight muscular frame, stood about 5'9" and talked slick and out of the side of his mouth. His eyes were like quicksilver that took everything in, but his eyes also said something else to me. This dude was bad news and had a rather dangerous kind of air about him. While we were talking another brother and a white dude walked up. The brother was introduced as "B Moe" (short for his hometown of Baltimore, Maryland); his true name was Howard Fern. He was as tall as me (6'1"), 190 lbs., and had a quick smile, which revealed two gold front teeth. One tooth sported a gold crown depicting a half moon and he seemed like he was pretty cool. The white guy was named William Shockley and he was from somewhere in California. He wore his blonde hair rather long and impressed me as being a surfer type white boy who wanted to be a "blue eyed soul brother." He, too, had a gold tooth in the front and wore African beads around his neck and a silver African bracelet around his left wrist. I then noticed that all three of these guys wore gold studded earrings in their left earlobes. It was getting late in the evening and near time for chow so, the guys told me to come along with them to the chow hall.

The chow hall quickly filled up with GIs and my three new friends made sure they introduced me around to all the boys. When chow was finished and we all walked outside, it was almost dark and the guys told me to come on with them out to the "flat lands."

As I followed I asked, "What are the flat lands?"

"We'll show you," replied Silky.

About a hundred yards or so from the main company area was a large sandbagged bunker sitting isolated in an open flat area. Sitting on top of the bunker were eight GIs who were rapping and listening to the Young Rascals singing "It's a Beautiful Morning" on a portable tape recorder. I climbed up on the bunker and was introduced to this new group of GIs: "Spam," Talley, Bruce, O'Malley, "Bird," Brown, Velez and Epstein. I introduced myself as "Rock" from Atlanta and immediately I was handed a "bomb!" The bomb was made by Velez. He had torn a page out of a comic book he was carrying and had filled it full of marijuana and rolled it. After rolling it he produced a short piece of coat hanger wire and wrapped it around the bomb to be used as a handle to hold the bomb as it was "toked." I was given the honor of firing the bomb up since I was the new kid on the block. This honor also had a veiled and dark meaning to it. It was a test. The group wanted to see if I was one of the boys: would I partake and could I handle the bomb. My willingness to smoke with the group would also help to allay any suspicions the group might have that I could possibly be a CID (Criminal Investigations Division undercover agent). CID agents were notorious for infiltrating units and finding out who used or sold drugs, dealt in contraband for black market profiteering, and gathering information on suspected subversives. Once these guys were satisfied that I wasn't a "Narc" I was accepted as one of the boys.

The next morning after I had breakfast, I went to the orderly room and reported to the First Sergeant for my duty assignment. The moment I met the "first shirt" I knew he was a racist. His name was Hanks and he was from Mississippi, spoke with a southern drawl which dripped with venom and he had a miniature rebel flag on his desk, so I made a mental note to avoid him as much as possible in the future. Hanks told me to go to warehouse number six and report for work to a sergeant by the name of Ralston. Ralston was a "buck" sergeant about my age (twenty-three years) from Wisconsin, and seemed like a pretty cool dude for a white boy. He gave me a tour of the warehouse explaining to me how everything was coordinated and how the files located in the front of the warehouse could tell me where to find items. The warehouse was stocked with all types of military hardware for trucks, tanks, artillery and other miscellaneous items. I was given a manifest list and had to pull ordered items from the shelves or bins and prepare them for shipment by trucks from the Red Ball Express. The Red Ball Express was a convoy usually made up of seven or eight, two and a half ton trucks (called deuce and a half's) which ran the roads in Vietnam like over the road truckers from one military base to another, delivering desperately needed equipment to troops out in the field. My new job in stock control management and supply was a very integral cog in the wheel of the war effort but I had to take my hat off to the guys who drove in the Red Ball Express. They usually drove at night through all kinds of "Indian Territory" with a partner-riding shotgun for protection. Some of the hazards they faced were snipers, bombs planted on the roads, mortar attacks and deadly ambushes. Everyone in the convoy had to cover each other's back.

After working in my new job for two weeks, I had developed a routine. I would quit working at four thirty p.m., cool out for an hour and eat dinner at five thirty p.m. About six o'clock p.m. I would meet the boys at the "flat lands" and groove on some music and get high. At the flat lands there was a lot of bonding taking place. We would sit for hours and talk about home, cars, women, what we had been into before the war and what each of us was going to do when we got back to the World. On a number of occasions, we got so deep into metaphysical discussions that I believe we came up with the answers to some of the world's most perplexing questions. Then, too, it could have been the influence of the marijuana, which made things seem to be what they really weren't. Sometimes, if I didn't feel like getting high at the flat lands I would go to the beer hall which was nothing more than an oversized hut where you could buy beer that was sometimes lukewarm. The beer was military beer, which was called "three point two beer" because the alcohol content was 3.2 percent, and you had to drink a case of it to get a buzz. It only cost fifteen cents a can and it seemed as if it would make you pee all night.

The music played in the beer hall was mostly country and western, hillbilly and redneck, but then so was the crowd that gathered there. At the flat lands you had the "potheads" and at the beer hall you had the alcoholics. I was very versatile; I fit quite nicely into either group and even though I liked all types of music, the stuff they played in the beer hall left something to be desired. "Yahoo!"

If I wasn't too drunk or high by eleven p.m., I would sit down on my bunk and write letters to my family and friends back in the

"World." I had a few lady friends I wrote to, but no girlfriends. I tried to be honest with myself and I didn't need any distractions, which could get me killed or hurt. I couldn't see myself being gone for a year and yearning for the day when I would return and see my true love standing on the sandy shore waiting for me. I did see many guys in 'Nam who did put stock in that kind of reverie; that is, they did until they got their "Dear John" letters. After receiving their correspondence, they usually got very drunk, cried, called on the name of the Lord, and pointed their M-16 rifle at their head and tried to do to themselves what the Viet Cong wanted to do. Usually someone close by would grab the weapon before the fool could kill himself.

A year and a half before I got to 'Nam I had dated a beautiful girl from Huntsville, Alabama who had attended college with me. Her name was Elizabeth Russell and we met when she became the queen of our junior class. We began dating and fell madly in love. We spent a lot of quality time together and many of our friends and acquaintances envied the special relationship that Elizabeth and I shared. Many months later when Elizabeth became aware that there was the possibility of me being drafted and going to Vietnam, she broke off the relationship. She had been my first true love and I had felt very angry, hurt, and confused by her decision. Months later, when the pain of the breakup had begun to subside, I decided that I would never ever allow anyone or anything to hurt me like that again.

During my third week in country I got a day off, so Spam, Bird, Epstein and Velez told me they were going to take me into town with them.

"Rock, get your rifle and a couple of clips of ammunition," Velez told me. He went on to say, "you won't need all of your other gear; we're going to be traveling light."

The town turned out to be a village named Phu Tai, which was about seven klicks from our base camp. We got there by hooking a ride with one of the convoys that was going that way. Phu Tai was a busy little place with an open market of vegetables, trinkets, and little old Mama-Sans cooking pots of strange looking foods. Most of the people were riding either bicycles or small Honda scooters and everything and everybody was all crowded in a three or four block area. All of the older women had on black, silk, baggy pajama pants, shower shoes, conical straw hats on their heads and dark brown/reddish teeth.

"What's wrong with these women's teeth?" I asked Velez.

"It's betel nut," he replied.

I asked, "What's a betel nut?"

"It's a type of nut they chew on like snuff or chewing tobacco and they get high off of it. It's an old custom and it turns their teeth brown," he said. "You want to try some?"

"Hell no!" I replied.

"Come on; let's get off of the street before the MPs make a sweep through here and see us," cautioned Epstein. "What do you mean?" I asked.

Epstein answered, "MPs regularly patrol village streets looking for soldiers who are AWOL from their units and if they catch you they lock you up until your Company Commander is notified." He went on to say, "After you get out of jail the Commander has the option of giving you a court-martial if he wants to. Areas like this are off limits to all military personnel."

We moved on following Spam down an alley to a back road. We turned down the road and stopped in front of a fairly large stucco house, which looked out of place in this little raggedy village. Talley pushed the door open and we walked in. When my eyes adjusted to the dimly lighted place after being in the glaring sun outside, I realized that we had entered a small bar.

"Lai Dai, GI. Come, come in."

When I looked to see who was talking, I saw a Vietnamese woman not quite five feet tall, about thirty-five years old although I found it difficult to determine the age of many of the Asian people I saw.

She was fairly attractive and dressed like an American female. She even had her hair cut in an American style, although many of the women I had seen so far wore their hair long and loose.

"Welcome. I, Mai Lin. What you drink?" She asked me.

"I'll buy the first round," Bird chimed in.

"Bird, you big time spender," she kidded him.

"Mai Lin, I love you darlin'," boasted Velez.

"Dong lai" (stop), sau my beaucoup (you lie big time) Velez," Mai Lin laughed.

Damn, I thought to myself, *these guys knew this chick!* "Come sit down," Mai Lin stated. We sat down at a table and at once a jukebox started playing the "Tempting Temptations" singing "My Girl." I was tired of drinking the usual 3.2 beer so I ordered some of the Old Granddad I saw on the shelf. The guys told me that Mai Lin's husband had been an officer with the South Vietnamese Army (our allies) and had been killed in action five years before. She had taken some of the money they had saved and invested in this tavern. Suddenly I looked up and entering the room were five young beautiful Vietnamese girls dressed similarly to Mai Lin. Their ages seemed to vary from seventeen to twenty, but it was still hard to tell. They came and sat down and started playing around and kidding with the guys and I could quickly tell that everyone knew each other. I was ceremoniously introduced to Kim, Mai Lon, Sallie, Mon and Lei. Sallie eased up beside me and started asking me questions about myself. I was really intrigued listening to the singsong lilt of her voice and amused by the way she fractured the English language. An hour later, I noticed that Spam had gotten up and was making his way towards a back room with Lei.

I leaned over and asked Epstein, "Where's Spam going?"

"He's probably going to take Lei to one of the back bedrooms to have sex with her," Epstein whispered to me. He went on to say, "I've noticed that Sallie seems interested in you, so if you want to have sex with her, just tell Mai Lin and she'll set you up in one of the rooms with Sallie. It will cost you 500 P."

"What's '500 P'" I wanted to know.

Epstein took his time explaining, "500 P is 500 piasters, and 500 piasters is Vietnamese money and is almost the same as three American dollars. Listen; give me five dollars in your American money."

I gave him five dollars and Epstein in turn gave me 750 P.

"Now," he said, "you're ahead of the game. The value of American money is roughly a 2 to 1 difference. Don't forget this valuable lesson in economics that I have just shared with you. I'm

Jewish, so trust me when it comes to money." We both roared with laughter. When I looked up again, Velez had disappeared with Mon. I surmised that they had retired to the rear area, too.

Suddenly, bright sunlight filled the interior of the bar from the doorway as three grungy looking GIs entered; two blacks and one white. None of these guys wore any type of rank insignia or nametag, but they all wore camouflaged, 173d Airborne patches on the left shoulder of their uniforms. The 173d Airborne Division was commonly known as the "Herd." Each one of these dudes also wore shoulder holster rigs with .45 caliber pistols stuck in them. *Bad news,* I thought to myself solemnly.

The trio entered and took seats on the far side of the room and gave a cursory nod as I acknowledged them. They ordered whiskey and sat stoically watching my two partners and the girls with us. Just as the juke box started belting out the first strains of Archie Bell and the Drells singing "Do The Tighten Up," I looked around at the faces of the girls and Mai Lin and I saw stark fear in their eyes. One of the black guys from the Herd walked over to our table completely ignoring Epstein, Bird and me, and reached across Bird and grabbed Mai Lon by one of her wrists and tried to snatch her out of Bird's lap. Meanwhile, Mai Lon had locked her other arm around Bird's neck in desperation. Bird got immediately pissed at the guy's intrusion and jumped up and said,

"Man, what the hell are you trying to do?"

"Screw you!" Shouted the guy from the Herd, as he stepped in close to Bird and threw an over hand right fist at Bird's head. Bird slipped the punch, dropped low and unleashed a right fist to the guy's mid section doubling him over, and followed up quickly with a chopping left hook behind the guy's right ear. All hell broke loose. The women were screaming, Archie Bell and the Drells continued to sing, Epstein was whipping on the other black guy from the Herd, and I had grabbed the white guy from the Herd when I saw him reach for his .45 pistol. I caught his hand before he could fist his weapon, twisted his arm behind his back, and shoved him face first into the wall. As I snatched him away from the wall to smash him into it again, Velez stepped through the doorway and threw a powerful uppercut to the guy's jaw that made a cracking sound. I saw teeth and blood fly out of the guys' mouth as he dropped to the floor like a sack of bricks. When I turned around to help Epstein and Bird, I heard a tremendous cracking explosion. Everything and everybody froze in place. Standing with his rifle still pointed toward the ceiling, which he had just blown a hole through, was Spam. This distraction gave the boys and me a chance to grab our rifles and use them to escort the three intruders back out the door they had entered earlier. After we had cleared the place out, we checked each other to see if any of us had been hurt and didn't know it. Everybody was OK. Mai Lin thanked us over and over again for taking care of matters and told us we could stay and didn't have to pay for anything. Nothing!

"You guys think we'll have any problems with those guys coming back?" asked Velez.

"I doubt it," croaked Epstein. "I don't think they want any more of us, plus, judging by their looks, I'm inclined to believe that they are probably AWOL from their unit and they can't afford to draw much more attention to themselves. It's not unusual for regular Army guys like us to have fights with airborne paratroopers like those guys. But, I'll bet that those guys have been AWOL a long time and the Army is looking for them. They're probably on the run and can't get out of the country to go home. So, they just wander from village to village raping, beating, stealing from the weak and moving on."

"Well I'm going back to finish what I was doing," stated Velez.

"Me too," Bird volunteered.

Epstein said, "Rock, go ahead and take Sallie on back to one of the rooms man, Mai Lin has said you don't have to pay!"

"Maybe later," I replied.

I didn't tell Epstein that I was really fearful of having sex with any of these Vietnamese women. Two months prior, during the jungle warfare training I had at Fort Benning, Georgia, to prepare me for coming to Vietnam, our training Sergeant had said,

"Men, be careful when having sex with the Vietnamese women. They could be communist sympathizers and they have been known to put glass slivers in their vaginas with the intent to do you some serious bodily harm! You can also contract a strain of venereal disease known as streptococci and gonococci that's so serious, it can get down into the testicles and cause epididymitis. The doctors can only treat it by throwing tetracycline, streptomycin and penicillin at it to try and slow it down."

Fearful? Hell, I was terrified!

CHAPTER THREE

First Patrol

For the next couple of weeks everybody in our base camp was kidding Spam about shooting a hole in the ceiling of Mai Lin's bar. His status had risen to the equivalent of Wyatt Earp's exploits at the "O.K. Corral." A couple of guys in camp had made it known that they too had run into the same wrecking crew we'd encountered at Mai Lin's, but nothing to equal the confrontation that took place with us.

A few days later I watched with interest as an MP jeep pulled into the compound with two MPs in the front and a familiar figure handcuffed in the back seat. When the handcuffed person got out, I realized that it was Silky! Five days before we had given him a big sendoff party. He had finished his twelve month tour of duty in 'Nam and had departed for Bien Hoa airbase 400 miles to the south to catch his flight home; back to "The World." What was he doing back here and why were the MPs escorting him? Velez was the company clerk in the orderly room and later that evening when everybody met up at the "flat lands," Velez filled us all in on the latest information. It seems that when Silky got to Bien Hoa and began out-processing to go home, a couple of CID Agents took him into custody for questioning. The CID guys had been investigating Silky and some of his close associates for a number of months and they had discovered that all of them had made large sums of money through black market transactions. They had been stealing generators, truck parts, and other miscellaneous materials from the warehouses and selling them to Vietnamese Nationals in the villages. The Nationals also had an elaborate black marketing network set up. These Vietnamese Nationals were some ruthless people and had the necessary financial resources to purchase a lot of hardware. It was also discovered that over a six month period of time Silky had deposited more than $40,000 into a bank account in

Harlem, New York, his home. Everybody was pissed at Silky, not because they were jealous, but because some of the miscellaneous items he sold were batteries; motor vehicle batteries, equipment batteries, all types of batteries. For a GI to sell batteries was a sin, because batteries were used to make booby traps and to set off bombs and all types of explosive devises which could be used against us or against troops out in the field. Silky had no morals or scruples. Then, I thought, *This is an immoral war!* But still, I couldn't forgive Silky on this one. He was taken before the Commanding Officer to be formerly charged, then put back into the jeep and taken back down south to stand trial before a court-martial. We never heard anything else about Mr. Ron "Silky" Owens.

I started to see some of the immorality of the war, when black newspapers published articles targeting the Selective Service Board and their practices. They had lowered the requirements for physicals and test scores. This act allowed for larger numbers of poor blacks, Latinos, and Appalachian whites to be drafted. Many of these draftees had previously been classified as mentally or physically unfit for military service.

I began to notice that the "first shirt," Sergeant Hanks, was starting to put my name on the roster for guard duty more frequently than I normally should have had to perform the duty, and I was starting to develop an attitude about it. I truly hated pulling guard duty. I was even starting to get paranoid about it. At night you had to pull two four hour shifts. The towers are far apart from one another, the terrain you watch in front of your tower is dark, desolate and hostile. You're out on the perimeter more than a half mile from the interior of the base camp and its activities. It's deathly quiet and when you hear a sound out in the night, every nerve fiber in your body screams silently as you try to figure out whether it's the enemy and is this the night he's coming for you? You constantly think about how you're on your own.

After pulling guard duty all night, you'd get the day off to recover. On these occasions I would hitch a ride to Troop Command thirty klicks away in Qui Nhon. At Troop Command there was a PX (Base Exchange) and you could buy personal supplies, goodies, magazines, all types of good stuff, and get film processed. When I'd completed my shopping I would walk around and visit the areas I had spent time in when I had first come in country. I'd see a few familiar faces and spend some time catching up on the latest gossip. On other occasions when I had some time off, I would go to the village of Phu Tai and visit Mai Lin's bar where there was usually a fairly large gathering of GIs from units in the surrounding areas. Many of them were temporarily AWOL just like me. It was no big thing as long as the MPs didn't catch you and you got back to your base camp before curfew went into effect at 1800 hours (six p.m.). It was really interesting meeting guys from every state in the US of A and making friends with people, some you might not ever see again. On many occasions some of my guys would drop in and some of the visiting GIs would scratch their heads trying to figure out why Mai Lin and her girls treated the boys and me so special. The visitors didn't know about the incident we had handled for Mai Lin when the dudes from the Herd had to be "taken down."

One evening after leaving Mai Lin's, I walked on the road which would lead me out of the village of Phu Tai and back to my Compound. As I walked, I constantly looked over my shoulder hoping for a military jeep or truck convoy to come along so I could get a ride. I didn't know why, but I had an uneasy feeling like something wasn't right. Sort of like a premonition. Suddenly I heard the villagers yelling to me, "Di Di, Medan!" "Di Di!" "Beaucoup MP come!" They were telling me; "Go quickly Black Man; many MPs are coming!" I looked back again and saw the MP convoy slowly threading its way through the village looking for wayward AWOL GIs. I started to sprint down the road before I was discovered. When the MPs were getting too close, I stopped in front of a door to a small shanty and busted the door open with the butt of my rifle. I quickly ran in and closed the door behind me. When I turned and put my back against the door and looked across the room, I saw an old Mama-San and Papa-San sitting at a table saying the blessing before they ate. Also at the table were a young woman and a young soldier in a South Vietnamese Army uniform and two children. The children looked to be about nine and ten years old, a boy and a girl. The old man heard all of the commotion outside and quickly assessed what my dilemma was and walked towards me.

He was saying something to me in Vietnamese, which I didn't understand, so I pointed my rifle at his face and told him to back away from me. His expression told me that he didn't have a clue as to what I was saying to him. Papa-San turned abruptly to the nearest wall which was made of plywood and slid the wall back to reveal a hidden compartment and then motioned for me to hide inside. I was very hesitant about following his suggestion, but the chatter outside seemed to indicate that the MPs were now searching house to house. Perhaps they had seen me. I climbed into the compartment and listened intently as the MPs made their search. I heard Papa-San's door open and the voices of the MPs as they came into the shack and searched for me. Papa-San kept chattering to the MPs in Vietnamese and I had the distinct impression he was telling them he hadn't seen any GIs. It was hot as blazes in the small compartment and I was sweating profusely. Twenty minutes later, everything got quiet and suddenly Papa-San slid the partition open and motioned for me to come out and he had a big conspiratorial grin on his face. He then motioned for me to sit down with his family at the table. I did.

Papa-San motioned to my rifle and his expression seemed to ask that I not point it at anyone in his house and I complied. He then put a book, pencil, and paper in front of me on the table. Using the book, he wrote in English the words "I YOU FRIEND." When I examined the book I found that it was a Vietnamese/English dictionary which had been published in 1926! I then searched through the Vietnamese section of the book and found what I was looking for. I wrote in Vietnamese "I AM FRIEND TO YOU." His family all joined him in gleeful laughter. Papa-San and I continued conversing with one another on paper for the next hour or so, until I felt comfortable enough to believe that the MPs had departed the area. I soon left Papa-San's and began my return to my Compound, but not before Papa-San made me promise to return at a later date.

Back in my Compound that same night, I thought about the events which had taken place at Papa-San's house. His name was

Huan and his wife was Xena; he had once been a soldier for the South Vietnamese Army and was now a farmer. The young woman was his daughter Kia, a teacher. The young soldier was her husband, Troung, and they were the parents of the two children.

During the next two weeks, I was able to spend more time with Huan studying Vietnamese and interacting with his family. The reason I had the time was because I was spending more and more time pulling guard duty. Therefore, my days were free. Huan had given me the name "Dat," which is Vietnamese for "Rock." Huan's family would greet me with big smiles and welcome me with open arms and the kids would grab on to my legs and hang on, each trying to show the other that "Dat" had come to see them. One day, Xena pulled me aside and showed me two pieces of jewelry; one was a small 24-carat gold statue of Buddha and the other was a miniature 24-carat gold crucifix.

She told me, "Both pieces are gifts for you. You wear in one of your ear lobes." I explained to her, "But I don't have a hole in my ear to put them in."

She said, "No sweat, Dat. I put hole in your ear."

After I had agreed to let her do it, I decided she should put the hole in my left ear lobe because that was the ear that all the brothers wore their earrings and adornments in and the rumor was you wore an earring in your right ear lobe to signify that you were gay. So I told her to definitely put the hole in my left ear lobe. She numbed my ear lobe with ice and then punched a needle through it, which made a little popping sound. She then pulled a white string through the hole and tied it into a circle. I wore the string for a few days until my ear healed and then Xena put the gold Buddha into the hole. I thought it looked pretty cool. I was surprised when I realized that both gold pieces were pure 24-carat gold, which made them very soft. I could detect the jealousy of other GIs who saw my Buddha and wished they had one.

Two weeks later, I again saw my name on the list for guard duty and I was pissed because my name was showing up on the list at a disproportionate rate compared to my white counterparts. I went directly to First Sergeant Hanks and complained to him about how frequently I had been pulling guard duty in the past few weeks.

Sergeant Hanks said, "Boy, you sound like you got a 'PP.'"

I didn't like his redneck sarcasm or his addressing me as "BOY."

I asked him, "What is a 'PP'?"

He said, "A 'PP' stands for Personal Problem."

I told him, "You're my personal problem and I'm not your boy. How big do they grow men where you come from?"

"Don't you talk to me that way!" He exploded.

"I'm not your boy and you need to understand that you're talking to a man," I retorted.

Hanks got so angry that he turned red in the face and a large vein stood out in the middle of his forehead.

"I don't want you to report for guard duty and you're dismissed," he said.

I left his office and went out to the flat lands where most of my partners were and tried to calm down by getting high.

Bird looked over at me and said, "Man, why are you looking so pissed off?" I told everybody about my run-in with Hanks.

Talley said, "Man, you've got to watch that peckerwood 'cause he can make life tough for you."

"Screw him," I said.

Epstein said, "Rock, Talley is telling you right. Hanks is a lifer. He's probably a high school dropout who came into the military and the military became his Mama and Daddy. He doesn't know anything but how to follow orders and try to screw over Blacks, Jews, and other minorities. He's been trying to mess over all of us who come to the flat lands. He has been heard to call us 'Communist, pinko, hippies' and has vowed to get us. So, watch your ass."

Later that night while sitting on my bunk writing some letters, I had that "funny feeling" again, like a premonition. Something was brewing in the cosmos, but what? I didn't know.

Two days later, Bird, Talley, Epstein, Spam, O'Malley, Brown, Bruce and I were given a set of orders transferring us to a newly formed unit. The unit was the 157th Guard and Reactionary Unit. The unit was set up about a mile and a half from our present unit on the other side of the Compound. The purpose of the new unit was to supply permanent guards to pull all of the guard duty for the entire Compound! When we weren't pulling guard duty, we were to go out on three-day patrols pulling tactical sweeps in the surrounding mountainous jungle looking for the enemy! I wanted to kill that cracker, Hanks!

A major commanded The157th by the name of Wilkerson and our sergeant squad leader/acting platoon sergeant was named Vickers. The "first shirt" was just as down and dirty as Hanks was; in fact they could be brothers and his name was Foley. Whenever the guys and I would come off of guard duty at 0600 hours (six a.m.), the first thing that Foley wanted us to do was fill sand bags.

He justified this duty by stating, "We're going to need more sandbags to reinforce our bunkers and to build up our AO (area of operation) for possible attacks and the coming monsoon season."

We would fill sandbags until lunchtime and then knock off for the day, only to return at six o'clock p.m. and report for guard duty. The handwriting was on the wall: the 157th Reactionary Force was a special unit put together for GIs who were considered troublemakers. To the best of my understanding, this unit was an illegal one because Troop Command Headquarters had no knowledge of its existence or its true purpose. The true purpose was racist in its intent, which was to expose certain individuals to enemy hostilities and hope that they are returned home or to the "Big PX in the sky" in body bags. None of the guys or I had an MOS (Military Occupational Specialty) of infantry soldier. We had all attended various types of military courses and were school trained in specialized areas of expertise. In order to get the school you requested you had to volunteer to serve an additional year in the military. I had been drafted for a two-year stint, but I had volunteered for a six-month course at Fort Lee, Virginia. I felt since the military had invested in training me, they wouldn't send me to Vietnam to die and waste their money. How wrong I was! When my tour of duty was up in Vietnam, I would still owe the military a third year of service.

With the guys, I discussed our predicament and we decided we would stick together no matter what the consequences. We were not infantrymen, but we had been trained in infantry tactics during basic training. Military law states: "You must obey the last order given by a superior; and if you disagree, you must lodge your complaint at a later time by going through the chain of command." The deck was stacked against us and there was no one who would readily intercede on our behalf. We were brothers and our survival depended on us covering each other's backs!

A few days later, I was told to go to the arms room to draw my weapons for my first patrol. Not only did I collect my weapons and ammo, but also two to three days' worth of C-rations. We were assembled into a squad of eight people, Bruce and Talley were the only guys I knew. Vickers was going to lead us on our first sweep through the mountains. We left out of the Compound at four o'clock p.m. and thirty minutes later our squad was moving single file through the mountainous jungle. It was hot as hell and giant mosquitoes that looked like miniature helicopters incessantly buzzed around my ears. It was nerve-racking. I took the little bottle of insect repellent that we carried stuck in the elastic band on the outside of our helmets and sprayed some of it all around my neck and ears. It seemed to help a little.

As the sun started to go down, I noticed that the natural jungle canopy made the heat dissipate but the humidity was stifling. An hour into our walk in the park, the point man gave a hand signal alerting us all to freeze in our tracks. Sergeant Vickers came up from the rear and cautiously approached the point man to confer with him. The rest of us now moved off of the trail and into the foliage beside the trail. Vickers gave us the all's clear sign and called us together to talk to us.

Vickers said, "Pearson here has discovered some tracks. They look to be a couple of days old. I don't know if they belong to the enemy or some village peasants out and about in this area."

"Sarge, how many of 'em is it?" asked a pimply-faced country sounding dude.

"Looks to be about four or five sets of tracks," answered Vickers. "If you look close inside the track you can see ridges imprinted in the dirt. The ridges are tire tracks. These buggers are wearing sandals with rubber on the bottoms made from old tires like on your car. We don't know what or whom we might have out here with us, so stay sharp men!"

I began to now take this trek through the jungle a bit more seriously. We moved out with me following Talley, who was three men back from the point man and Bruce two men behind me. We walked on in this formation for another hour and everyone seemed rather tense, to say the least. The point man brought us to a halt and again Vickers moved up front and called us together.

"All right men, we're going to move off the trail to our left and go into the bush about 200 meters and start setting up our night defensive position. OK, move out," Vickers said.

We moved quickly and found a favorable location to set up. Bruce and Talley set their positions close to mine. A couple of other guys went out away from the main body to set up a small perimeter around us ringed with trip wires and claymore mines. This procedure is like insurance. It's an early warning system. If any enemy approached our night perimeter and hit a trip wire, they were going to touch off flares, which would illuminate the area like a giant strobe light. The claymore mines were explosive devices that were filled with 700 steel balls set in an explosive bed and detonated by remote control. It's a rectangular cast iron box with spikes fitted to the base for stability. Once detonated, its contents are sprayed in a 60-degree fan-shaped pattern that's lethal up to a range of fifty yards.

A couple of guys were put on the perimeter to pull the first watch and we all would take turns rotating every two hours. Talley and I were going to pull a watch together at 0300 hours (three a.m.). We decided to get some sleep, but first we decided to eat some of our C-rations.

"What'cha got you wanna trade?" Bruce asked me.

"I've got nothing I wanna trade. What kinda meat you got?" I asked.

"Looks like I got ham and lima beans," Bruce replied. "No way, man! I got beef and for dessert I got fruit cocktail." I said.

At this point Bruce knew that his efforts were useless. When someone lucked out and got a delicacy like fruit cocktail in their C-rats, it meant that GOD truly loved them. What really blew my mind was that many of the C-rats we were given in Vietnam were processed and packed in their boxes in 1944. This information was on the cans. These same C-rats were prepared for GIs during World War II, but when you used your P-38 (a miniature can opener most of us wore on our "dog tags") to open a can, the food inside was pressure packed and just as fresh as it was when it was packed in 1944. Amazing, I thought.

At 0300 hours I was awakened to pull my watch. Talley and I pulled the watch until 0500 hours. During our watch we spoke to each other in soft, low tones talking about Vietnam, life, and love. Talley shared with me the fact that he was worried about his relationship with his girl back in the World. He hadn't received a letter from her in over a week and a half, which is an eternity in 'Nam. I told him to just be cool; maybe the mail had gotten screwed up or something. I tried to cheer him up 'cause the last thing we needed was for him to be out in the jungle with tears in his eyes and little men with tire track sandals slipping up on our asses. As daybreak shimmied up on the horizon, our watch ended uneventfully.

We moved out of our perimeter area around 0600 hours, after cleaning up all traces that would indicate we have ever been there. I was assigned the dubious duty of walking point. After a couple of hours out in front everybody else, I settled into a kind of natural rhythm. I realized that I had the responsibility of the whole squad resting on me. Suddenly my reverie was interrupted by that "weird" feeling again! Something was not right...something was out there...in front of us. The hair on the back of my neck bristled. I signaled everyone to move into the bush on both sides of the trail to take up firing positions. Coming down the trail towards us were five Korean soldiers in full battle gear. These guys were our allies known as ROKs (Republic of Korea Soldiers). The tension was lifted. Vickers called out something to them in Korean and they halted. Then Vickers ventured out onto the trail and approached them. They exchanged what looked to be amiable dialogue, and then Vickers signaled our squad to come out of our positions. We formed up a couple of yards from Vickers as he continued to converse with the ROKs. It was then that I noticed two of the ROKs had a string of wire around their necks with three or four human ears on them. *Unbelievable,* I thought to myself. This was a mean looking bunch by any estimation. They had a cold, deadly, slant-eyed look which was hard to read, and an air of arrogance. They were some "bad mamma-jammers!"

Vickers finished his conversation with the ROKs and they moved on down the trail. I asked him what was going on?

He said, "The ROKs were working their way back to their base camp two mountains further behind us and that three days ago they had encountered a VC raiding party. There had been a firefight with them and they had confirmed a body count of four dead VC."

I asked him, "Sarge, why did they have those ears strung around their necks like that?"

"Whenever the ROKs have a confirmed kill they cut off the enemy's ears and turn them over to their superiors for a bonus. The ROKs are paid a bounty for each pair of ears they show up with," Vickers answered.

Vickers called to a white guy named Herron and told him to bring the radio up front to him. Vickers called in our grid coordinates to headquarters and gave them the information that he had received from the ROKs. After he had finished, he told us that we were going to alter our course, so we wouldn't follow the route the ROKS had used.

We continued our patrol for a few more hours and after breaking for a quick lunch we again moved out. Shortly afterward, I heard voices off to my left and halted the squad and called Vickers forward. When he got to my position he told me that he heard the voices also. He motioned for me to follow him forward. We scampered to the edge of a clearing and crawled a few yards more and scanned the area. We had happened upon a small hamlet with tribesmen! Vickers told me to go get the other guys and to meet up with him in the hamlet. I carried out his instructions and when the squad and I found him in the hamlet he was talking with a couple of the tribesmen.

"Who are these people?" I asked Talley.

Talley told me, "'These are Montagnard hill tribesmen. They number only about a million compared to South Vietnams total population of about eighteen million. They are guerilla fighters and they're on our side."

"What race are they?" I asked Talley, because these people had very dark skin color but had oriental features.

"I guess they're Cambodian and mixed with some African ancestry." Talley said. "'They occupy more than half of Vietnam's countryside; the Vietnamese prefer the Delta and the coastal lowlands where rice is easily cultivated. These tribesmen are primitive and so are their weapons, but they can kick ass and take names with the best of them. These tribesmen dominate the high plateau region of South Vietnam, which is the prime strategic target of the communists. Dominate the Central Highlands and you can cut South Vietnam in two."

"Well damn! Thank you Professor Talley for such enlightenment," I joked with Talley.

I noticed that even though these people seemed deprived of many amenities, they were a very proud group and the women were attractive. *Must be those soulful genes*, I thought to myself.

After we had rested awhile, we again moved out. The rest of the day was uneventful, and towards nightfall we set up our perimeter and procedures as we had the night before. I had drifted off to sleep in what I learned was called twilight sleep. Twilight sleep is not a deep sleep, but a type of sleep that allows you to completely relax in a state sort of like suspended animation. The body receives the rest it needs, but your mind's level of consciousness never totally surrenders to sleep. If something or someone approaches you or if your built-in radar picks up a perceived threat or intrusion of your space, you are instantly awake, aware of where you are, and ready to do battle. That's exactly what happened to me at about 1:30 a.m. While deep into my twilight sleep, I heard a twanging sound that signaled that the enemy had touched off a trip wire. I immediately sat up arid grabbed my rifle just as the first flare went off illuminating the area. All hell broke loose! The claymores were detonated, their loud explosion ripping open the night quiet Small arms fire was popping everywhere;

suddenly the guy in charge of the "pig" was laying down a constant chatter of machine gun fire into the jungle night, aimed in the direction of where the penetration had first been felt. Everything was happening in surreal speed. I remember thinking that Vickers probably wouldn't try to call for an artillery strike because we were fighting too close to the enemy. Then I wondered how many of them were out there trying to kill my young ass. Next, I heard the steady "whump whump" of the "blooper" as a dude named Hix was firing the 40 millimeter grenades as fast as he could fire and reload. Orders, curses and instructions were being yelled at the same time by all of us. Fifteen minutes later, the enemy broke contact and the commotion started to abate. When everything had quieted down and the firing had subsided, we took a head count to see how many of us had been wounded or killed. Everybody checked out as being OK. I considered that a blessing!

Vickers next said, "Rock, take Talley and Bruce with you out about a hundred meters into the area where the attack came from, and scour that area for a body count. Watch your backs and look close for anything that might be of importance, like maps and stuff, which the enemy may have left behind. GO!"

We cautiously eased out into the terrain spread out from one another about fifteen meters apart. Forty meters out, I motioned for Bruce to approach my area. When he came up, I showed him some blood drops, which began to increase into a blood trail as it, moved away from where I was standing. The trail continued for another thirty meters and then disappeared. All around you could see broken blades of palm tree fronds and tamped down grass which, to me, indicated about twelve to fifteen VC had hit us. Looking to my left, I saw something flat and black under a bush, so I leaned down to observe what it was. It was a backpack with the support straps cut away and frayed with blood on them. Perhaps the pack had been blown off the back of the VC that had left the blood trail.

"What's in it?" Bruce asked.

"Looks like some pictures and other personal stuff," I replied.

"Wait! What's that?" Talley had joined in.

"It's a map with grid coordinates on it," I supplied.

"Come on, let's get the hell out of here," Talley implored.

We got back and gave the gear to Vickers and he immediately got on the horn to headquarters and gave a report. Headquarters gave us new coordinates, which we were to follow on our left flank that would bring us back to our base compound in a shorter amount of time. We moved out glad to put that place behind us.

We got back to our base camp at 6:30 p.m. After cleaning ourselves and our gear we ate and sat around with the other guys from the 157th, telling over and over again what had transpired on our first patrol. We talked, joked, and kidded each other for hours, I guess to let off some of the tension. Everybody's nerves were tightly strung, so this was good therapy. Finally, at 1:30 a.m. I dropped off to sleep.

CHAPTER FOUR

Winning and Losing

A week later, Hanks assigned me to pull guard duty at tower number eleven. Everyone hated duty at tower eleven. It was located at the weakest part of the perimeter and like many of the other towers it was a "listening" post. It was weak because it was in a very dark, remote sector and farther away from the center of the base camp activity than any of the other posts. Being a "listening" post meant if you hear anything, don't ask yourself questions just start shooting. Post eleven faced about ten acres of fields and rice paddies, which flowed, in a flat pattern to the base of a mountain. There were three very small, thatched grass hootches in the distance, which always appeared empty. This open area was called "Kimchee" by the Vietnamese people. The truck dropped me off at Post 11 at two a.m. to relieve a brother from South Carolina, named Ollie. Ollie was waiting at the base of the tower as I approached and he yelled to the truck driver telling him, "Go on without me; I'm going to stay here with Rock while he pulls his shift." The truck driver complied with Ollie's wishes, but I was confused because Ollie should not have been at the base of the tower until I had properly relieved him of duty and secondly, why would he want to stay at this spooky place any longer than he had to? Ollie's nickname was "Geechee" and he was from Charleston, South Carolina. Geechee believed in such things as "Miz Rudolph" the Voodoo Priestess, monkey feet, and potions.

When I asked, "Geechee, why are you staying here with me?"

Geechee said, "Man, I've got a bad feeling about this place. When I started my watch at ten p.m., I kept seeing figures moving back and forth out in the distance by those grass huts."

When I looked in the direction Geechee had indicated, I saw two small grass huts about a half a mile away.

Geechee continued, "At first I thought my eyes were playing tricks on me, but now I'm not so sure. I didn't want to shoot and draw attention to myself, so I came and sat down at the base of the tower and watched the area. I've seen you around and I think you're a pretty cool dude so I ain't gonna leave you out here by yourself. We can sit down here at the base of the tower and still get the job done."

Considering the fact that Geechee knew "Miz Rudolph" and that my sixth sense was tugging at me, I agreed with his suggestion. We went up in the tower and brought the "pig" down and set it at the base of the tower with our other weapons. We took up comfortable sitting positions on the ground and settled in.

Geechee and I discussed how each of us had ended up in the Army. Geechee had been born on Tybee Island, Georgia and had been raised there by his mother and grandmother along with his two brothers and one sister. He started working at an early age with the men of the island on a shrimp boat in an effort to help his family. His mother worked as a domestic in the beautiful, big houses of the rich and famous elite of Hilton Head, South Carolina, while his grandmother took care of his siblings. He became very proficient as a fisherman and loved the work and the freedom of the ocean. Geechee had a ninth grade education. He had only attended school during the winter months. All other months were spent earning a living.

His mother told him he was born with a "veil over his face." Some babies are born with a thin membrane covering their faces as they exit the birth canal. The doctor then removes it. In Geechee's case, it was removed by the mid-wife who had delivered him. In island parlance being a "veiled baby" meant that Geechee was gifted at birth with the ability to one day have premonitions, to know things before they happened and see things others could not.

At the age of fifteen, Geechee had tried unsuccessfully to talk his shrimp boat captain and crew into not going out on a fine and beautiful day of fishing. He refused to go because he had a bad feeling about the trip. Late that evening, a terrible storm swept through the island and surrounding waters with lashing winds and lightning which flashed indiscriminately in every direction. The violent storm decimated the boat and crew of twenty men. Only two crewmembers survived and their injuries were so severe, that they were never able to return to their chosen livelihood. On another occasion, Geechee had begged and pleaded with the principal of the school he had attended in an effort to get the school closed for the day because he saw a fire coming. The principal refused, but Geechee stood his ground and was adamant that a fire was imminent. Finally, the principal called for the Tybee Fire Department to come and check all of the wiring. When they did, one of the firemen discovered a bomb, which had been placed in a storage area with enough sticks of dynamite to wipe out half of the small island. The FBI later concluded that some very unscrupulous land developers were looking to acquire new properties for an annexation of the Hilton Head Resorts. The developers had hired local Ku Klux Klansmen to do the dirty work of scaring off the black land holders and killing off the rest. Island people began to look upon Geechee as some kind of Shaman or something. Over the years after this incident, Geechee was able to forewarn of other impending calamities and was also able to advise people of some good, positive and profitable things which would benefit them. Eventually, he met a weathered, sage, old island woman called "Miz Rudolph." She explained some things to him concerning his "gift" and he came into some understandings that he didn't bother to explain to me and I didn't bother to ask.

"Unfortunately," Geechee said, "I wasn't able to foresee that I would be receiving a letter from 'My Uncle Sam' saying 'Greetings, You're In The Army Now!'" We both laughed at the irony of it all.

Geechee then wanted to know my background. I told him I was twenty-three years old, which was older than the median age for most guys in Vietnam. The reason being was that I had been in college when I was drafted. My mother was a fourth grade school teacher and my father was a dining car waiter for Southern Railroad. Once a week my father traveled from our home in Atlanta, Georgia, to New Orleans, back to Atlanta, to New York and back to Atlanta. I have a brother named Michael who is fifteen months younger than I am and he had recently left college and joined the Air Force. As a young child and until coming to 'Nam, I had traveled extensively up and down the East coast visiting relatives in almost every state. I could travel for free because the Railroad would give me and my immediate family members free travel any time we requested it.

As a kid, I was a C student and did just enough to get by in school, but my real interest and talents were in art–drawing and painting. When I was about to enter the ninth grade, my mother decided that I was the kind of little boy that she didn't want me to play with. So, to help me get some discipline, she and my father decided to send me to a boarding school in your state, South Carolina. I attended a school named Boylan-Haven-Mather Academy.

Geechee said, "Hey! I know where that is. It's in Camden, South Carolina. I've got relatives there."

I proceeded with my story. I got there in late August to begin the school year. When I entered the dormitory I was greeted by the Dean of Men who also stayed in the dormitory on the same floor where I had been assigned. "He told me that his name was Robert C. Hill and that he didn't like anybody from Atlanta." I quickly realized that I had better steer clear of Hill if I was going to make it at the school. Hill was a short stocky guy built like a fireplug and had been a Marine Corps Drill Instructor. He harassed me day in and day out, so I reached a point where I determined "this was war." I started booby trapping his room door by putting a bucket of water overhead, which would spill on him when he entered. On a couple of occasions, I stuck a water hose in his window in the middle of the night and turned that sucker on full blast. I sometimes took the valve stems out of all the tires on his car, leaving him with four flats. I'm sure Hill knew it was me that was causing him so many problems, but to him it was a man to man, or a brother to brother thing of pride and his goal was to catch me in the act of doing something wrong.

I was a member of the football team and played the positions of halfback and defensive left corner back. I also made the basketball team where I played forward. The coach was named Perkerson and he had a brother in my class named Stan who was a gifted athlete in both sports. I played second string in both sports behind Stan, so I didn't get much playing time. I had a few bright moments on the field and the basketball court, but I never felt that Coach Perkerson provided me with the type of guidance, preparation, and coaching that was necessary for a young athlete to reach his potential. All of his efforts were spent coaching and living through the heroic exploits of Stan. So, I remained on the second string. As I was telling Geechee about this, it brought to mind and old football joke:

First guy says: "What position do you play on the football team?"

Second guy says: "End, guard, and tackle."

First guy says: "All three positions?"

Second guy says: "Yeah. I sit on the end of the bench and guard the water and tackle anybody that tries to get to it!"

Eventually, Dean Hill reached the breaking point. Six months after entering Mather, Dean Hill contacted my parents at the beginning of the second semester and informed them that he was sending me back to where I had come from. He said, "Your son's lack of discipline is unacceptable for a Methodist Institution of this caliber." I was hurt, shocked, and disappointed. I thought those people were specialists who were going to discipline me and show me the error of my ways and put me on the straight and narrow. Their brochures had definitely been very misleading.

I returned to my old high school and in my tenth grade year I tried out for the track team as a high hurdler and low hurdler. I made the team and was marginally successful accomplishing mostly third place finishes. Again, I had a coach who didn't think I had much potential, so he didn't waste a lot of time trying to train me. My coach also didn't know anything about teaching the fundamentals of hurdling. When he passed out the uniforms for a big track meet, he would give me the raggedy, second hand ones. I started studying films and reading books of some of the world's greatest hurdlers like Harrison Dillard, Ralph Boston, and my idol, Lee Calhoun, who set a new world record and won the gold medal at the 1956 Olympic Games in Melbourne, Australia.

During my eleventh grade year, I won every 120-yard high hurdles and 180-yard low hurdles race until I got to the final track meet of the season—the City Championships. When the local newspapers and TV stations started writing articles, and interviewing me, my coach started telling everybody he had always known about my potential and how he had spent endless hours teaching me the fine art of hurdling.

In 1964, my senior year, I was undefeated in every race I competed in leading up to the City Championships! All of my wins were so impressive that many people, including myself, just knew that I would win the championship. However, two weeks before the meet was to take place, the Atlanta School Board announced that for the first time ever the City Track and Field Championships would be integrated! I quickly heard about a white guy named Al Edwards, a hurdler extraordinaire, who attended Dykes High School across town. I went to see this guy run in his last tune up track meet before the City Championships were to take place. I was shocked when I saw him win the 120-yard high hurdle race! He was very muscular and athletically built, with graceful and powerful cat-like movements when he ran. He was mature and confident looking, with a hint of prima donna arrogance and he was fast as hell. Man, the dude was bad with a capitol B and to my regret, I knew in my heart of hearts that I could not beat Mr. Al Edwards.

For the next two weeks, I trained extra hard and pushed myself to exhaustive limits. I figured if I could make a very impressive second place finish closely behind Al, I would be noticed by some of the college scouts and still have a chance at being offered a scholarship. The day of the City Championships arrived and it was a beautiful, warm and sunny day in May. I looked up in the stands and saw a beautiful sight: thousands of spectators; black and white all mingled together, laughing, smiling, and cheering at the first integrated high school sporting event ever held in the city of Atlanta. The event was taking place months after Lester Maddox, the avowed white racist owner of the Pickrick Restaurant, had given out ax handles to Ku Klux Klansmen in his restaurant parking lot, which were to be used to beat a group of blacks who had planned to desegregate the restaurant by seeking service there. Black leaders, realizing the potential for death and bloodshed, called the demonstration off, but the city "Too Busy To Hate" was left with an ugly, unsightly scar. Perhaps, the City Fathers felt that the integrated City Track Championships might be the balm to soothe the wound of racism.

The hurdles event was announced and I reported to the starting line for my lane assignment. I was assigned lane number two, and Al Edwards drew lane number three. As we were warming up we made eye contact and instinctively I knew that he knew who I was. At that moment I thought to myself, *If I believe that this guy can beat me, he will. By believing I can't win means that I am defeating myself by at least fifty percent.* At that point, I made up my mind that I was going to win. I was not going to be denied the championship. I signaled to my brother Michael who was sitting up in the stands, letting him know I need to talk to him.

When he approached, I told him, "Sit on the first row down by the eighth flight of hurdles and when I come past, no matter whether I am winning or losing the race, I want you to yell at me and get my attention."

Mike said, "OK, but why?"

I answered, "Because, all season I have been winning by such a large margin that no one has been close enough to push me to my full potential. This has caused me to slack off when I get to the eighth hurdle. When you yell at me that will get my attention and cause me to focus and reach deep within. I've got to push myself." The starter called the race, "RUNNER'S COME TO YOUR MARKS!"

This is it, I thought silently as I said a prayer.

"GET SET!"

I coiled and tensed every fiber of my being, like a clock you wind to within a half of a tick before it's about to burst open, spewing cogs, wheels, springs and intricate parts everywhere.

BANG!

We exploded out of the starting blocks. As I powered forward preparing to clear the first hurdle, I saw that Al was ahead of me by three steps and peripherally, I could see that the other six competitors were nowhere near us. This was a two-man race between Al and me. The only thought going through my head was *concentrate, concentrate, concentrate.* By the sixth hurdle, nothing had changed in our positions, the roaring of the crowd was deafening and Al was still ahead by three steps. At the eighth hurdle, Mike leaned over the railing and yelled into my ear "FIGHT HIM; FIGHT HIM, ROCK!" Then something happened which I had never experienced in running before or since and to this day I still do not fully comprehend. The noise of the crowd ceased to exist; there were no sounds anymore. I felt like I was in a timeless, soundless vacuum where everything was happening in surreal slow motion. Then, I realized that I had caught up to Al and we were running side-by-side, stride for stride. I continued to concentrate and stayed focused on the finish line two hurdles away. Out of the corner of my right eye, I saw Al turn and look at me with shock and disbelief on his face, and the silence in the vacuum was punctured when I heard him utter a "HUH!?" His break in concentration caused his steps to falter and he became entangled with his hurdle and began to go down with it. Time froze. I mean time literally froze; everything stopped. Out of the corner of my left eye, I saw very clearly a man five feet away from me down on one knee, wearing a wide brim hat with a credential stuck in the band which read "PRESS." In front of his face he held a big camera like the ones used by newspaper reporters. The silence was again punctured; this time by the big camera as it issued a loud "CLICK!"

The next instant everything around me was now in real time and I was dipping my chest to break the tape at the finish line and I was all alone. After stopping, I turned to walk back to the finish line and I felt like I was in a daze, then I began to realize that I had won! The many hours and years of training that I'd invested in track had finally paid off. All the years of self-doubt, insecurity, and the pain and humiliation of losing "the big races" became insignificant as I thought about what I had accomplished historically. In the 120-yard high hurdles event I had become the first African-American record holder in the first integrated track meet in the state of Georgia. The commentator on the P.A. system announced, "Morocco Coleman has just broken the old record of 14.9 seconds and has set a new record of 14.1 seconds."

I looked up into the stands and the crowd was going wild. Both black and white were cheering me enthusiastically. I later discovered that it didn't have anything to do with color. The response I received was for the phenomenal performance I had given, which I had no idea that I was capable of. One of the greatest moments of my life was when I looked up in the stands and saw the pride beaming on the faces of my mother, father and grandfather. They had never been to any of my track meets before that day.

The following day, on the front page of the Sports Section of the Atlanta Constitution Newspaper was the picture that the reporter had captured when time stopped. When I looked closely at the picture I could see my brother Mike, leaning over the railing yelling for me "to fight."

During that summer, I received track scholarships to a number of colleges, but I decided to attend North Carolina Central University in Durham, North Carolina. NCCU was the same institution my idol Lee Calhoun had attended and my coach would be Dr. Leroy Walker, the same coach who had coached and trained Lee! I entered NCCU in 1964 and under Dr. Walker's tutelage I set my sights on two goals in track. First, I wanted to compete at the Penn Relays in Philadelphia, Pennsylvania. The Penn Relays is a very prestigious track event, which features competition between the cream of the crop and the best of the best athletes from around the country. My second goal was to compete in the 1968 Olympic Games that were to be held in Mexico City.

Suddenly, my storytelling was interrupted by a sharp metallic sound, which I heard far out in the night distance in front of us. Both Geechee and I turned to look in the direction of the sound at the same time. From the area of the nearest hut we saw a small ball of fire with a tail of flame coming towards us rising in an upward arc. Time seemed to move in slow motion as I struggled to position myself behind the .60 caliber machine-gun, while Geechee began firing his M-16 on full automatic. We were spewing out a stream of bullets in a continuous pattern towards the area where the ball of fire was coming from. The ball of fire got closer and bigger and I heard a "whooshing" sound coming from it. Slow motion time disappeared and reality time checked in. Reality time

45

told my senses that the ball of fire coming straight at us was A ROCKET! The rocket was fired from a LAW (Light Anti-Armor Weapon) which was a smaller version of the bazooka used in World War II. As it closed its distance to us, it started to arc higher and we ducked as it passed over us. A loud crunching "VROOM" sound punctuated the night and burning splinters of wood and shingles started to rain down on us. The LAW had struck the roof on the tower above us and exploded, spraying debris all around and leaving the frame of the tower leaning at an odd angle sort of like the leaning tower of Pisa. Reinforcements arrived shortly afterward and began firing indiscriminately into the darkness. Oddly enough, there was no return fire from the enemy. "Victor Charlie" had fired his rocket and made a hasty retreat into the night. Later, I had time to think about how close I had come to being up in that tower when the rocket came through it. During the ordeal my reflexes and training took over, and instinctively I did all the right things, but afterwards I was shaking like a leaf on a tree. The terror of knowing that the specter of life or death can take place within the blinking of an eye is a very sobering thought. I also began to wonder, *How did Geechee know that something bad was coming?*

For the next two days all anyone talked about was how lucky Geechee and I were to have been able to scramble down from the tower in time to avoid being hit by the LAW. We didn't tell them we had not been up in the tower when all hell broke loose. If our superiors had known this fact, we could have been court-martialed. I did share the truth with my "tight man" Talley.

I told him, "Man, I had a strange feeling when I was in the truck on the way to that tower."

"What kind of strange feeling?" Asked Talley.

I went on to say, "Well, I felt like something bad was in the cosmos waiting to happen but I didn't know what. I was even more concerned when Geechee volunteered to stay with me. It was as if I had a premonition of things to come. Lately, I have been having these feelings, which seem to warn me of some impending danger, or I see something before it happens. I guess you think I'm going nuts from being in Vietnam too long."

I felt comfortable sharing this information with Talley, because he was college educated, intelligent, and a deep thinker whom I respected.

"Rock, these feelings you're having are different from what Geechee experiences. His experiences are probably culturally biased and border on some form of the occult or mystical. Maybe he is just truly gifted. I can't really say. But, have you ever heard of the term synchronicity?"

"Nope. What is it?" I asked.

Talley said, "Synchronicity has been defined as coincidences that are so unusual and meaningful that maybe they can't be attributed to chance alone. Some say that when fabulous coincidences occur maybe we should look at such coincidences as evidence that life is filled with meaning and mystery. Have you ever been sitting quietly and you thought about someone you hadn't seen in ten years, who lived in another city a thousand miles away and suddenly the phone rings and it's them calling you? Or, you're planning to take a trip to Tahiti, a place you've never been to before, and your name is selected in a contest and...You win a free trip to Tahiti! Is it possible that there's a sort of universal plan behind all of these 'accidental coincidences'? These opportunities that present themselves seem to help us heal or evolve into more fulfilled, aware, spiritual people."

"Does synchronicity have anything to do with Albert Einstein's theory of relativity?" I asked.

"Yes," replied Talley. "Einstein believed that space and time are not separate entities, but are linked and a part of a larger whole he called the space-time continuum. Einstein's protégé, a quantum physicist named Bohm, took this idea a giant step further. He said that everything in the universe is part of a continuum. He believed that despite the apparent separateness of things, everything is a seamless extension of everything else. For instance, a whirlpool that forms in a river possesses individual characteristics of size, depth and direction flow-but even if you look very carefully, it's impossible to tell where the whirlpool ends and the river begins. Most of us don't see ghosts, or have E.S.P., but most of us do experience synchronicity. And to believers, synchronicity quite simply tells us there is some kind of God. Some scientists believe that there is space, there is matter, and the matter interacts with space. The space, the matter, and we are all wonderfully connected and bound together by gravitational and even by electromagnetic interactions; there really is a web in which we're all caught together. Every atom in your body is drawn downward toward the earth. No one has yet been able to definitely correlate the significance of all this, but gravitational connections certainly exist."

"Talley this stuff you're telling me is very cerebral, but I think I'm following what you're saying," I announced.

"Think of it this way," replied Talley, "that we in the universe are an orchestra, and an existing higher intelligence is the conductor of I the orchestra. When we don't pay attention to the conductor, we play our instruments randomly and everything is chaos. When we listen to our own inner wisdom, we are really paying attention to the conductor and figuring out his intentions; then, we're somehow able to create our own amazing coincidences and the song falls into place in a most amazing way. If we personally realize that synchronicity is at work in our lives, we feel connected rather than isolated and estranged from others. Paying attention to meaningful coincidences helps us understand that we are a part of something greater than ourselves."

Talley had given me a lot to contemplate. Later, as I was sitting on my bunk writing some letters home, Geechee broke my concentration.

"So what happened?" He said. I looked up at him perplexed. I had no clue as to what he was talking about.

"What happened when?" I asked.

"Before we were attacked by that rocket the other night you were telling me about your two goals. Did you achieve them?" Geechee asked.

"Man, you must be part elephant 'cause you don't forget anything," I said. I began to tell him my story where I had left off. In my freshman year I became a member of the North Carolina Central track team. Each of the previous three years the team had won the Conference Championships and boasted having two Olympians on the team, Edwin Roberts (200 meter champion) and

Norm Tate (triple jump champion). Dr. Walker was an excellent coach and taught me the finer points of being a high hurdler. He also taught me how to run the 400-meter hurdles event and win. I was able to become a much better and stronger hurdler. The only event freshmen could participate in at the Penn Relays was the one mile relay. Our one mile relay team consisted of three guys who were so fast you would have thought they had afterburners tied on their behinds. The lead off leg was Leary Rivas from Trinidad; the second leg was an excellent hurdler named Paul Wilson from Plainfield, New Jersey; and the anchor leg was "Chuck" Copeland from Raleigh, North Carolina. Dr. Walker held try-outs to determine which freshman would win the coveted spot to run the third leg on the one-mile relay team. I defeated all of the competition and won the spot on the relay team. I was ecstatic, but at the same time a little disappointed because I realized that I was the slowest member of the group. In our initial practice each one of us had to run 400-meters (one time around the track) and passed the baton to the next team member as if we were in actual competition. Rivas led off and was clocked in 48.8 seconds; on the second leg, Paul was clocked in 47.8 seconds; on the third leg I turned in a time of 51.7 seconds and passed the baton to Chuck who blistered the distance in 46.9 seconds. My teammates gave me a lot of moral support and told me I'd get better as I got more experience.

Dr. Walker explained that we had run a respectable 3:15.7, but in order for him to even think about taking us to the Penn Relays we would have to run at least a 3:10.0 or better. He said if we couldn't meet this standard, it wouldn't make any sense to take us because the competition would "chew us up and spit us out." We had two upcoming track meets, which would offer us an opportunity to try to meet the standard.

The following week we ran in a big track meet at Duke University and our freshman mile relay team won handily in a time of 3:14.0. My teammates congratulated me for lowering my individual time to 50.5 and running a stronger race than the week before. The next week we traveled to South Carolina State

University in Orangeburg, South Carolina, to participate in the South Carolina Relays. On the day of the track meet, the stadium was overflowing with spectators and there were many world class athletes in attendance that had come to "strut their stuff." You could feel the electricity in the air.

Shortly before my teammates and I were to run, they took me to a section under the stadium and told me not to worry about anything and to just remember everything I had learned recently. They told me to just give them my best and they in turn, would give me my first goal–the Penn Relays. We said a prayer and stepped back out into the sunlight and walked to the starting line for the beginning of the one-mile relay.

When the starter fired his gun to start the race, Rivas exploded out of the starting blocks like a man possessed. By the time he reached the 200-meter mark he was leading the pack of other runners by ten yards. As he approached the 300-meter mark, he had increased his lead by another two yards and was running a masterful race. When Rivas neared the 400-meter mark, he reached down into his bag of tricks, pulled out all of the stops, and managed to give Paul an extra two more yards of daylight. As I watched Paul running down the back straight away, I thought to myself, *He looks just like one of those big Budweiser Clydesdale horses prancing towards freedom.* When he rounded the last turn, I stepped upon the track to await the baton exchange he and I would share. Paul had maintained the same amount of distance he had inherited from Rivas and as I looked into his face as he approached me, I noticed that he was smiling. I couldn't believe it!

I took a quick look at the other runners to size them up, because with the lead Paul was bringing me they would soon be my pursuers. At that instant, I realized that one of my soon to be pursuers was a guy I hadn't seen in four years. It was none other than Stan Perkerson, Coach Perkerson's brother from my old Mather Academy boarding school days! He happened to look up see me just as I turned to take the baton pass from Paul. I sprinted the first 110 meters as if my life depended on it and as I closed in on the 150-meter mark I suddenly heard footsteps closing in fast behind me. The stadium crowd jumped to their feet and started screaming and yelling; they sensed that I was about to be caught from behind by the fast approaching runner. The footsteps got louder and closer. At the 200-meter mark I had to make a decision. Did I have enough strength to fight off this challenge coming fast from behind? Will I be committing too much energy too soon? Will I be strong enough to get the baton to Copeland? The guy behind me was now breathing down my back! Suddenly, standing on the field to my left was my upperclassman teammate Terry Amos. Terry was a short, gruff, and outstanding runner that nobody messed with. In his gravelly voice he yelled at me, "You better not let him catch you, dammit!" I don't know if it was my fear of Terry or what, but my mind was made up. I reached down into my soul and thought, *Damn the torpedoes and full steam ahead!* I was jolted by a burst of energy and I felt as if I were running on air. As I pulled away from my pursuer I could actually feel his energy drain from him to me. Without looking back, I could feel him wilt away to nothingness. The immediate response of the crowd told me that they couldn't believe what they were witnessing. When I rounded the curve at about the 330-meter mark, I heard and felt the presence of another challenger coming. This challenger's footfalls sounded stronger and his presence was much more pervasive than that of the previous runner. I lowered my head, pumped my arms and legs as if they were pistons and I felt my body shift into a gear of overdrive that I had never experienced before. I had increased my lead by five more yards. When I looked up again, I was fifteen yards from Copeland and he was waiting for me to bring him the baton; on his face was a big, wide, shiny toothed grin. When I passed the baton to him and turned to the inside of the track to get out of the way of the runners coming in behind me, the crowd literally went into pandemonium.

Copeland was so powerfully built that he made his run look as if he were gliding around the track. I had given him a very comfortable lead and he was taking full advantage of it. By the time he had cleared the finish line, he had increased his lead by more than ten yards. Rivas, Paul, and I waited at the finish line for Copeland to congratulate him. The four of us were hugging and yelling as Dr. Walker came over to us and he had a big smile on his face. He told us that we had won with a winning time of 3:08.7, which was a new stadium record, and that I had run the fastest 400-meter relay leg of my life with a time of 47.6. This news coupled with the adrenaline rush I was still experiencing, made me feel as if I were intoxicated. We were going to the Penn Relays!

As we continued to rejoice, a man who looked vaguely familiar to me walked up and asked, "Son, why didn't you ever tell me you could run like that?" It was then that I realized that the man was Coach Perkerson. I answered him by saying, "Well Coach, you never gave me the opportunity to show you or to tell you." After spending a couple of minutes chatting with my old coach, his brother Stan, walked up and said, "Man, after all of these years you didn't have to come on my home turf and embarrass me like you did." It was then that I realized that Stan had been the last pursuer who had been unable to out run me. I was elated as I thought about how I had come back to South Carolina and redeemed myself athletically. It was like "coming full circle."

The next week our team made the trek to Philadelphia, Pennsylvania, to compete in the Penn Relays. In addition to trophies, members of the winning one-mile relay team would receive gold watches with red, white and blue watchbands on them. Instead of numbers on the face of the watch, there were letters which spelled out "PENN*RELAYS*." I desperately wanted one of those watches. On the day of the track meet, the weather was overcast, dark, cold and wet. It had rained earlier that morning and the cinder track was a little loose. My three relay legs and I had a meeting among ourselves to plan our strategy for the upcoming mile relay event. Our strongest competition would come from the one-mile relay teams of Morgan State and Maryland Eastern Shores. Both teams featured excellent lead off legs and they both were from Trinidad, Rivas' home. Rivas told us he had run against both guys throughout his high school career and had always defeated them. We all told Rivas not to be cocky concerning those guys and to get out front and stay there. Copeland was going up against the anchor leg from Morgan State. His name was Ray Pollack and he was as devastating a runner as Copeland was. Copeland said that he wanted to get the baton at the same time that

Pollack did and then he would show, once and for all, who the baddest 400-meter runner was. We then went into one of the beautiful buildings on the campus of the University of Pennsylvania and began to warm-up by jogging through the halls until it was time for our event.

When we stepped onto the track to run, it was a cold, ugly April day. When I looked up into the stands, I was awestruck. I'd never seen that many spectators at a track meet before. The attendance was announced as being nearly 40,000. I'd never run before a crowd this large.

When the gun fired to start the race, Rivas and his two homeboys from Trinidad immediately lead the pack. Going down the back straight away Rivas had a slight lead, but then Rivas slowed somewhat and to my horror I realized that he was toying with his homeboys. It was obvious that Rivas could have easily pulled away from them if he wanted, but instead, he wanted to play with them and at the right moment, he intended to turn on the after burners, pull away in grand style and humiliate them. I was furious. Just as Rivas turned on the speed to make his move, his two homeboys moved up on both sides of him and effectively boxed him in. Rivas fought frantically all the way to the three hundred meter mark, trying to break out of the box and all to no avail. He had used up precious strength and energy and had begun to panic. In a situation like that, when you panic it can do some strange things to your adrenaline. Rigor mortis had started to descend on Rivas; his muscles began to tie up and he ended up ten yards behind his two friends. When Paul took the baton he ran a valiant race, but the distance he had to overcome was just beyond the realm of feasibility. By the time Paul handed off to me, he had cut the leaders edge by three yards. When I reached the 220-meter mark I had caught the two leaders, but the energy I had expended in order to catch them began to take its toll on me. Like Rivas, when I reached the three hundred-meter mark I began to tie up and as I came off of the last turn I could readily see the disappointment on Copeland's face. I was sorry that the mail I was delivering to him was not the mail he was looking for, but at least he was getting a third class delivery...which translated to a third place finish in the race. Needless to say, we were all very disappointed and we wanted to kill Rivas.

I learned a very important lesson that day. We had won big time in South Carolina the week before and we were riding on a crest after our win, but each race in life is full of its own different dynamics. We must assess those differences and make the necessary adjustments to triumph. What won for you yesterday may not be the formula for you to win tomorrow. Each race is different, but you must never forsake your winning attitude.

In my junior year at North Carolina Central I received a letter telling me to report to the 1968 Olympic Trials at Lake Tahoe, Nevada, for tryouts in the 400-meter hurdles event. I was about to realize my second dream and goal to participate in the Olympics. As fate would have it, the next day I received a letter from an uncle I didn't even know I had...His name was Sam and he wanted me to join him for military basic training at Fort Benning, Georgia. I had been DRAFTED!

After completing my two months of basic training I was given a thirty-day leave then sent to Quartermaster School at Fort Lee, Virginia near Petersburg, Virginia. My course was to last two months and I had been there about a month and a half. One Saturday morning as I was coming back on Post, after spending a drunken night partying in Petersburg, I noticed a large crowd at the Post Stadium. I walked over and asked a Colonel what was going on. He explained that the Army was hosting the All Services Track and Field Championships. I asked if I could participate. They Colonel asked what event I was interested in and I told him the 120-yard high hurdles and the 220-yard low hurdles. He then asked if I had any experience and I quickly told him I had a little bit of experience. He cleared me to run, so I went and got my college track uniform and running shoes, which I always kept with my other gear. I also grabbed some aspirin for the throbbing hangover I was nursing.

I won both events very easily and then I found out that the track meet was the trials to qualify the winners to compete in the All Army Nationals that were to take place the next weekend. So, for the next week I trained diligently. My thoughts were: *If I win the Army Nationals, maybe I could represent the US Army in the* 1968 *Olympics and still be able to realize my second goal.* Well, I set new meet records while winning both events in the finals and I talked to a number of military officers in an attempt to represent the Army at the Olympic Trials. "My request had to go through a lot of different channels and while I was waiting for an answer, my 'Uncle Sammy' sent me over here, Geechee, my man, to help you win this war." Geechee looked at me perplexed for a moment, and then we both burst out laughing.

On the morning of April 4, 1968, I was about to climb onto a truck, which was going to take me and my squad out to the landing zone. From there we were going to board a chopper at the "LZ" that was going to fly us to the starting point of our next mission. As I got on the truck I heard a news bulletin on the radio that the guy next to me was listening to: "...This is the Armed Forces radio network, Voice of America. I am sad to report that the Reverend Martin Luther King Jr. has been killed in Memphis, Tennessee. He was gunned down at the Lorraine Motel in Memphis by a lone, white gunman using a high powered rifle..."

I sat there stunned. I couldn't believe what I was hearing. I was on my way back to the jungle to put my life on the line for good old Americana and good old Americana had turned into a jungle and killed the greatest black leader of my generation. "...The Reverends Jesse Jackson and Ralph Abernathy were at his side as he was felled by a single shot..." I was pissed off to the highest point of pisstivity. I looked around into the faces of everyone near me and I saw that all of the white GIs were looking down as if embarrassed, and all of the brothers were looking shocked, hurt and angry. I stood up and shouted, "What have you crackers done?" No one said a word. I reached out and grabbed the first white guy I could get my hands on and I began to pummel him with a maddening fury! Somebody grabbed me and pulled me off of him yelling, "You're killing him, Rock!" Sergeant Vickers ran up and said for everyone to get off the truck. All of us black GIs were told that we were not going on the mission and to turn our weapons in at the arms room. We did, and I later found out that almost every military installation in Vietnam had given their black soldiers the same instructions. Many of the commanding officers were afraid that black GIs would start shooting and killing white GIs *en masse*, which would then create a war within a war. The pain and anger of Dr. King's assassination had caused many black soldiers to become very distrustful of our white counterparts. As a result, black soldiers were very vigilant and committed to protecting each other's backs. Paranoia was rampant among both groups of soldiers. The news reports we received from back in the states made us aware of the riots and the burning that had occurred in many cities throughout America. For three days, all black GIs were confined to their installations until further notice. These trying circumstances started to subside and I began to notice that in working their way through the pain of Dr. King's death, the brothers seemed to exude a strong sense of solidarity towards one another.

A week later, I was back in the bush on patrol. On one particular occasion we had made contact with the enemy and had been involved in a fierce firefight. When the enemy eventually broke contact, we swept the area to ascertain a body count. We only found two bodies, but we also found something else. The Viet Cong had left leaflets scattered all around the area which read:

"GO HOME SOUL BROTHER! THIS IS NOT YOUR WAR. WE ARE BOTH MEN OF COLOR. DONT LET THE WHITE IMPERIALISTS MAKE US FIGHT ONE ANOTHER. GO HOME SOUL BROTHER!"

I was speechless. I looked around at the rest of the squad to judge their reactions and I saw that all of the brothers were looking at me, as if to say; "You know it and I know it...Victor Charlie is right."

After this incident, I began to hear rumors from GIs in other units who said there had been incidences in which only the black GIs had been allowed to escape from ambushes that had been sprung on unsuspecting patrols. I didn't know how true these rumors were, but I did notice that the number of black GIs being exposed to combat situations had indeed increased.

CHAPTER FIVE

Sergeant Walker; an Enigma

In the middle of the month of May, I had just returned from my tenth patrol when Velez came running up to me all excited. "Rock, didn't you tell me you could type?" He asked. I told him, "Yeah, I took typing in high school 'cause I had to take an elective subject to assure that I graduated and the typing class was where all the girls were. But, after I got into the class I liked it and I learned to type. Why'd you ask?"

Velez said, "The guy in the orderly room who has been the company's legal clerk is getting ready to go home for good and we need to find a replacement for him. We now have a new First Sergeant that happens to be Puerto Rican like me, and he told me to look around and see if I could find a good man to fill the position. Are you interested?"

"Hell yeah!" I replied. "I'll do anything to get off patrol duty. What do I have to do?"

"Let me talk to the First Sergeant and I'll let you know what he says," Velez assured me.

Late that night, Velez came by my bunk and told me to report to First Sergeant Rivera in the orderly room the following morning at eight a.m. The Sergeant wanted to discuss the position with me. I was excited at the prospect of being able to get out of patrol duty and being able to perform a duty which I might enjoy.

I reported to Sergeant Rivera at the appointed time as ordered. I wore my best pair of boots, which I had shined for the first time since I had been in 'Nam, and a freshly washed fatigue uniform. Sergeant Rivera was a rather short, stocky man with black hair and a swarthy complexion. His eyes kind of twinkled when he looked at you and I decided right away that I liked him.

"So, you're Coleeemeen. You typeee?" He asked.

"Yes, First Sergeant," I answered.

"Good. Here you study this," he said as he handed me a book. I looked at the book in my hand and saw that it was the Uniform Code of Military Justice...The military's Legal Bible, which contained about 118 articles and covered every type of legal offense common to the military.

"Sit at that desk over there and study," Rivera told me. I did. At noon, Sergeant Rivera told me to go and have lunch and when I finished I was to come back and study some more. I did. At the end of the day, the sergeant told me to leave and report back in the morning at the same time. At chow that evening, Velez came and sat next to me and told me I had gotten the job. He said Sergeant Rivera was satisfied that I was the man for the job. I asked Velez how the sergeant decided on me with such limited interaction. Velez told me that the sergeant was one of several men who had survived an ambush in the Mekong Delta. Rivera had been assigned to a tank unit and they got hit hard. He was one of the few survivors and had been awarded the Silver Star for his bravery. He had been in the military for twenty years and had seen it all and prided himself on being able to read the caliber and character of an individual. Thus, he had made his decision...I was going to be his legal clerk. So, I became the legal clerk for the 629th Supply Unit, a company of six hundred men.

I studied the UCMJ diligently for two weeks and even utilized all of the research materials I could get my hands on in an effort to learn as much as I could about military law. When I felt that I was ready to handle some actual cases, Sergeant Rivera sent me to Troop Command Headquarters in Qui Nhon to see a colonel. The colonel asked me some questions; finger printed me, had me fill out some papers, swore me in under an oath and then told me that I was now working under the auspices of a Secret Clearance. I was given carte blanche to examine any records, documents or other pertinent information which I deemed relevant in the performance of my new job.

The primary responsibilities of my new job were to gather information about charges brought against military personnel and to prosecute military personnel when the charges were substantiated.

Much of the job consisted of investigations, research and filing of charges. I prepared Article 15's (summary punishments imposed by the Company Commander), bad discharges, and court-martials. In a short amount of time, I became very proficient at my job and I took a lot of pride in the expertise I had begun to develop in military law. In many ways my new job was synonymous, in the civilian world, to a paralegal clerk. Of course, the military has its own way of doing things, so the job was more than just paralegal work. On many occasions I stayed in the orderly room all night working on cases. Most of the time when I worked late into the night, Velez was in the orderly room with me working on his multi detailed reports. I especially liked working on complicated cases with the JAG (Judge Advocate General Corps) Officers; they were the lawyers assigned to the cases. Some of the lawyers had started asking for me by name to work on their cases with them. And to my surprise, my case work and all reports were reviewed and acted upon by Colonel Schlosinger, who was now heading up all Troop Command legal matters. I had only seen Colonel Schlosinger briefly when I had first gotten to Qui Nhon the night we got hit, but he sent me a note praising my work and offering words of encouragement.

A month into my work I began to notice something that disturbed me. There appeared to be a disproportionate number of black GIs who had been targeted for some type of legal action. In my company of approximately six hundred men, almost half were black, and of that number more than a third were facing some form of legal punishment.

My old unit, the 157th Reactionary Force/Guard Unit, now had a Military Police (MP) Unit attached to it. When I looked into the matter, I found that all of the MPs appeared to be your everyday garden variety rednecks and good ole' boys. The so-called justice they dispensed seemed questionable at best. I began to think about those leaflets "Victor Charlie" had left in the jungle; the rumors about the brothers caught in ambushes; the fearful reaction of Company Commanders who disarmed black soldiers in the middle of a war when Martin Luther King Jr. was killed; the information we had received that riots had erupted back in the states after King's murder; and now, a large number of black GIs being charged with crimes. I pulled the records of a sample group of seventy-five black GIs who had been charged with crimes to examine the validity of their charges. I discovered that fifty-two of the cases were for minor infractions such as: insubordination; being in an off limits area such as a bar; wearing an earring while in uniform; wearing hair in an afro style and considered too long for regulations; smoking of marijuana; being AWOL for a couple of hours after sneaking off to one of the villages to have sex. But, the most profound charge I found was that a number of soldiers who had been charged with damaging Government property after it was discovered that they had contracted a venereal disease. The Government property in question was the bodies of the soldiers! These somewhat minor infractions and charges were bumped up to the levels of Field Grade Article 15s, court-martials and in some instances dishonorable discharges from the military. The punishments didn't fit the crimes. Some of the fifty-two soldiers in question were making the military a career and were facing the possibility of losing everything they had worked years for. These stupid mistakes made by the black soldiers would not only devastate the soldiers, but their dependent families as well. I was haunted by the fact that in my opinion the punishments didn't fit the crimes.

The twenty-three other cases in my sample were definitely serious offenses. The charges against those black GIs consisted of rape, murder, extortion, assault on military personnel and whole sale distribution of all types of drugs.

There was a prison/stockade facility named LBJ in Vietnam for American soldiers. The initials didn't stand for Lyndon Baines Johnson (past President), but for Long Binh Jail. It was located down south and in most instances if you were given a six month sentence to serve there, you would do your six months, return to a unit to make up the lost six months, and then complete whatever remaining time you had on your original tour of duty. Of course this extended amount of time in Vietnam increased your chances of not making it out alive.

I began to agonize over the dilemma I was privy to. My dilemma was should I try to help the GIs with the less serious charges? Should my decision rest on my legal obligation of upholding the universal military law, or should my moral obligation come first in attempting to uplift and help those GIs who had made mistakes, which were classified as misdemeanors? The probability was that many of the black GIs who had fought proudly and honorably for their country might be stigmatized for life once they returned home, due to the racism exacted upon them by the military system of justice in Vietnam. I remembered hearing someone say that the system of JUSTICE for the black GI in Vietnam was exactly that...JUST US. I began to rationalize by asking myself, *Is it really morally wrong to kill someone? Is the killing in war exempt from moral turpitude, or does a declaration of war justify killing?* The system drafted me, sent me to Vietnam, gave me a gun and told me to go out and kill a man who hadn't done anything to me; I didn't even know him.

After a few days of contemplation, I made my decision. I would do what I could to help those GIs with the less serious misdemeanor charges, regardless of race, creed or color. The GIs who had crossed over the line and were guilty of felonies would have to fend for themselves. *The die is cast*, I thought aloud.

For over a month, I had been making charges disappear against those individuals I could help. I had a couple of older sergeants to come and ask me when they could expect to have to answer certain charges they had pending against them. They were worried because they were career men and had children in college and mortgages and they were facing financial ruin if found guilty of the charges pending. When I told them they didn't have any charges pending, they didn't understand what was going on. I told them I had made the charges nonexistent, but if they divulged to anyone what I had done for them, I would make their charges reappear and they would be prosecuted to the fullest extent of the law. I began helping many of my fellow soldiers by using my position in this manner and to my knowledge no one ever told the wrong people what I was doing. Many of the soldiers were so grateful for what I had done for them, that they began to bring me money, offers and special deals on some hard to get items and even some contraband items. I wouldn't accept any of them. I would, however, accept a bottle of good liquor because it was so hard to come by. I would share it or give it to the boys.

Troop Command assigned a new commanding officer to the 629th. He was a young; baby faced, white captain named George Olson. Captain Olson gave me a court-martial case and told me to prepare it for prosecution. When I sat down at my desk to look over the package, I realized that the guy being given the court-martial was a buddy of mine named Horatio McCallum. McCallum was a dark skinned guy who stood about five feet eight inches tall and bore a striking resemblance to the comedian Jack Benny's sidekick, Rochester. McCallum was a very funny guy and always jovial, so it was difficult for me to believe he had gotten into such a situation. McCallum was being charged with disobeying a lawful order. He had been ordered to go up into one of the guard towers to pull guard duty and he had refused, stating that he was medically exempt from having to perform the duty. Even after numerous threats had been foisted upon him repeatedly, he steadfastly refused to do as ordered. I realized that if he were found guilty at his upcoming court-martial, he would be facing at least six months at LBJ. I went and found McCallum at his regular work station and asked him what the heck had transpired to get him into this kind of trouble. McCallum unbuckled his pants and let them drop to the floor. He then showed me a seven-inch scar on the front of his right thigh, which extended from near his groin towards his knee. He said that when he was a teenager back in Harlem, New York, he and some friends robbed a store and a policeman had shot him in his thigh. As a result of the shooting, he had to have a plastic tube implanted in his thigh. The implant never bothered him, but recently his leg had begun to bother him so he went to see the doctors at the 67th Med Evac Hospital. The doctors gave him a complete medical exam and determined that the rigors of Vietnam had aggravated his medical condition and he was given a permanent profile which exempted him from performing any duties which required prolonged running, jumping, stooping or climbing and no heavy lifting. McCallum had given his profile to the commanding officer that Captain Olson had replaced, yet there was no record of the profile having ever been received. I readied McCallum's court-martial papers as instructed. I next went to the 67th Med Evac and talked with the doctors and got a duplicate of the profile. The day before McCallum was to be transported to Qui Nhon for his summary court-martial; I sat down and explained to him how to present himself before the court and how to present his reasons not obeying the order he had been given. I gave him the duplicate copy of the profile to show the judge at his court-martial. I told him not to worry about anything and that he would be found innocent of the charges because he was legally exempt from having to perform the duties in question. The next morning I took McCallum to the orderly room to report in and be transported to Troop Command Headquarters for his day in court. Waiting to transport him were two MP Staff Sergeants from my old unit, the 157th. They both stood about six foot, three inches tall and each of them weighed about 230 pounds. Both were rednecks to the core. I gave McCallum some words of encouragement and then I left him as I made my way to the chow hall for some breakfast.

I got my food and joined Talley, Bird and Velez as they ate. We were discussing McCallum's pending court-martial, when a white guy named Ricks ran up to us all excited and said, "Rock, you better get over to the orderly room quick!"

"What's wrong?" I asked in a concerned voice.

"Man, those MPs are beating up on your boy McCallum!" We all jumped up and sprinted towards the orderly room. When I rushed upon the scene I couldn't believe what I was seeing. McCallum was on the ground flat on his back and one of the MPs was sitting astride his body with both hands intertwined in his jacket collar, and was slamming McCallum's head viciously on the ground. The other MP had grasped one of McCallum's legs and was jerking and dragging him along the ground. I grabbed the sergeant that was slamming McCallum's head into the ground and pulled him off of McCallum. No one standing around bothered to help me. I then pulled McCallum up off of the ground. He was sweating, crying, cursing and bleeding from superficial cuts he had sustained. I pushed McCallum towards Talley and told Talley to calm him down. Then I turned towards the nearest MP and asked, "What the hell do you think you're doing?"

He stammered, "We were trying to get him into the jeep to transport him, but he refused to get in and tried to run away, so we had to subdue him."

"Those assholes are lying Rock!" McCall screamed aloud, as he continued to curse the MPs and call them every vile name he could think of.

When I looked over at McCallum, I noticed for the first time that he had been handcuffed with his hands behind his back throughout the beating. I told McCallum to calm down and to go on to his court martial and when he returned later we were going to bring the two MPs up on charges of assault.

With the help of my boys we calmed McCallum down sufficiently enough to get him into the jeep and on his way. As I turned to walk off, a tall, ruddy-faced, new lieutenant I had never seen before said, "Corporal Coleman, I'd like to have a word with you." I was angry as hell and even angrier when I realized that the new lieutenant had been standing there watching while McCallum was being assaulted and didn't intercede. I committed an unthinking and dangerous error as I turned to the lieutenant and said, "Man, get outta my face; you ain't got nothing to talk to me about." I then turned and walked away leaving the lieutenant dumfounded.

Later, that same day while anxiously awaiting McCallum's return, I was approached by a GI I didn't know and he said to me, "Rock, Sergeant Major Walker wants you to report to his hootch at seven o'clock p.m. sharp."

"What does he want to see me about?" I asked the GI.

"I have no idea what it's about; he just told me to be sure that you got the message."

After the guy left, I was perplexed as hell trying to figure out what the sergeant major wanted with me. Sergeant Major Walker was a brother with a café au lait complexion, six feet four inches tall, in his early fifties, sported a bald head and was built like Hercules. He was the highest ranking NCO (Non-commissioned Officer) I had seen since I'd been in 'Nam. He always wore a crisply starched, fatigue uniform and airborne jump boots which were always spit shined to a high gloss. Nobody seemed to know exactly what Sergeant Major Walker's job was. He didn't talk much, was a loner and you usually saw him just walking around the company area kind of observing things. It was rumored that he was a high ranking CID Officer. In any case, I had the distinct impression that Sergeant Major Walker was not a man to be messed with and I had no idea what in the hell he wanted to see me about.

I reported to his hootch at the appointed time and knocked on the door. I was apprehensive as I waited for a response and also concerned because McCallum had not returned from his court-martial. Maybe his court proceedings had been lengthy and he had to stay overnight in Qui Nhon and would return in the morning.

"Enter!" Sergeant Major Walker bellowed.

"Corporal Coleman reports as ordered Sergeant Major," I said.

"Sit down soldier," the sergeant major ordered.

The flickering light supplied by five large burning candles illuminated the small hootch. Sergeant Walker was sitting in a wooden chair, which was tilted back on its two hind legs. He had his jump booted feet crossed at the ankles and perched upon a small wooden table that separated us. When I sat down he asked me, "Do you drink liquor?"

"Yes, Sergeant Major," I replied. He then reached down near his chair and produced two bottles of Johnnie Walker Scotch, one red and one black. He slammed both bottles down on the table, then produced two canteen cups and told me to pour myself a drink. I poured a small amount into my canteen cup. Sergeant Walker then looked me in the eye and in a very stern voice he stated, "You said that you drink liquor. Now, I want to see you pour a serious drink of liquor."

I was more than happy to oblige the Sergeant Major. We worked our way through three fourths of the first bottle while discussing women, sex and politics...and then politics, sex and women. I found the sergeant major to be a very learned man who had been around the world and could intelligently discuss almost any subject. He was very wise. Suddenly, he changed subjects and said, "That was some dumb and sophomoric bull crap you pulled today!"

"What are you talking about?" I asked completely confused. Sergeant Walker responded. "The disrespect you showed that lieutenant today. That's what I'm talking about. You very easily could have been brought up on charges for disrespecting an officer. What you did was inexcusable!"

I couldn't understand why he was so upset about my actions. I knew what he was saying was exactly right and I knew that I was lucky to have gotten away with it. But, I told Sergeant Walker, I had been angry with the lieutenant for idly standing by and allowing those MPs to brutally attack a defenseless, handcuffed man.

"Bull!" Sergeant Walker bellowed. "Don't you understand that you can't afford to draw attention to yourself? Look, you might think that you have all the non-commissioned and commissioned officers around here fooled, but not me. I know what you're doing and how you're doing it.

"Sergeant Major, what are you talking about?" I inquired uneasily.

Sergeant Walker elaborated, "I know all about you protecting some of the soldiers around here from court-martials, Article 15s, and other bogus and biased and trumped up charges. I know everything you're doing. You have chosen wisely as to the ones you should help. You have learned your craft well, which allows you to handle these matters discreetly and not leave a paper trail that leads back to you. Many of the men who need your help or will need your help have found a purpose in their lives since coming into the military. When they return home they just might be able to contribute something meaningful to their families, their communities or to society as a whole. But, if they are kicked out of the service with a dishonorable discharge or some other black mark on their record, they might be ruined for life and never able to pick themselves up to get back into the race. Many of these men have also performed above and beyond the call of duty that their country has asked of them in this stinking, god-forsaken war. I have fought in World War II, Korea, and now Vietnam and I have seen what war can do to a person. I have seen young men perform outstanding and heroic feats on the battlefield in defense of their country and go home to die in shame and poverty because of a careless, unthinking act of youthful stupidity, such as your actions earlier today with the lieutenant. Whether you know it or not young man, you have a mission to even the playing field and get these men home–the ones you can help."

Astonished at how much Sergeant Walker knew about me I asked him, "What did I miss in covering my tracks that allowed you to find out what I was doing?"

Sergeant Walker explained, "You didn't miss anything. I've been around the world three times and I've seen everything in it five times. I watch, I look, I listen, and I learn. I saw what you were doing in my mind's eye. Then I started watching what you were doing. Listen son, as you continue to do what you're doing, it's very important that you remain vigilant in making sure that you cover your tracks. If any higher ups discover what you are doing, you will truly regret the day you were born and you will pay one hell of a price to the piper. You cannot afford to draw attention to yourself by disrespecting superior officers or any other such nonsense. You've got to move, think, and act above the crowd."

"It seems that what I am doing is almost as important to you as it is to me. Why are you so concerned that I succeed in my mission?" I asked.

"That's none of your business." Sergeant Walker stated solemnly. I looked him straight in the eye and asked him, "Sergeant Walker, who are you and what are you?"

"That's none of your business either." He again stated solemnly. He continued, "I will tell you this I will be leaving Vietnam in three months to go home. During those three months, I want you to keep doing what you're doing, remember the things I have told you and always be cautious and stay above the fray. When you leave out of here tonight, I will never speak to you again or even acknowledge your presence. I won't know you and you won't know me. But, I will be watching you from afar and covering your back. As long as you walk this mission as I have told you to, no harm will come to you and I will be protecting you from the shadows. But, once I leave, you will have no one to depend on except your own understanding. Understood?"

I had met a lot of people in my life, but never a Sergeant Major Walker. I was convinced of the man's sincerity. And underneath his gruff exterior, I knew in my heart of hearts that I could trust him. I wondered to myself, *why did he come into my life at this particular time and did it have anything to do with the meaningful coincidences in our lives that help us to understand that we are a part of something greater than ourselves, which Talley had told me about?* "Yes. Sergeant Major, I understand." I replied.

The next day I almost went ballistic when I found out why McCallum hadn't returned. McCallum had been sentenced to six months of hard labor and sent to LBJ. The judge hearing his case had dismissed the charge of disobeying a lawful order when McCallum produced the medical evidence exempting him from the duty. But, the two MPs who had transported him were fearful that McCallum would surely bring them up on assault charges, so they implored the judge to hear some other relevant testimony. They told the judge how dangerous a person McCallum was and how he had attacked them in an attempt to escape. He was further accused of cursing the MPs and making threats on their lives. The racist judge took the information under advisement and right there on the spot found McCallum guilty of assault, terroristic threats, and disrespect on non-commissioned officers. The charges stood, and within a matter of hours McCallum was sent on a military flight to LBJ to begin serving his time.

I was furious, but then I thought about Sergeant Major Walker's words and I realized that I would have to fly under the radar screen on this one. I began to use every legal tool, contact, and resource at my disposal. McCallum had been abused by a "kangaroo court." He had presented himself before the court to answer his original charge and was prepared to successfully defend against the said charge and was found innocent. The tactic of introducing new charges put him in a position where he had to defend himself against charges which hadn't been properly filed or received due process. The whole procedure was illegal and was a miscarriage of justice. I fought with everything I had; two weeks later I was able to assist in McCallum's release from LBJ and his return to our unit.

Upon McCallum's return, all of the gang gathered around him yelling and jubilantly celebrating his safe return. I informed McCallum that I had filed charges against the two MPs that had assaulted him and the charges were pending. We all then went to the flat lands to continue celebrating. McCallum later pulled me aside and, with tears in his eyes thanked me profusely for everything I had done for him. He even said that he would name his first born child Rock, in deference to me. I told him the child would surely have a hard row to hoe if it was a girl!

At eleven o'clock, I left the party at the flat lands and went to my bunk. I was restless and a bit agitated. I thought about what could have happened to McCallum had I not helped him. I thought about the other fifty or so GIs I had helped. I thought about the meaning of Reverend King's death and the long tentacle of racism which seemed to stretch from the US of A all the way across the span of 14,000 miles to touch the war torn country of Vietnam. I needed to get some of these things off of my chest, so I began writing a letter to John H. Johnson, the publisher of the largest black magazine in America, *Ebony* magazine. I decided to write Mr. Johnson because he had always impressed me as being a man of integrity and fairness, and was willing to publish the truth. In my personal letter to Mr. Johnson I told him about the racism and bigotry that I had witnessed in Vietnam, perpetrated by many white officers and soldiers. I talked about the racist terms which, these same GIs used when referring to the Vietnamese people by calling them "slopes" and "gooks;" names just as derogatory as the word "nigger." I addressed the disproportionate numbers of black GIs, compared to white GIs, which were being put into combat situations and the disproportionate numbers of black GIs that were being court-martialed and railroaded off to prison in Vietnam. I wrote until I had gotten all of the anger and angst out of my system. I then asked Mr. Johnson if he would use his political influence to get a Congressional Investigative Committee to look into the allegations I was making him aware of. Because of the fact that I had been specific about locations, units, and incidences in my letter, I was hesitant about signing my name to the correspondence. Finally, I said to myself, *The hell with it! If I'm bold enough to say it, I should be bold enough to sign it.* So I did.

CHAPTER SIX

Illegally Legal

A month later, I was having a very esoteric conversation with a guy I had grown to have a lot of respect for. His name was Jesse Frazier. Jesse was built like the boxer Joe Frazier. He was about the same complexion and he possessed great, quick, winning smile. He always had a positive attitude no matter how adverse circumstances and situations were around him. He didn't drink, smoke, or visit the brothels of the working girls of Vietnam. He spent a lot of time writing to his girlfriend, also named Jessie, and reading his Bible. Jesse was from Kansas City, Missouri, and he was a surprisingly regular kind of guy. Jesse made it clear to everyone that he planned to get out of Vietnam alive and in one piece, because he put God first in everything in his life. Needless to say, he was a very spiritually grounded individual and he practiced what he preached.

I was intrigued by Jesse's knowledge of the Bible and his level of faith. He was truly a believer. I explained to him that I believed in a supreme power I called God but that I had my doubts about of a lot of things. Jesse told me that was a normal reaction for people who had not come into the many truths of religion. Then, Jesse said something that was confounding to me, but I would never forget it. He said, "Rock, you are a deep thinker and you like to help people. Evidently the Lord has something that he wants you to do. One day there will come a time when he will let you know exactly what it is you are to do. And when it happens, you'll know that you know." To break the tension of the moment I joked, "Man, you and Talley need to have a dialectical conversation. Has he ever talked to you about his theories on synchronicity?" Before Jesse could answer I looked toward the door as two people walked in. One of the figures in the doorway announced, "Hey Rock, this guy's looking for you." Suddenly I realized it was Punchy! I ran over to him and we grabbed each other in a bear hug.

"How in the hell did you find me? How did you get here? How long are you going to be here?" I asked in a string of questions.

"Whoa, hold on man, you're going too fast!" Punchy exclaimed. "My commander gave me three days off, so I decided to come and try to find you. I checked with the people at Troop Command Headquarters and they told me what unit you were with. Once I got the basic information, everything else was easy. I got on Highway One and started hitching rides and here I am."

I hadn't seen Punchy since we first arrived in Vietnam. I introduced him to Jesse and a couple of other people that were in the area at the time. I then anxiously asked him, "Where are Dino and Cedric? Have you seen them?"

"Naw Rock, I haven't seen them. We stayed together at Bien Hoa for about a week after you were shipped out and that was the last time I saw them."

"Well, I hope they're both doing OK. I've heard that Dong Ha is just a few klicks from the DMZ (Demilitarized Zone) and things are hot and heavy up there and that's where Dino was going. Ban Me Thuot, Cedric's destination has a lot of enemy activity going on there, but not as bad as Dong Ha."

I took Punchy around the base camp with me and introduced him to everyone I thought he needed to meet. Later when we had finished eating chow, we retreated to the flat lands for a party in Punchy's honor. The next day some of the boys and I took Punchy to Mai Lin's Bar for libations and more partying in Punchy's honor. At one point I was having a conversation with Mai Lin and she told me something rather disturbing.

She said to me, "Rock, this village is the birthplace of the sworn enemy of my people here in South Vietnam and he is also your enemy."

"Who are you talking about?" I inquired.

Without batting an eyelash she said, "Ho Chi Minh."

I looked at her in disbelief as I said, "You're telling me that the communist leader that controls North Vietnam was born in this village. I don't believe you."

Mai Lin then handed me an old history book written in English and French, which chronicled the life of Ho Chi Minh. I read with rapt attention as I discovered that Ho Chi Minh was born about 1890. Ho had gone to Europe in 1917 as a ship's cook and while abroad he became a staunch communist, seeing in Marxism a philosophy that offered hope against colonialism. He then joined the French Communist Party and traveled throughout Europe and studied, but later spent most of his time in the Soviet Union living his life as a political exile.

He returned to Vietnam in 1941, but then fled to southern China when the Japanese invaded. His birth name was Nguyen Ai Quoc but in China he adopted the name which he made famous: Ho Chi Minh, "He Who Enlightens." He led guerillas against the Japanese and occupied Hanoi when they surrendered in 1945; fought a guerilla war against the French until he defeated them in 1954; directed a new guerilla war in the South from 1959; and finally took on the US military machine. His goal was to one day unify all of Vietnam and come home to claim the village of his birth in the Central Highlands...Phu Tai!

The information I read gave a glimpse of just how ruthless and mercenary Ho Chi Minh was. This information partly explained why the Viet Cong and the North Vietnamese Army were such formidable opponents for American soldiers and our allies. The information Mai Lin had shared with me was very enlightening.

Two days later, I watched sadly as my buddy Punchy packed up his gear and left my base camp and headed back to his unit two mountains away. We promised to stay in touch with each other. I noticed that most of my friends regretted that Punchy had to leave. Punchy had made a lot of friends in a short time, but that's the kind of guy he was.

For the next three days, I had been experiencing a sense of foreboding. At first I thought it had something to do with seeing Punchy and being reminded of home, but that wasn't what was bothering me. I started having the "weird feelings" like I had before, but I couldn't figure out what was nagging at me. I then began to feel like I was receiving a warning that something bad was coming...like something was riding on the wind. I withdrew from my friends and stayed close to the compound as I tried to work my way through whatever it was that had me uptight. Around eleven o'clock one night, I decided to take a walk around the perimeter of the compound. I felt that the two-mile stroll in the night air would maybe clear my head and lighten my mood. At the conclusion of my trek I felt a little better, but the "weird feelings" hadn't passed. On the third night of my walking ritual I had walked maybe a quarter of a mile when I sensed something behind me. When I turned abruptly and looked behind me I saw a figure move quickly into the shadows of the jungle foliage. I didn't know what it was that I had seen, but I continued walking as if I hadn't seen the telltale movement. As I walked, I adjusted my eyesight utilizing the night vision techniques I had learned on my jungle patrols and watched for the shadowy figure to reappear! *There! I saw it,* I thought to myself. I had clearly seen the shadowy figure of a man tracking me and aiming a rifle at my back! I moved deftly into the jungle foliage and waited for whoever it was that was stalking me. Then I saw him! Less than two yards from my hiding place I saw a white soldier with green camouflage paint on his face and an M-16 rifle in his hands. His eyes were scanning the night trying to determine where I had gone. I was unarmed, but my decision was made. I jumped out of the darkness from my adversary's rear, slashing my right forearm around and across his windpipe, choking off his oxygen, my left hand flashing around the left side of his body to grasp his rifle. I then tightened both holds that I had on him and kicked both my feet out behind me, making my body prone in the air and forcing his head and neck forward. We both hit the ground with me still in the prone position and the GI on his back with my arm still across his throat and his head locked forward. While he was disorientated and fighting for air, I spun around in front of him and snatched the rifle from his hand. Once I had possession of the rifle I threw it across his neck and continued to choke him with it as I yelled into his face, "Why are you following me! Why in the hell are you following me?"

His eyes were bulging and filled with fear. Suddenly, a jeep roared up, seemingly out of nowhere, with its bright headlights bathing us both in its glare. In a matter of seconds two men had run up to me and put .45 caliber pistols to my head, yelling at me to release my opponent now! As I looked up at the two men, I realized that they both wore MP patches on their shoulders and another thing I realized was that these were the same two MPs who had assaulted McCallum!

The MPs made me stand up and threw me into the back of their jeep along with the injured GI and drove quickly to my company orderly room. With their pistols still pointed at me, they escorted me into the orderly room and told the duty officer to send for my Company Commander and First Sergeant immediately. When my CO arrived the MPs began explaining to him that I had been apprehended while trying to sneak out of the compound through an opening in the perimeter wire.

My CO asked, "For what purpose?"

"Sir, many of the men sneak off to the villages down the road to frequent the prostitutes and to buy illicit drugs and black market contraband. And we have reason to believe that's where Coleman was headed," stated one of the MPs. Then the GI who had been following me spoke up; "Sir, I observed this man from my guard tower as he attempted to climb over the perimeter wire near my tower. I felt it was my duty to stop him before he breached the secured perimeter area. When I tried to stop him he put up a struggle."

"He's lying!" I yelled as I ran across the room and grabbed him in the collar and snatched him up from the chair he was sitting in. One of the MPs grabbed me and my CO shouted, "Coleman! Stand at ease!" When I heard his command I stopped, gathered myself and returned to my seat. For the first time I looked at the GIs nametag and saw that his name was Van Walde.

I sat there listening to Van Walde as he continued to tell lies about my activities. I heard a roaring sound from inside my head, which blotted out all semblances of reasoning and in a blind fury I swung a fist which caught Van Walde on the side of his head and sent him sprawling to the floor. When he hit the floor I began to stomp and kick him. Immediately the First Sergeant grabbed me and shouted, "Coleman! I'm giving you a lawful order to cease and desist!" The cease and desist order was not one to be taken lightly, so I complied as ordered. But as the First Sergeant pulled me away I stated in a deadly serious voice to Van Walde, "Motherfucker, you pointed a loaded weapon at me, but you didn't get to pull the trigger." The thought flashed through my mind that I had survived the enemy pointing guns and trying to kill me for months while on patrols and here's a guy wearing the same uniform as me trying to accomplish what the enemy couldn't do; kill me..."I'm going to kill you motherfucker, if it's the last thing I do!"

A hush fell over the room. Then, my CO told the MPs that he would handle the situation and dismissed them and Van Walde. When they had departed the CO said to me, "I believe you're telling the truth. Go cool off and get some sleep. You're dismissed."

I went to bed, but I couldn't sleep. I tossed and turned most of the night trying to make some sense out of the madness I had experienced at the hands of Mr. Van Walde and company. I tried to figure out why he had been stalking me in the first place. I had never seen Van Walde before so I ruled out the idea that maybe he had a personal vendetta against me. Perhaps the same two MPs that attacked McCallum were trying to retaliate against me for filing the charges against them. How did the MPs know to show up at such an isolated area of the perimeter when I jumped Van Walde? I came to the conclusion that I had been set-up for something and maybe Van Walde was being used as a hit man to take me out. But, things went wrong for them when I went on the offensive. The idea of Van Walde being a hit man was not too far-fetched. I had heard of instances where officers who were hated by their men had been "fragged." "Fragging" usually took place when the officer sat down in the latrine to take care of his personal business and someone would roll a live grenade underneath his toilet seat, blowing the officer into another dimension. I didn't feel that they knew anything about what I was doing to help GIs with their legal problems, because they could solve that concern by simply removing me from the position. A lot of questions continued to occupy my mind.

The following day, the First Sergeant and the CO discussed with me the activities of the previous evening. They told me to forget about it 'cause it would all probably blow over.

The next day we received a new clerk in the orderly room. He would be assisting and learning the duties which Velez performed, because Velez was getting "short." Getting short for Velez meant that he had less than thirty days before he would be going home to a life of civilian existence. The new guy's name was Harry Preston from Pennsylvania. He was a corporal like me, average height and build, white and rather clean cut. Something about his clean-cut visage bothered me and I started getting that "weird feeling" again. By the third day I realized that Harry had begun to get under my skin by asking me a lot of personal questions and going out of his way trying to be my friend. I decided to make the thirty-mile trip to Troop Command to satisfy my curiosity. At Troop Command I used the authority of my secret clearance to take a look into Harry's personal records. What I found blew me away! Harry Preston really was from Pennsylvania and had graduated from Valley Forge Military Academy as a Second Lieutenant! He was presently a First Lieutenant and his military job specialty was intelligence. Harry Preston was a CID Undercover Operative, a commissioned officer, and masquerading as a lowly corporal. I presumed that I was who he was interested in. But why?

On the way back to my base camp I thought about the words of wisdom Sergeant Walker had given me. I also thought about the fact that Sergeant Walker had left a few weeks earlier to go home and enjoy his retirement from the military. Something was closing in on me. What was it and why?

When I got back to the orderly room and sat down at my desk, Harry looked over at me and asked, "Where you been, Rock?"

I looked him straight in the eyes and stated, "I've been checking on a guy from Pennsylvania, who grew up, at 423 Maple Street; had a mother named Mary Preston; the guy graduated from Valley Forge Military Academy; and is a First Lieutenant working for CID. I suggest that you go and tell your superiors to send somebody else for the assignment 'cause your cover's blown."

Harry looked at me with a stunned expression on his face. He then reached down and cleaned out his desk and packed his belongings. He stood up and looked at me with vengeance in his eyes, turned, and walked out the door exiting the compound. I never saw him again.

The next morning at mail call, I received a letter from a girl named Sandi McFallen. Sandi lived in Philadelphia, Pennsylvania and I had met her in Greensboro, North Carolina, where she attended Bennett College. Sandi was very much involved in the Black Power Movement and in her letter to me she said, "Right on brother. I'm glad to see that there are still some brothers who are committed to making the truth be heard. I just got the enclosed information and thought you would want a copy of it. Stay strong brother! Sandi." When I saw what the enclosure was my heart stopped! Sandi had sent me a copy of the letter I had sent to John H. Johnson, Editor and Publisher of *Ebony* Magazine. Johnson had published my letter in the latest issue of *Ebony* in a section entitled Letters "To The Editor." I was in a near panic state as certain realizations hit me. I quickly decided that I would go to the nearest PX, which was in Qui Nhon, and buy up all of the latest issues of *Ebony* before too many people found out about the article. When I got to the PX, I was in for another shock. The shelves were stocked with more *Ebony* magazines than I had ever seen since arriving in Vietnam. And to make matters worse, I didn't have enough money to purchase the vast amount of *Ebony's* I saw.

The latest edition of *Ebony* had eight black men on the cover and each wore a military uniform depicting war in which black soldiers had fought: The Spanish-American War, The Revolutionary War, The War of 1812, The Civil War, World Wars I and II, Korea, and Vietnam. The publication was an August 1968 Special Edition of *Ebony* magazine dedicated to: The Black Soldier. A profound thought hit me *My ass is grass and the lawnmower is on its way.*

I went back to my compound and entered the orderly room and sat down at my desk. While sitting there I began to analyze my predicament. The letter I had written contained information which could haunt me. I had divulged information such as my unit, location, names, dates and other pertinent information, which could be used against me. My musings were interrupted when an MP Captain entered the orderly room accompanied by the two MP Sergeants from the other night. They strode purposefully to my

CO's office and entered. A few minutes later, they exited just as purposefully as they had entered.

A couple of minutes later, the CO motioned for me to come into his office. When I entered he handed me some papers and said, "Here. Look these over. Hell, you do them every day." When I looked at the papers I saw that they were court-martial papers addressed to me. I was going to be tried by a Special Court-Martial. This was serious! I knew that there were three types of court-martials: Summary, Special, and General. McCallum had only received a Summary Court-Martial and a General Court-Martial could send an individual before a firing squad. And I was getting one somewhere in-between. My charge sheet stated; On September 25, 1968, you did communicate to Corporal R. Van Walde, "I will kill you motherfucker or words to that effect." In essence, I was being charged with communicating a threat to kill someone.

The CO said, "The captain that came in here was the CO of the MP unit and he told me that your threat devastated Van Walde so badly that he had a nervous breakdown. He took your threat very seriously and he has been evacuated to a hospital in Japan that specializes in psychological disorders. I've confirmed this information as being true by checking with Troop Command. The MP Captain is alleging that you have damaged governmental property (Van Walde) by your irresponsible actions. Coleman, I'm required by law to relieve you of your duties until your court-martial has been adjudicated one way or the other. Do you understand?"

"Yes Sir. I understand." I answered.

"You will be allowed to use the free time to prepare for your court-martial, which is scheduled to take place here on October fifteenth at eight thirty a.m. If I can help you in any way let me know. You're dismissed."

"Thank you, Sir." I replied and I walked out.

I told the boys what was going on; they all offered encouragement and to help me anyway they could. Even some of the older sergeants I had helped with their legal problems quietly told me to let them know if they could help me with anything. The word spread like a wild fire and even white GIs made their support known to me. One night I was walking around the perimeter in deep thought, analyzing the reasons for my predicament and thinking what to do about the situation I was in. "Sergeant Walker, where are you now when I 'sho nuff need you?" I asked aloud. I walked along watching a beautiful moonlit night sky filled with twinkling stars and smoking a joint. As the cannabis sativa began to expand my consciousness, everything associated with my dilemma started to become clear. It was as if I were experiencing a vision of true understanding. I was then able to assemble the pieces of my perplexing puzzle. There were people in high places that knew I was doing something to help many of the soldiers with their legal problems, but they couldn't find a paper trail or evidence directly linking me to any improprieties. Then, they had become aware of my letter which had been published in *Ebony* and feared the possibility of a Congressional inquiry. So they decided to promise the world to Van Walde and use him as a pawn to put a bullet in my back. But that plan failed. Whether it was true or not about Van Walde having a breakdown, it gave the higher ups a clean and tidy way to dispose of me. By finding me guilty in a Special Court-Martial they could ship me out to a prison in Vietnam, separating me from people who knew me, and I would mysteriously disappear somewhere along the way during hostile enemy activity. Very neat, clean and sanitary...end of problem.

Now that I had determined the type of battlefield I'd have to fight on and who the enemy was, I had to determine which weapons I would need to select from the arsenal of life and wisdom in order to successfully engage the enemy and win.

I decided that I would defend myself at my court-martial. I had determined that I couldn't afford to trust anyone and that I trusted myself more than I could possibly trust a military officer supplied to me by the same Army that had set me up. I began doing the research, which I knew would be necessary for my defense at trial and I began to assemble and interview my potential character witnesses. I had concluded that my defense would be based on an aggressive response to an acute traumatic episodic stimulus or in laymen's terms...temporary insanity. In my testimony I planned to show the court that Van Walde lied to my CO in the orderly room about my actions in an effort to hide the fact that he was trying to shoot me; when I realized the reason for his lies, my mind had flashed back to when I was on patrols and the enemy pointed and fired weapons at me with the intent to kill me. The thoughts attributed to the enemy trying to kill me versus Van Walde trying to kill me became one and the same. When the full import of Van Walde's actions hit me, the accompanying trauma caused me to lose control. My faculties, which govern my rational thinking and actions, were not functioning. I knew that my defensive strategy was very weak, but the hand had been dealt and I would have to play the cards I was holding. On the night before my court-martial I said a prayer and asked God to guide my steps when I walked before the judge the next day.

When I reported for my court-martial, I quickly realized that the judge assigned was a "full bird" Colonel named Woodruff. He was a white haired, grandfatherly looking gentleman and exuded an air of nobility. The attorney for the prosecution was Major Tom Irving; a shrewd, nattily attired officer who appeared to be very efficient and competent.

The proceedings of my court-martial began with the reading of the charges being brought against me. After the charges were read aloud before the court, I was presented with the original charge sheet for my records. Suddenly a silent voice screamed at me, "ERROR!" My mind's eye confirmed the error. I held myself in check as I prayed that no one had observed what I had glimpsed.

The first witness that the prosecution called was one of the two MP Sergeants. He testified before the court, under oath, by further embellishing the lies he had told to my CO on the night of the confrontation. I squirmed in my seat as I listened to the sergeant weave his tale of untruths sprinkled with liberal doses of innuendoes in an attempt to assassinate my character. When he completed his testimony I began to cross-examine him by asking, "Sergeant, how were you able to arrive at the scene of the altercation so rapidly?"

His response was, "We were patrolling the area and saw you jump out of the darkness and began attacking Corporal Van Walde."

I continued my line of questioning relative to the sergeant's response to my first question, and when I was satisfied that I had laid some ground work for potential damage, I concluded my cross examination of him.

The second MP Sergeant was brought into the court and he began to testify echoing the same rehearsed lies as his counterpart that had preceded him. The prosecutor concluded his line of questioning. Under cross examination, I asked him the same question that I had asked the first MP and his response was, "We were patrolling a different sector of the perimeter and we received a radio message telling us to check out a disturbance at the location where we found you attacking Corporal Van Walde."

"So, Sergeant, you're saying that you did not just happen to pass by the area and see me attacking Corporal Van Walde?" I asked.

"No. I told you we received a radio call." He replied in an irritated tone. The prosecutor tried to cut off the sergeant's response to the question by objecting, but the damage had been done.

The judge then wanted to hear the testimony of Corporal Van Walde. The prosecutor spoke up and told the judge that Van Walde had a nervous breakdown, which necessitated him being sent to a psychiatric facility in Japan. While in Japan he had been given a medical discharge from the US Army and sent home.

In an effort to attest to my character and creditability I paraded a host of witnesses before the judge. Talley, Bird, Velez and Epstein were my primary witnesses followed by some of the guys I had been on patrols with. My closing character witnesses were Sergeant Vickers and Colonel Schlosinger who both gave me glowing accolades as a very dependable and capable individual and very high marks as an outstanding soldier.

I began to get a little nervous because, so far, no one had yet discerned that an "ERROR" had occurred and my thoughts were, *Will they realize in time what has happened?* I was sworn in before the court and subjected to a brutal cross examination by the prosecutor. I utilized every tool I possessed to maintain my cool against the prosecutor's onslaught. When it was finally over I felt relieved and comforted in the knowledge that I hadn't committed any faux pas which could be used against me.

It was now time for me to present my defense before the court. Another thought flashed through my mind, *I'm about to make or break my case and it all depends on me. If I can't impress the court with my brilliance, then I had better dazzle them with 'BS'. But, no matter what happens...don't let them discover the ERROR!*

I presented the court with a forty-five minute diatribe of everything, which took place when I first saw Van Walde on the night in question. I then put the burden of proof on the court by showing that Van Walde had put me in a posture of self-defense, or the essence of fight or flight. The element of fear, which he evoked, propelled me into a reactionary state of mind, which was synonymous with my combat training.

Judge Woodruff peered at me with a perplexed look on his face and then called for a recess for one hour. I left the court and when I got outside I was immediately surrounded by many of my partners who wanted to know how things were going inside. I sat for a while smoking and talking with the guys. Then Talley suggested that we go and have lunch. After we had finished eating we walked around talking for a while. Talley pulled me aside and asked confidentially, "Rock, do you feel like you have a chance of a possible acquittal?"

I replied, "Man, I don't really know. But I'll tell you this, at the beginning of my trial I saw an error occur in the proceedings, and so far it seems as if nobody else saw it. It was the kind of error that can get me out of this mess if it's not discovered before my trial is over."

"Hell man, what was it!" Talley exclaimed.

I answered, "The judge forgot to..."

Suddenly, a court officer was frantically motioning for the other respondents and me to return to the hearing because the judge was about to re-enter the court, so I left Talley standing there.

When I entered the judge had me to stand before the court. "Corporal Coleman I have given my decision careful deliberation and I have reached a verdict. First, let me say I fully understand the reasons you have given the court as to why you found it necessary to physically engage Corporal Van Walde, but it is a fact that you did communicate to Corporal Van Walde a threat to kill him and you did in fact assault said individual therefore, I find you guilty as charged. Your sentence shall be a reduction in rank two grades to the equivalent of Private E-2; forfeiture of two-thirds of your base pay for the duration of six months; and you are to be confined to jail for six months at hard labor at the Long Binh Jail in the Republic of South Vietnam. When you are released from jail you are expected to make up your six months of jail time here in Vietnam plus serve the remaining two and a half months remaining on your original tour of duty, at which time, you are to be evaluated for the possibility of a dishonorable discharge. Your sentence is to be carried out in three days from today. Court dismissed."

For the next three days people kept coming up to me offering words of encouragement. Some were even shocked to have learned that I had been found guilty. I appreciated the concern shown by my comrades, but it didn't change the fact that I was facing time in jail. I wrote letters to friends back in the states telling them of my dilemma and I began the process of putting all of my personal business in order.

The day before my departure to LBJ a white guy I didn't know approached me and asked if he could have a few words with me. I asked him what did he want to talk to me about and he said, "Your brother."

"What about my brother?" I inquired.

He said, "Coleman, I work in an office at Troop Command and I handle all of this areas communications...Telex's, short wave radio and field telephone communications. For the last week and a half I've been receiving a communications hook-up from an Air Force installation at Cam Ran Bay, South Vietnam."

"Where's Cam Ran Bay?" I asked.

I found out that the guy's name was Wilkes and he answered, "It's about seven hundred miles from here. It's down south. Anyway, your brother, Michael, is in the Air Force and he's stationed down at Cam Ran. He's been here in country for about two weeks and every time he has tried to call you by phone I have

84

relayed his calls out here to this god-forsaken place. But, each time I have patched the call through to your unit, someone would answer and say that there was no one here by your name. I knew better because I've seen you at Troop Command a couple of times working on some of your legal cases and I remembered hearing your name. Somebody here in your unit wants to keep you from knowing that your brother is here in Vietnam. Your brother seems to be a pretty cool dude, so he and I have gotten to know each other over the phone. He trusted me enough to give me some information to pass on to you."

"What did he tell you?" I asked anxiously.

Wilkes continued, "Your brother is an Air Force Special Agent which is the equivalent to the Army's CID and he was stationed at an Air Force Base in Minnesota when he found out that you were going to receive a court-martial. He knew that according to the 1954 Geneva Convention Act that two surviving brothers in a family could not both serve in a combat environment so he volunteered for duty in Vietnam. His plan was to report for duty in Vietnam and let his superiors know that he had a brother already here. Once it was known that two surviving brothers were serving, the Army would have to send you home. The objective was to get you sent home before your court-martial could take place. But, somebody wanted to make sure that you didn't find out about any of this. Here, take this number and call me tonight at ten o'clock and I will patch you through to your brother."

I couldn't, for the life of me, understand why Wilkes had put himself on the line like that for someone he didn't even know. When I asked him why? He said, "Man, you helped a partner of mine get out of some serious trouble and to this day he talks very highly of you. So I respect you and what I'm doing for you and your brother is only the right thing to do."

"Wilkes, what can I do to repay you for what you done for me?" I asked him.

He said as he was leaving, "Pass it on brother; just pass it on."

I contacted Wilkes at ten o'clock as arranged and he quickly patched me through to my brother whom I hadn't seen in about a year and half. We quickly caught up on the latest information, which we needed to discuss. When Mike asked about my court-martial, I filled him in on the particulars. And I also told him that I had a PLAN. I told him not to worry about me and that I hoped to see him very soon...in fact, I planned to see him within a couple of days.

The following morning I reported to the orderly room to be transported to LBJ. When I entered the office the CO was waiting for me with some papers he wanted me to sign. Outside the door were the same two MP Sergeants from my trial and they were waiting to do the honors of transporting me to jail.

The CO said to me, "Coleman, the judge that tried your case had his head up his ass and forgot to get you to sign these papers at the trial, so I need your signature on them. Just sign all six copies right here. I looked the papers over and then signed all six copies. When I handed them back to the CO he had a big smile on his face as he said, "You know, people said you were a pretty smart black guy, but you're not as smart as they thought."

"What do you mean, sir?" I skeptically replied.

"Well you see, it was imperative that you sign these court-martial papers 'before' your trial started but the judge forgot to do it. So without your signature on these documents before your trial commenced represented a miscarriage of justice. No signature on these papers would have meant that you were tried illegally, but I just got you to sign them so nobody will be the wiser." Then he laughed. He was about to tell the MPs to come in to take me away when I stopped him.

I then said to him, "Sir, I am as smart as they told you I was and I do happen to be black."

"What are you trying to say?" He asked with a confused expression on his face.

"Well sir, you just had me to sign six copies of my court-martial papers and to check off one of two boxes which asks the question 'do you ACCEPT trial by court-martial' or 'do you NOT ACCEPT trial by court-martial'. But, what you have overlooked is the fact that at the beginning of my trial you and the judge presented me with the original charge sheet from which these copies were made and on my original charge sheet is your signature and the judge's signature dated for the day of the trial. Absent from the document is my signature and my consent to be tried by court-martial. This means that I was tried illegally and that makes you and the judge co-conspirators. I have also sent the original charge sheet to a very influential individual within the continental borders of the United States and if I am not heard from within the next thirty-six hours, I have requested that a full scale congressional investigation be made concerning my 'kangaroo court-martial' and as to my whereabouts." The CO looked at me with shock on his face. Then a look of anger replaced the shocked look as he wanted to know, "What would it take to make this right?"

I told him, "I want my record cleared of all and anything relative to me ever having had a court-martial. I also want some time to go to Cam Ran Bay to visit my brother who has recently arrived in country, which I think you already know about." His attempt at ignorance concerning my brother's phone calls was not well acted out.

He stated, "I'll allow you to go for three days to see your brother."

I informed him that it had been over a year since I had last seen my brother and I felt that a five day visit to see him would be just fine and he agreed. The MPs were dismissed, and as I turned to leave, the CO implored me not to discuss the very delicate information concerning my court-martial with anyone. I just stared at him as I left.

When I got outside I basked in the glow of the morning sunshine and thought about what had just transpired. I had realized at the opening of my trial that Colonel Woodruff and the CO had erred in not having me sign the documents. This was the important information I had glimpsed during the trial and I had done everything I could to keep the trial moving quickly to its conclusion, hoping at every step of the way that no one would realize the costly mistake the court had made. They dealt the cards unaware that they had gifted me with a royal flush.

CHAPTER SEVEN

Was He The Son of God?

Two days after my last conversation with the CO, I arrived at Cam Ran Bay, South Vietnam. Mike had secured a jeep from his base commander and was at the airfield to pick me up. I was surprised at how much my little brother had matured in the past year and a half. We laughed and kidded each other during the long ride to the sector of Cam Ran Bay, which supported the Air Force's military operations. Cam Ran was a gigantic military complex where almost every branch of the military service was represented. Part of Cam Ran was a peninsula, which jutted out into the Red China Sea. The ocean waters surrounding the landmass were pristine and the white sandy beaches were beautiful. Cam Ran was the place where Bob Hope, James Brown, Ann Margaret and many other entertainers stayed and performed for the American soldiers when they came to Vietnam. The area was considered as one of the safest and best protected bases in South Vietnam due to its natural geographic configurations, but during the TET Offensive of '68 the area had been hit hard by mortar and rocket attacks.

Mike took me to the hooch he lived in which turned out to be a small bungalow house he shared with four other airmen. I couldn't believe the layout they had. Everyone in the house had comfortable mattresses on their beds; they had a stove, a refrigerator stocked with plenty of beer and booze, food from the PX and even a television. I knew that the Air Force lived large, but not this large.

During the course of the day Mike took me around to meet his superior officers and many of his partners. They, black and white, turned out to be a great bunch of guys. Almost everyone seemed to regard me as an anomaly because I wore a Korean Army officers' utility cap I had acquired in a trade with a ROK soldier and they had all heard that I had been in combat. These factors seemed to cause some of the airmen to accord me a special respect and a bit of star status. I even discerned the same reaction from a few of the officers.

For the duration of my stay at Cam Ran I enjoyed all of the luxuries that the Air Force had to offer, but I was never able to let go of my "jungle mentality." I was always vigilant for any signs of trouble or inordinate circumstances, which might require my survival instincts to take over.

When Mike was taking me back to the airfield at the end of my visit, I explained to him how important it was for him to take care of himself and make it back home in one piece. I felt bad that he had volunteered to come to 'Nam to get me out of the country and out of a court-martial. I was going home in less than a month and a half, while he would have to stay for nine more months to complete his tour of duty. He assured me that he would take care of himself, that everything would be fine with his tour. If he had it to do all over again he would still come to 'Nam to try and get me out. At that moment I realized how much I had always loved my little brother, even if we did have knockdown, drag out, fights when we were kids. Mostly over important issues like who drank the very last drop of Kool-Aid out of the container and then put the empty container back in the refrigerator.

When I returned to my base camp everything was about the way I had left it. I quickly caught up with the boys to hear the latest scuttlebutt. I learned that Talley, Bird, and Velez were all going to be leaving during the next week "to catch an iron bird back to the World." They were going home and would be getting out of the Army since they had successfully completed their military obligations. I was going to miss them and I had to admit to myself that I was a little jealous, but my time to go home was coming soon.

The day after the boys had departed I was a bit down in the dumps. I had a month and one week left in country. The company commander seemed to ignore my presence. I didn't have a job to go to and all of my superiors seemed as if they didn't want the responsibility of trying to figure out what to do with me. So, I just kind of drifted around the base camp and stayed out of everybody's face. It seemed like everybody wanted me and the stigmas associated with my court-martial to just disappear. That's what I did.

The following morning I went to the orderly room and got the clerk to give me a signed slip authorizing me to leave the compound to go to Qui Nhon to see a doctor for problems I was having with my arches and ankles. I loaded a backpack with essentials I would need, grabbed my rifle and ammo and took off.

The doctor's examination revealed that, due to my activities while on patrols, my arches had fallen and that I had also sustained hair line fractures to a couple of bones in my right ankle. The doctor bandaged both ankles, gave me some medication and put me on bed rest for three days. He also placed a T-3 profile in my medical records, which stated: no prolonged running, jumping, stooping, or extended physical training.

On the way back towards Long My Valley I stopped in Phu Tai and went to Huan's house. When I arrived he and his wife Xena were excited to see me and I realized it had been quite a while since I had last visited them. After I had stowed my gear Huan told me had a surprise for me. He took me next door to where he had added on a large room to his little shack. Inside were six GIs sitting around drinking beer and talking with a Vietnamese girl and a Cambodian girl that I quickly identified as prostitutes. Xena was supplying the GIs with reefer and selling them beer from a cooler behind a newly built makeshift bar. I became pissed off because I had been the first American GI to befriend Huan and teach him English. Now he had other American GIs in his life and didn't value our friendship. I was jealous because I felt that I had to take a back seat to his new found friends now that he had become an entrepreneur. I was wrong. Huan began to grin at me and took me to the back part of the house to show me another room. In the other room was a portion of an American parachute which covered the ceiling and was suspended from the four corners of the room which created an artistically beautiful, billowing, draped effect. On a table was a new stereo radio acquired from a military PX and hanging, suspended, off to the side of the room was a hand woven hammock. Huan smiled and said, "This your room. I build for you. You stay here."

I couldn't believe what Huan was telling me. He had known that I would be coming back to visit him and he wanted me to feel as if I were part of his family. This was perfect, because I had come here with the intent of staying in his village as long as I could until the time came for me to go back to the World. I had already rationalized that nobody in my base camp would miss me; their attitude seemed to be "out of sight out of mind."

For the next two weeks I moved very easily throughout the village and among its inhabitants. It seemed as if the villagers understood that I was a personal friend of Huan and his family and was to be accorded the status of special guest in their village. I spent a lot of my free time at Mai Lin's bar where I caught up on what was happening back at my base camp by talking with and gleaning information from GIs who frequented her bar on a regular basis. It appeared that my absence was not drawing any real attention, especially since it seemed that a number of the people involved in my court-martial or those who were aware of what had transpired had rotated back to the states or would soon be leaving. From this information I presumed that people had their own personal priorities to concern themselves with and what was going on in my life was of little or no consequence to them.

While swinging in my hammock with my eyes closed one night at Huan's house, I was sipping on a beer and listening to some nice music on the Armed Forces Radio Network. I was luxuriating in the cool breeze wafting through the open window right next to me, which was in sharp contrast to the humidity and scorching heat of the earlier part of the day. Suddenly, I felt an eerie, familiar sensation, which I immediately identified as present danger! Without telegraphing any quick movements, I deftly reached below me and fisted my rifle, which I always kept at the ready. I snatched the rifle forward and aimed it at the window opening where I had perceived the threat emanating from. The barrel of my rifle came to stop four inches from the chest of a young Vietnamese man clad in a black pajama type outfit worn exclusively by my adversary the dreaded Viet Cong. The man, who was accompanied by four others, had a machete' poised at my neck and he wore a look of surprise on his face when he understood that he had a 5.56 millimeter bullet aimed at his chest which could produce a muzzle velocity of 1,000 meters per second. We were both facing what was known as a standoff. My adversary spoke first saying, "We know that you are called Dat and that you are friend to Huan. But we live and work in this village and we have work we must do. We have missions to carry out just as you. We have let you stay in our village and we no bother you. You are in way of what we must do." I quickly understood that these men walked around all day as regular citizens of the village, but at night they became the enemy. My presence in their village after dark made it difficult for them to go on their raiding parties to attack American military positions and return unobtrusively as if nothing had happened.

I told him, "I realize that you have to do what you have to do. I have many GI friends in the mountains around here and at the nearby military outpost. As long as you do not attack bases nearby, you don't have a problem with me seeing or knowing anything." The man removed his machete from my neck and I in turn removed my rifle from his chest He conferred with his fellow VC and said that we had a deal. They disappeared as silently and swiftly as they had appeared. As I lay there listening to the amplified, pounding sound of my heart as it tried to find a quieter and more normal syncopated beat, I thought to myself, *I hope and pray that the chance encounter I just had will in some way spare the lives of some unsuspecting GIs and keep them from harm.* Many years later, I would remember that night and wonder if I had made a small contribution in preventing some of the military installations in my sector from coming under attack during the short period of time that I lived in the village of Phu Tai.

Two days before I was to catch my "iron bird back to the World." I reported to the orderly room to receive my new orders. The new orders allowed me to begin the procedures necessary to depart the Republic of South Vietnam on January 30, 1969. All of my boys had already departed for home weeks before, so I was the last of the old guard to depart. On the day of my departure the CO pulled me aside and with renewed concern in his tone asked me again what he could do to make things right He was referring to my court-martial and he wanted to be assured that I didn't plan to bring some type of future legal actions against him. I told him that my new orders instructed me to go home and take a thirty-day leave and then report to Fort Stewart Army Post in Hinesville, Georgia. I didn't tell him that I had seen an article in the latest *Jet* magazine, which had covered a race riot that had taken place at Fort Stewart when some rednecks had displayed a rebel flag on the wall in the mess hall. I knew that if I left Vietnam and went to a situation such as the one existing at Fort Stewart, it wouldn't be long before I would be facing another court-martial for doing something I might regret for the rest of my life.

I told the CO that I would have exactly one year of active duty left to complete in the military after my thirty-day leave was up. I suggested that maybe he could use his influence to get my orders changed and get me assigned to Fort McPherson, Georgia which was ten minutes from my home in Atlanta, Georgia. He told me, "That would be impossible! Many high ranking officers can't even get that kind of assignment."

"Well, I'm sorry we couldn't work something out, sir." I replied.

"Wait! Hold on." I'll see what I can do. I can't make any promises, but I'll see what I can do."

I told him that I thought he should try very, very hard. I then left Long My Valley for the last time in my life and headed for the nearest airfield in Qui Nhon to catch a flight that would take me to Bien Hoa Air Base in South Vietnam, where I'd rendezvous with an "iron bird" which would take me back to the "World."

I arrived at the Bien Hoa airfield in the late afternoon. I approached an Army private who looked as if he worked at the airfield and I asked him, "Where do you report to in order to get a flight going home?" He directed me to a building next to a hangar and told me to go in there and show the clerk my orders and they would direct me from there. I followed the guy's instructions and I was told by the clerk that my flight back to the World would depart at eleven o'clock p.m. "Damn!" I said loud. I looked at my watch; the time was 6:15 p.m. I didn't know how I was going to survive having to wait four hours and forty-five minutes to get out of Vietnam. The clerk told me that there was a beer hall across the road and he showed me an area where I could stow my gear until flight time.

As I started walking across the road to the beer hall someone called out, "Rock!" I turned and saw a familiar face approaching me. It was Punchy! "Man, what's up? Where are you going? What are you doing here?" I asked excitedly.

"I'm getting out of here and going home." Punchy laughingly replied.

"Yeah, me too. I was going over to the beer hall across the road. Have you checked in yet to find out what time your flight leaves?"

"Yeah, my flight leaves at eleven o'clock p.m. When do you get out of here?" Punchy inquired.

"Eleven o'clock p.m., too. I guess we're going back to the World the same way we came here together!" I told him. "Well, let's go get a drink."

We sat in the beer hall listening to jukebox music, drinking beer and talking about what we were going to do when we got home. Three guys we didn't know asked if they could sit at our table with us. After they joined us we found out that we were all going to be on the same flight. The beer hall closed at nine o'clock p.m. so we all wandered back over to the airfield and collected our gear. A sergeant directed us out near the flight line and told us to make ourselves comfortable.

We sat down on the metal tarmac and leaned our backs against our duffel bags and tried to get comfortable. We were seated under a very large metal shed with about 300 other GIs, all of whom were awaiting Continental Airlines flight 1127. I noticed that everyone was speaking in subdued voices. You would think that a crowd of GIs who were on their way home from a one-year tour of duty in Hell would be making all kinds of noise. Then it dawned on me. We were all quiet because we were afraid. We were afraid that we would wake up from this dream and realize that we weren't really going home at all; or Victor Charlie and the North Vietnamese Army might pick this particular night to launch a massive attack on the airfield and we're sitting ducks who have turned all of our weapons in; or something goes wrong and we don't get out of here alive. Fear can do some strange things to a person's psyche.

Suddenly, we heard a loud, bellowing, yell. We all looked in the direction of a short, stocky, black guy that had jumped up near the left side of the shed. He kept yelling "We've got to go home! We've got to go home! Don't you know who I am?! Don't you know who I am?!" Then he let go with a blood-curdling scream and began shouting again over and over, "Don't you know who I am?! Don't you know who I am?!" The brother then started running back and forth among us yelling, "We've got to go home! Don't you know who I am?! Don't you know who I am?!"

Everyone's anxiety level was already at the breaking point and the guy's weird outburst didn't help matters. I felt sorry for the guy. I thought to myself, *Here's a guy that's put his life on the line in Hell for a year and now as he's about to be freed to go home, he has a nervous breakdown and cracks up.*

Everybody moved back away from the guy because we had no idea who he was or what he was capable of doing. A few minutes later three MPs surrounded the guy and each one had his billy club in his hand as they approached him. The MPs tried talking to him, all to no avail. Then all three MPs grabbed him and wrestled him to the ground and cuffed his hands behind his back. As they attempted to drag the guy away, he again started yelling, "Don't you know who I am?! Don't you know who I am?!...I AM THE SON OF GOD!"

The scene became deathly quiet. Then I saw one of the MPs draw his billy club back, and in a blur of forward motion, I watched as the billy club streaked to the side of the distraught fellow's head and the night captured the horrific sound...CRRAAACK! The guy slumped to ground and he looked like he was dead. The crowd started to surge forward toward the MPs. The MPs pulled their pistols and aimed them at us and told everyone to back off. Two jeeps pulled up with MP reinforcements and they quickly threw the limp body of the hapless guy into one of the jeeps and sped away. We all looked at one another with dazed expressions on our faces. A thought occurred to me, *Was that guy really the Son of God? Was he being beaten and persecuted for returning and speaking the truth? Was the truth that we ALL needed to stop the killing, leave the killing fields, and go home?* I wondered. After the shock had worn off, we all sat back down and tried to understand what we had just witnessed. A couple of GIs went to the flight counter to see if they could sort out what had happened. When they returned they said that nobody would tell them anything.

Twenty minutes later, a sleek beautiful jet plane bearing the Continental Airlines logo came to a stop near the shed. An air cargo person had us to line up according to the seat numbers we had been given earlier. When I boarded the plane I was struck by the beauty of the flight attendants. These were the first American women I had seen in a long time. The next thing that struck me was that Punchy was already seated and his seat number was the same as mine...just as it was when we boarded our flight coming to Vietnam.

When everyone was seated the plane began to taxi on the runway. The pilot gave a perfunctory greeting over the speaker system and introduced the flight attendants. He explained that we were going to experience some heavy G-forces because of a quick lift-off and a very steep angle to gain altitude; that is exactly what happened as we took off. I looked back out of the window as we struggled for altitude and saw tracer bullets and what could have been small rockets streaming ineffectively at the plane. When I shifted my gaze to the front of the plane towards the cockpit, I noticed that I was looking up in order to see the cockpit door. We were really climbing and it was all right with me. When the plane reached a safe altitude, the pilot leveled the plane off. When we all realized that we had broken ground contact and had leveled off safely, a roaring chant welled up from all of us as if it were one loud voice.

An hour later we all seemed to let the tension seep out of our bodies and sleep became the order of the moment. The flight would be nearly twenty hours or more. The flight also became confusing because we flew through many different time zones: night to day then day to night. Even more confusing, time wise, was when we flew through the International Date Line and in mere seconds the day of the week changed from Sunday to Monday.

We stopped for refueling in Yokota, Japan, and Anchorage, Alaska. Our last stop was the airfield at Fort Lewis, Washington, at five o'clock am. When we left the plane and stepped on to the tarmac, it was covered in a sheet of ice and in the distance there were four feet of snow. We all had on light weight jungle utilities and we had landed the day after one of the greatest snowstorms to have ever hit the State of Washington. Every one of us was nearly freezing to death.

We were herded quickly to a mess hall where we had breakfast. Then afterwards we were herded to a facility where we were all issued new winter Army clothing. Punchy and I caught a commercial flight out of Washington and then caught a connecting flight out of Chicago, Illinois, heading home to Atlanta, Georgia. We arrived in Atlanta at ten o'clock p.m. where many family members and friends greeted us.

We had formed a motorcade of five cars when we left the airport and headed for home. I rode with my first cousin, Stephen Johnson, who was from St. Albans, New York, and a student at Morehouse College. Stephen wanted me to ride with him so he could show me his new sports car, a dark green, 1967 MGB-GT. When we got on the expressway Stephen began speeding and quickly pulled away from the motorcade. I looked over at the speedometer and saw that it read eighty miles an hour.

I told Stephen, "Man, your car is really fast, but you need to slow it down."

He jauntily replied, "Don't worry I can handle it."

Before I realized it, I had grabbed Stephen by his collar and yelled in his ear, "Slow this damn car down!"

Stephen looked at me like he had seen a ghost and quickly decelerated. I got a grip on myself and settled back in the seat. I noticed Stephen cautiously looking over at me out of the corner of his eye. All at once, I felt guilty and ashamed for my outburst against my cousin. I was feeling very edgy and I realized that I was experiencing fear—fear of being killed in a speeding car on the way home from the airport after surviving a war filled with mayhem, death, and destruction 14,000 miles away. I apologized to Stephen and he eagerly accepted my offer. But, I was still concerned about my uncharacteristic behavior and I rationalized it away by blaming it on jet lag.

When I arrived at home it was a great feeling being back on familiar turf and surrounded by people you cared about and who cared about you. We socialized for a couple of hours, during which time my aunts, uncles, and other relatives questioned me as to how my brother was doing when I last saw him, and what was combat like in Vietnam. My response to the latter question was somewhat evasive. I didn't really want to talk about that facet of my tour in 'Nam.

I finally got to bed around two o'clock in the morning and I was dead tired. I dropped off to sleep almost immediately, but sometimes later I woke up sweating, shivering, and sitting straight up in the bed. As I struggled to get my bearings as to where the hell I was, I realized that I had been having a nightmare. My dream had been about one of the patrols I had been on in 'Nam when two of the guys in my squad had been killed. On that night we had made contact with a Viet Cong element and they were giving us all that we could handle. The fighting was fast and furious and we were getting hit with mortars and rockets and the two unlucky GIs were near the point man in a forward position when they got hit. When the fighting was over and we went forward to help the wounded, I saw that both of the guys were dead and the one whose nametag read Richards was decapitated. His head was two feet away from his body. But in my nightmare I looked at his head and his eyes opened and he said to me, "Hey man, please put my head back on my body, I gotta go home!" That's when I woke up. The Fear. I got up and had a good stiff drink and, before getting back in the bed, I turned on the TV in my room and turned the sound down low. The next morning I discovered that having the TV on during the night seemed to relax me and allowed me to drift off into the "twilight sleep" I had learned and practiced in the 'Nam. To this day, I still leave the TV or radio on when I sleep.

CHAPTER EIGHT

The Pentagon Sends a Wire

During the second week of my thirty-day leave, my dad and I went to a Chevrolet auto dealership to see if we could find me a new car. While overseas I had saved up enough for a down payment, but I didn't have a clue as to what kind of car I wanted. When I walked into the dealership and looked in the showroom window, I knew exactly what car I wanted. The first car I was to ever own was beckoning to me from the showroom window. It was a brand new Verde green, 1969 Chevrolet Camaro 327 with a light green vinyl top. After a couple of hours of tense negotiations with the salesman, I had my new car.

The next day Punchy pulled up into my driveway and blew his car horn. When I went out to greet him he yelled out of the window, "How you like my new ride?"

"It's outta of sight man!" I yelled back.

Punchy had just bought a brown over brown, 1969 Plymouth Road Runner and it was hot! Punchy was going to be starting a new job in two weeks and I sure envied him. He had finished his military obligation and had been honorably discharged, but I still had that other year to complete. For the next week we rode around town and made sure that we cruised through the campuses of Morris Brown, Clark, and Spelman Colleges a couple of hundred times a day, girl watching.

On the last day of my leave I hadn't heard anything from the military about changing my orders to Fort McPherson, Georgia. Regulations stated that I must obey the last order given and the last official order I had been given was to report to Fort Stewart, Georgia. I surmised that the CO had lied to me. I loaded up my car, bid my family farewell and departed for Fort Stewart. Ten minutes later as I was about to enter onto the highway, I remembered that I left some money at home. So I turned around and headed back. A block from my house I stopped to make a left hand turn onto my street when I heard a squeal of tires indicating that somebody's car was skidding out of control. I looked up in my rear view mirror and saw an old man rapidly closing in behind me as he struggled to control his older model car that looked like a Sherman tank. Before I could react I heard a loud crash as the old man's car plowed into the back of my brand spanking new car! I was shaken up but got out of my car to survey the damage as the old man carne up to me and began to profusely apologize stating, "I'm sorry son; I just didn't see you." After the police cited the old man and my new car was towed away to the dealership for repair, I called Punchy and had him take me to the MP Station at Fort McPherson. I met with the MP Commanding Officer and explained to him what had happened to my car and that I was reporting to him so I wouldn't be considered AWOL when I didn't show up on time at Fort Stewart, which was five hours away. The MP CO asked for my orders and I told him they were in the trunk of my car, which was smashed up so badly that I couldn't get my orders out. The CO tried for two hours to contact the CO of the unit to which I was supposed to report, but every time he called the phone would go dead on the other end due to a communications problem at Fort Stewart. Finally, the CO told me to go home and as soon as contact was made with my new CO an MP vehicle would be dispatched to my house to pick me up and transport me to Fort Stewart. When I returned home and was about to enter the house, an MP vehicle pulled up to the curb and an MP approached me and asked me to identify myself. When I did he handed me a telegram from Western Union and turned to leave.

I asked him, "Aren't you going to transport me to Fort Stewart?" He said over his shoulder as he kept walking, "I don't know anything about that."

As I stood there confused I opened the telegram and saw that it had been sent from the US DEPARTMENT OF DEFENSE, OFFICE OF THE PENTAGON, ARLINGTON, VIRGINIA.

2 MAR 69 CORPORAL T.M. COLEMAN RA 53451786
You are to report at the earliest convenience to the 3d
Communications Detachment Fort McPherson, GA STOP If
you have already reported to Fort Stewart, GA disregard
telegram STOP

I couldn't believe it! My orders had indeed been changed and I
was now going to be stationed at Fort McPherson, Georgia, which
was only a few minutes from my house. Fantastic! I learned a
valuable lesson from the accident that wrecked my new car; behind
every dark cloud is a silver lining. Had the accident not occurred I
would have reported to Fort Stewart in South Georgia and it would
have been too late for the telegram to help me. It just goes to show
you that sometimes the one who puts you in the mess ain't
necessarily your enemy (the old man that hit my car), and the one
that gets you out of the mess ain't necessarily your friend (the CO
at my court-martial). When I reported to the 3d Commo
Detachment the next day, I met the Operations Officer and the
First Sergeant. The "first shirt" was named Roy Gilmer and I liked
him right off the bat He had an engaging personality and he wasn't
a stickler for a lot of the formalities associated with rank and
everyone I met who worked in the Communications Center was
professional and pleasant. They appeared to have a great working
environment Sergeant Gilmer called me to his office and said,
"Coleman, I'm going to put you in charge of our supply operations
here in the Commo Center. You will be 'The Man,' but in order for
us to do that I'm going to have to get you promoted to Sergeant.
So I'll put that request in before the close of business today, and
they usually give me what I want without any hassle. I've looked
over your records and I was impressed by your soldiering abilities.
Now, since you live in Atlanta you will be paid separate rations for
food and for living at home and not on post. You will report for
work at eight o'clock a.m. and we knock off at four thirty p.m. Any
questions?"

"No, First Sergeant." I answered.

"Coleman, call me Roy," he said.

"OK, Roy." I responded.

"Good. Now, take off the rest of the day, go home and get yourself situated, and report back in the morning at eight o'clock."

On January 30, 1970, I departed Fort McPherson Army Post for the last time no longer a member of its cadre. I had become an Honorably Discharged Vietnam Veteran. I had attained the rank of Sergeant (E-5); received all medals and decorations to include the Good Conduct Medal; and was awarded a service connected disability of ten percent. My newly acquired freedom meant that I had to join the civilian work force, so I began to earnestly seek gainful employment.

CHAPTER NINE

How Did Talley Know?

In early February of 1970, I was walking through downtown Atlanta on my way to the Personnel Office of the Atlanta Post Office. I had been told to report for a possible position as a mail handler. I found out that my veteran's status would give me priority consideration for jobs within the postal system and I had immediately applied for both the mail handler and the clerk carrier exams. The mail handler exam was the only test being offered at the time and I successfully passed it. As I walked along, someone walked up beside me and said, "Hey Rock! Where're you going?" I looked over and saw that it was Punchy. I told him I had a meeting down the street and he said he was going in the same direction so we continued walking and discussed my recent discharge. When we reached the steps of the Post Office I told Punchy I would see him later 'cause I was going inside. He turned to go up the steps with me, stating that he had to attend to some business in the Post Office also. Well, as fate would have it, both of us had been told to report for employment with the postal system. We ended up working at the same location and on the same shift.

We worked at the Bulk Mail Center and the pay and benefits were very good, but the work was heavy, hard and demanding. On the first day, I discovered that Punchy and I were two of a total of fifteen newly hired Vietnam Veterans. After working for only a few days, I further discovered that all fifteen of us were routinely told to perform the dirtiest and hardest job assignments available. Many of the white supervisors were racists, and like many of the nonveteran employees, they didn't give a "flying flippy" about Vietnam Veterans or "that damn war they fought." The supervisors were very disrespectful to many of the employees and constantly used threats and coercion against them, which blatantly pushed the limits of decency. There were even instances when I witnessed supervisors yelling and screaming at employees.

The fifteen of us became very close and we decided that we weren't going to accept any forms of racism. We determined that we would perform our jobs without complaint, but we weren't going to bow and scrape. We would give the supervisors their proper respect...And they were definitely going to give us ours. We were men who had paid our dues and we weren't asking anybody to give us anything. We were not going to be yelled at, threatened, intimidated, disrespected, or treated like children...slavery had long been over.

When I asked some of the other employees why they accepted the abuse, their only response was, "Y'all Vietnam Vets are crazy and just gonna cause trouble." I came to the conclusion that most of the employees had not been in the military and they had been working for the Post Office a long time. Many of them had started working right out of high school and because of the good pay, benefits, and the life style the job afforded them, most employees were willing to accept the abuse.

During the month before Christmas, the supervisors would wait until fifteen minutes before the shift ended to tell all employees that mandatory overtime had been put in to effect. This caused a hardship on employees with childcare issues, personal business matters, and family issues that needed to be taken care of. The supervisors were not concerned with the personal concerns of the employees and would threaten to suspend anyone who could not stay and work.

I had noticed on my check stub a deduction which was being made for union dues. I had not joined the union, and when I inquired about the deductions no one could give me a straight answer as to who had authorized the deductions, so I made it my business to attend the next union meeting. At the meeting I asked about the rules governing mandatory overtime and the union representative informed me that superiors must notify employees two hours in advance when mandatory overtime was to be instituted. I shared this new information with my veteran counter parts and the next day when my supervisor called for mandatory overtime fifteen minutes before the shift ended, I informed him that I would not be staying. The supervisor began to threaten me with a three-day suspension if I didn't stay. I felt the anger rise in me, but I held my emotions in check and when my shift ended I started walking towards the sign in/out clock. As I walked across the floor of the cavernous building, all eyes were on my actions, all of the machinery came to a stop and the only sound that could be heard was my footsteps as I approached the clock. When I reached the clock, there were five supervisors and the facility Post Master standing between my time card and me. The Postmaster muttered under his breath to me, "Coleman, don't try to do this. If you do I'll fire you."

I took a deep breath and said, "According to Postal Regulations you are in violation of your own regulations. You did not give ample notice, specifically two hours' notice of mandatory overtime. Therefore, I must leave at this time." I brushed by him and retrieved my time card and clocked out. A cheer went up from the other employees and a line quickly formed at the time card rack as many of the employees rushed to clock out as I left the building.

The following day, overtime was announced two hours before quitting time. And, it was no longer mandatory; it was optional. Workers were congratulating me for helping them and a union representative approached me to ask if I would attend the next union meeting because there were some people who wanted to meet me. I told him I would be there.

When I attended the union meeting I was introduced to some of the shop stewards and the Regional Director. These gentlemen cut right to the chase and made it known to me that they admired my tenacity, character, and willingness to challenge the system and stand up for what was right. They said that they needed more employees like me and that they were willing to offer me a position as the shop steward for my facility. They looked at me expectantly and mistakenly thought that I was flattered and honored by their offer.

I smiled at them and asked, "Who authorized the union to deduct wages from my salary for union dues?"

The Director, a guy named Harry Wilson replied, "Well, Mr. Coleman, we have asked the facility Post Master to assist us in this matter because many of the employees don't know of the valuable services behind the scenes which we provide to help them. So, we're sort of helping them to help themselves, if you know what I mean. We would love to have you on our team and we're prepared to compensate you financially if you choose to join us in the capacity of shop steward."

I measured my words carefully as I looked Wilson in the eye and told him, "Mr. Wilson, you are full of crap. I know for a fact that you and the union have been deducting $7.00 every two weeks from my pay check and the pay checks of fourteen other newly hired veterans for a couple of months and none of us has authorized you to do so. That's $210.00 per month. I wonder how much more you're collecting from the other employees? The travesty in all of this is that you have stood idly by while management violated the employee's rights by making them perform mandatory overtime and not giving them ample notice. You were fully aware that employees you were deducting union dues from were being forced illegally to work overtime and you did nothing to assist them. I don't trust you or your organization, so the answer is an emphatic 'no', I don't want to be a shop steward and I want the union to stop deducting dues from my paycheck immediately." Before anyone could reply I turned and left. A few days later when I reported for work, a new guy came up to me and said, "Coleman, I'm Ron Bally and I'm your new supervisor. I have a special assignment I want you to work on, so just follow me. "

I regarded him cautiously as I followed him and thought to myself, *He knew my name and who I was the moment I walked through the door.*

He took me to the area known as the Customs Section and began to show me what the job requirements were and how to perform them. My responsibility was to stand beside a small, slow moving conveyor belt that paraded various sized parcel post boxes. All I had to do was stamp each box with a red rubber stamp that read INSPECTED BY CUSTOMS. All I had to do for eight hours was to stamp boxes.

Bally said, "Periodically you might have a box to come down the line which might look suspicious. When that happens you are to open the package and inspect it for contraband or other types of illegal materials. If you find something illegal, let me know immediately."

Two weeks later, I was starting to really like the customs position. I no longer had to perform the hard and heavy work of unloading mail trucks or catching the heavy mail sacks off of the large conveyor line. Bally didn't stand around watching me like the other supervisors did with employees on the line. Everything was going fine...Or so I thought

Some of my veteran buddies had started the habit of walking by my work location talking loudly amongst themselves. Their conversations were meant to be loud to make sure that I heard them as they made statements like: "Yeah, Rock sure must be eating a lot of cheese with the big bosses to get that good job," or "I wonder who he's been brown nosing to get such an easy assignment?" Their comments got my attention and caused me to realize that Bally and the union were working together in an effort to make me look like they had me in their hip pocket. Some of my fellow employees had begun to think that I was standing up to management to make things better for everyone, but they were wrong. I was standing up for myself. Management and the union thought that I was trying to establish myself as a leader and spokesman for the employees. And, they were wrong also. I was standing up for myself and what I knew to be the right thing. I had begun to exist on the job in a "gray area" and I wasn't comfortable with it. So, the next day when I reported to work and Bally told me to work customs, I told him that I couldn't do it. When he asked me why, I told him that the job I had been hired for wasn't customs. I reminded him that I had been hired as a mail handler and I would appreciate it if he would send me back to the department I had been originally assigned to. We had a very heated discussion about the matter and when he saw how serious I was, he relented and sent me back to catching mail sacks off of the line and unloading trucks. I didn't really want to go back to my old assignment, but I had started to feel like a sell-out to myself and there was a principle involved called pride.

Punchy and I decided to pool our resources and we got an apartment together. We had a lot of card parties at our apartment and quite a few social functions in the apartment complex to include swim parties. There were always people in and out of our crib and plenty of single women dropping by to visit.

Everything was going great, except for the job. My supervisors started giving me leave slips to fill out if they felt I should have returned from the restroom two minutes sooner than I did. If I returned from my breaks three minutes late, I had to sign a leave slip. My name came up on rotation to unload trucks more than anybody else's did. It became very evident that I was being targeted for a harassment campaign because I wouldn't be the "token" for Bally and the union. I decided to fight fire with fire, so I contacted the Office of the Post Master General in Washington, DC. and lodged a formal complaint against my department and superiors for illegal labor practices, which they exacted against myself and other employees. Within a month, two investigators, a black female and male, were dispatched from Washington to review my complaint. They came in at the beginning of my shift and they interviewed all employees one by one. They spent about ten or fifteen minutes with each employee and requested to see me last. As I walked towards the office after being told that the investigators were ready to see me, Bally strolled up beside me and said, "Coleman, I hope you aren't going to go in there and say the wrong thing to those people, especially about me. You knoow that I have been good to you and I've tried to look out for you." When I ignored him he became angry and told me that I'd better give him the leave slips that he had given me over the last couple of months. When I continued to ignore him his last words to me were, "You're going to regret doing this!"

When I stepped into the office with the investigators, the female spoke up by asking, "Mr. Coleman, what makes you so important around here?"

I was taken aback by her statement and asked, "What do you mean?"

She replied, "Almost everyone we have talked with so far has mentioned your name and said that we should talk with you about what's going on around here."

I told her she might be interested in these, as I handed her the fifteen leave slips, which I had illegally been told to sign. She looked over the slips and then looked at me with an incredulous expression on her face as she asked me to have a seat. I talked with the investigators for more than two hours.

Within days after I talked with the investigators, charges were brought against some of the management staff and others were transferred to other postal facilities.

For the next two weeks, the remaining supervisors were very civil towards the employees, but one could detect an underlying tension in the air. One morning, I reported for work after a night of partying and suffering with a headache which was the aftermath of a hangover, when suddenly a supervisor named Jones stood in front of me and began yelling at me. I didn't have a clue as to what had provoked such an outburst from him, and as he continued his harangue I couldn't decipher what the hell he was talking about. But I did know that he had pushed my last button. Before I realized what had happened, I had gotten right up in his face and said to him,

"Jones, I told you to never yell at me and if you try it again I will kick your ass!"

Jones looked at me with a shocked expression on his face as he blubbered; "You can't talk to me like that I'm a supervisor and I'll see to it that you're fired!"

By this time I was so enraged that I yelled in his face, "You can't fire me 'cause I quit!

"You can't quit!" Jones retorted.

"Just watch me!" I yelled over my shoulder as I strode purposefully towards the office. I went into the office and requested a leave form, which I quickly filled out and in the section that requested how much leave was to be taken I wrote "indefinite."

The news of my confrontation with Jones had spread quickly throughout the building, and when I walked out of the office all eyes were on me as I angrily made my way to the door leading to the parking lot. The rage that engulfed me made me feel like I had in the 'Nam when you watched somebody dying and there wasn't a damn thing you could do about the precious life which was slipping from their body. I got into my car and drove to the bank that I used and cleaned out my account. Then I went home and packed all of my clothes and loaded them into my car along with my stereo and all of my record albums. My next stop was at the nearest liquor store where I purchased a quart bottle of cognac and then I drove to the on ramp of the Interstate and took 85 North. I was getting out of Dodge! I didn't know where I was going, but I knew that I had to leave. I drove north and sipped on the cognac for about three hours when I realized that I was getting too drunk to drive so I pulled into a rest area somewhere in South Carolina and went to sleep. When I woke up it was late afternoon and it took me a minute to orient myself as to where the hell I was. Once I had gotten my bearings, I took stock of my situation: I had quit a pretty good paying job with career potential and good benefits; I had no idea where I was going or what I was going to do; I was feeling anger and an inner pain and hurt. Turmoil. I felt like something was stalking me like when I was in the "bush." I was still having nightmares associated with my experiences in Vietnam, but they were manageable when I used alcohol to sort of numb myself. But, as I sat there in my car looking out at the highway I understood that I wasn't very happy with my lot in life. I decided that I would keep driving north until I got to Washington, DC, and when I got there I would look for a job. So, DC it was and I headed out.

I arrived in DC early the next morning and the first thing I did was to buy a roll of toilet tissue at a Safeway grocery store. I then went to the nearest Post Office and wrote my resignation to the Atlanta Post Office on two sheets of toilet paper and had the clerk to notarize it. I then sent the notarized document to the Post Master in Atlanta by registered mail.

My grandmother had two sisters that lived in DC, Aunt Lucille and Aunt Nett (short for Johnetta). Ever since I was a small child they would compete with each other to see which one of them could shower me with the most love. They are two great ladies. Uncle George was married to Aunt Nett and he was a man's man. He and I would on occasion, slip down to the cellar to drink from his well-stocked bar and talk trash until the wee hours of the morning. Uncle George was a super guy and I felt a lot of pride when I was with him. Aunt Lucille's husband was Uncle John. Uncle John was just as super as Uncle George was. The only big differences were that Uncle John didn't drink and he was a man of few words, but he would lay some heavy wisdom on you. Uncle John liked to go to the horse races, and when I was about eighteen he would take me with him. I remember that the first time he took me to the track there were ten races that day. At the start of each of the first nine races, Uncle John would give me a $20.00 bill to bet on the horse I felt would win. I lost on each of the nine races I bet on, but he was winning big time. He would coach me and give me pointers and show me things to look for in picking the horses. On the tenth and final race Uncle John gave me a $20.00 bill and utilizing some of the tips that he had given me, I bet on a horse named Mr. Personality. Mr. Personality Won, Placed, and Showed! When I collected my winnings, I thought I was wealthy and I tried to pay Uncle John back with some of my winnings but he adamantly refused, saying that I had earned what I had won and it was my money. I left the track with $960.00 and for an eighteen-year-old that was wealth untold!

After visiting with my aunts it was decided that I would stay with Aunt Lucille and Uncle John while I looked for employment. The first night I was with them their son, Marion, came by to visit. Marion was about ten years my senior. He was short, stocky, and powerfully built, light complexioned and sported a big gapped tooth smile that could charm the bird's right out of the trees. As a child I had never met Marion because I was always told that he was away in boarding school. I could tell right away that Marion had a good-natured slyness about him and that he knew his way around in some tight spots. Later that night, Marion and I decided to go out to a couple of clubs. Before we left, I could tell that Aunt Lucille was a little apprehensive about me going out with Marion; almost like she thought he might get me into some kind trouble. I told her we would be fine and we left.

Once we were in my car Marion told me that he didn't have any money, so I told him not to worry about money. I would cover everything. Marion, like his dad, was a special kind of guy and I liked him. I asked Marion what school he'd been away to. He said that his mother told everybody he had been away in school, but in reality he had been in prison for something he'd been charged with when he was a young man hanging out with the wrong crowd. He said the school he was attending was "Hard Knocks University!" We both roared with laughter. As we continued talking I discovered that Marion was wise like his father and had a great sense of humor. I was glad to have a cousin like him.

We decided to stop at a liquor store to get something to sip on. When we walked into the store I saw a very familiar guy standing around begging patrons for spare change. The guy was disheveled and wearing an old army field jacket. When I got close enough to him to look into his eyes, I could see what the ravages of heroin had done to him. I was disbelieving and hurt to the core when I realized that the junkie before me was Talley! I grabbed him by both shoulders and tried to talk to him but his eyes would only flicker on me for a moment and then drift into Never Neverland. When I finally got him to realize who I was he said, "Yeah. Hey, Rock man. Man, you know you did real good in 'Nam when you put that dude's head back on his body." Suddenly my breath tightened into a big knot in my chest and I thought I was about to go insane. Fear gripped me as I asked myself, *how in the world did Talley know about my nightmare that I had never told anybody about?* I had to get out of there and away from Talley, my friend, my main man...Talley...The Junkie. Later, while riding along in the car, it occurred to me that out of the thousands of liquor stores in the District of Columbia, I had picked the one where Talley would be. Was it just a coincidence, or was there a reason for me to find him in the condition he was in? Was there something greater for me to understand after seeing him and did this encounter have anything to do with the concepts of synchronicity which he and I had explored at length back in the Nam? Again, I asked myself, *how did he know about the guy's head that talked to me in my nightmare?*

Marion asked me to make one more stop before we got to the club. He wanted to go to a neighborhood bar where he was to meet a guy who owed him some money. When we got to the bar the owner told Marion that the guy would be coming by shortly. There was a pool table near the rear of the bar, so Marion and I decided to shoot a game of pool while we waited. When it comes to shooting pool my game is less than average, but on that particular night it seemed as if my long absence from the game had improved my skills. While soundly defeating Marion on our second game, a guy walked over and challenged me to shoot him a game of pool for twenty dollars. My better judgment told me not to do it, but my daring nature caused me to accept the challenge. The bartender held the bet as I proceeded to break the balls. My strokes and cuts on the ball were better than even I had reason to anticipate and in short order I had soundly beaten my opponent. The guy immediately began re-racking the balls and with clenched jaws growled, "Let's shoot again double or nothing."

Once again, I soundly defeated him and collected my money from the bartender. The guy who owed Marion showed up and paid him, but as we were leaving trouble began to brew. The guy I had beaten playing pool came up to me and demanded his money back stating, "Man, you hustled me. I know a pool shark when I see one. You ain't walking out of here with my money; so hand it over or I'll kick your ass!" I glanced quickly at Marion and made eye contact. The look in his eyes told me all I needed to know— that he had my back covered and to go ahead and deal with the issue at hand. I told the guy facing me that if he wanted his money he was going to have to take it from me. He then made a very stupid mistake: he tried to throw a sucker punch to my face, but he may as well have been working for Western Union 'cause he telegraphed his intent too hastily. I sidestepped his punch and unleashed a flurry of punches of my own. I don't know how many unanswered punches I threw until the guy crumpled to the floor in a comer, bleeding and semiconscious. Just as I turned to exit the place, I saw Marion crack a pool stick over the head of a guy who had decided to sneak up on my blind side. We made it to the car and got out of the area quickly. Marion was laughing as he said, "Damn, Cuz! You're pretty rough. You beat that man two times. Once, on the pool table and once on his head!"

I was glad we had gotten out of the bar all right, but I didn't feel good about what had happened. I felt as if the fury I had unleashed on the guy in the bar was a culmination of the anger, pain, and rage I felt after seeing what that damn war had done to a good man like Talley.

While driving along a new song I hadn't heard before came on the radio. Marvin Gaye was singing a song entitled "What's Going On." The song was about war and hate being conquered by love. *Very appropriate*, I thought to myself as I drove on into the night. I also began to ask myself, *what's going on with me?* I asked the question because I had started to feel as if I were becoming unanchored or disconnected from the true purpose and direction that my life was supposed to take. The feeling I experienced felt like being on a patrol in 'Nam and getting separated from your unit and being unable to find your way back to friendly lines. You're lost, alone, scared, and not tethered to anything familiar. I thought about the problems I had with Van Walde in Vietnam; I thought about my many confrontations at the Post Office; I thought about the physical confrontation in the bar I had just unwittingly been involved in. I concluded that I needed to get a grip on myself and try to figure out why trouble seemed to always find me.

Marion and I hung out together for the next week or so, as he showed me the ropes and how to negotiate my way around DC. During the day I would follow up on job leads and interviews. I soon started hanging out with some of my friends from college whom I had been able to locate. A couple of days later I went back to the liquor store where I had seen Talley hoping to find him. I wanted to see what I could do to help him get off of the streets. I didn't find him so I cruised the neighborhood and searched for him. All to no avail.

I spent four months in DC actively seeking employment, but none was forth coming. My money and my patience were running low. Regretfully, I made a decision to return to Atlanta and look for employment. I had developed some great friendships in DC, and I really loved the excitement of the city. But I felt it was time to return home.

CHAPTER TEN

They Were Killers,
But Not From the 'Nam

Shortly after my return to Atlanta, I received two interesting letters through the mail. One was from a governmental agency in Washington, DC, and they were requesting that I report for a job position which I had applied for while in DC. The second was from the personnel department of the Atlanta Post Office informing me that I had abandoned a government position and that I could never again work for the federal government.

The next day, I went to the personnel office of the Post Office and spoke with the personnel director. She explained that I had left my position vacant for more than thirty days, at which time the postal system determined that I was AWOL and terminated my employment My records had also been flagged, indicating that I was barred from ever working for the federal government again. I reached into the folder I was carrying and produced a return receipt from the certified letter I had sent to the Atlanta Post Office formally tendering my resignation. The personnel director went to the files and found my letter. When she opened it and read my notarized resignation written on the two pieces of toilet paper she looked at me with an embarrassed expression on her face and said, "Well, sir! We seem to have made an error in terminating your employment. I will personally rectify this mistake."

I thanked her and left. Later that week, I received a letter from the post office reinstating my eligibility for government employment in the future. A lesson I learned in the military had once again served me well—always document

One day, while I was trying to decide what kind of work to look for, my cousin Cheryl Drake, suggested that I try my hand at teaching. Cheryl was a fourth grade elementary school teacher and she informed me that her principal was looking for a supply teacher to work with fifth, sixth, and seventh grade boys in an after school program. I told her that I was interested and she got me an interview with the principal, an affable gentleman named "Bruiser" Jones. Mr. Jones had been one hell of a football player in his day. We hit it off immediately and, twenty minutes later, he hired me. My job consisted of tutoring the boys in the basic core courses and coaching them in athletics. I enjoyed working with the kids and they were eager to learn. Most of them seemed starved for the attention of an older male or a father figure. As a result, I became pretty close to my charges. We sometimes had rap sessions and they would want me to tell them stories about my running track days or my time spent in Vietnam. When it came to stories about Vietnam, I gave them the PG rated ones; I didn't want to lay heavy grown folks stuff on 'em.

The year was 1973 and life was great! There were fantastic parties every weekend and the slogans we spouted in our youthful vigor were "flower power," "peace," "free love," "black power," and "power to the people." Life was fantastic! Our parents and the generation older than them had come to the conclusion that we "baby boomers" had totally lost our minds. We were the generation that challenged the system. We vehemently began to oppose the war in Southeast Asia. We had our own music, our own way of dressing, talking, and dancing. In fact, I like to think that we truly changed the course of history and set some new standards.

Six months after I had begun teaching, I was offered a job with the county Juvenile Court Detention Center. I took the position and became a detention officer. When I was offered a choice of assignments, I elected to work with the youths fifteen to seventeen years of age. My new director, Mr. Charles Johnson, suggested that I work with the younger boys because the older boys were more apt to take advantage of a new employee, and on occasions had violently attacked them. I assured Mr. Johnson that I felt I could handle the older boys and any problems which might arise.

I was assigned seventeen of the older boys, all of whom were facing charges of armed robbery, rape, assault or murder. When I entered the detention area for the first time to meet my newly assigned group, a young man that I intuitively knew was one of the group's leaders immediately approached me. He engaged me with a big smile as he introduced himself to me as Clarence Mims. He asked me my name and if I were his new detention officer.

"My name is Mr. Coleman and, yes, I'm your new detention officer and you'll report to me," I answered.

"That's great! I know we're going to get along just great," young Mims enthused. Mims began to pat both hands on his chest and then on his pants pockets as if looking for something he couldn't find. He then said to me, "Doggone it! I must have misplaced my cigarettes somewhere around here. Can I get one from you?"

I calmly spoke in a very low tone so Mims' buddies couldn't hear as I said to him, "Young Mr. Mims, you know and I know that you are not allowed to have any contraband and that includes matches and cigarettes. Now, there's something else I want you to know. If you ever try to run another one of your little ten-cent con games on me, they will have to call an ambulance to take both of us to the nearest hospital. You will be going to the hospital to get patched up and I will be going with you so the doctors can remove my foot from out of your ass! Do I make myself clear?"

I watched his expression change as his brain told him that he had made a bad mistake and had chosen the wrong detention officer to play mind games with. "Yes, Sir," he blurted as he scrambled backwards to rejoin his partners.

When his buddies asked him what I had said to him, I overheard Mims tell them, "Man, his name is Mr. Coleman and he ain't to be fucked with; he don't play!"

A few days later I realized that the incident with Mims had gained me a modicum of respect from the group. In working with my group, I treated each one of the boys the same and with dignity. I found a very interesting dichotomy. Even though the boys were charged with some serious adult type crimes, after everything was said and done, they were still really just children. They were kids from broken homes, growing up quickly or raising themselves in an urban jungle where the rules of the jungle dictate that survival is of the utmost and the battle cry is: "BY ANY MEANS NECESSARY!" This metaphor of the jungle brought to mind something I had once read. On the windswept plains of Mother Africa live the lion and the gazelle. Each morning when the gazelle awakes, he wakes up running for he knows that the lion will be on the hunt for his morning food. The gazelle must run; his survival depends on it. Each morning when the lion awakes, he wakes up running, for he knows that he must run to capture his food. His survival depends on it. In Mother Africa, it doesn't matter whether you are a lion or a gazelle. When the sun comes up, you'd better be running.

I had to remain cognizant of the fact that the boys were children trapped in the bodies of young warriors. I gave them their "young person" respect and I expected my "adult person" respect. As time progressed, I established a very good rapport with the boys. They trusted me and they knew I cared about them and that I would do what I could to help them work towards turning their lives around. I instituted rap sessions with them and talked with them individually about their personal concerns and problems. I enjoyed my work, but I never forgot where I was and whom I was dealing with. There was a part of me deep down inside that I had brought back from Vietnam that would never let me drop my guard and forget that these kids were quite capable of killing someone. And, they could do it without the slightest bit of provocation and at the drop of a hat. I sometimes worried about how I might react if I were ever faced with a serious threat from the warrior side of the boys' psyches. I was secretly afraid of what I might do instinctively and I never told anyone about some of the demons that sometimes visited me in my sleep at night.

Six months later, the judges, probation officers, the psychologist, and Mr. Johnson let me know how impressed they were with the progress I had made with many of the boys regarded as incorrigible. The psychologist and the judges had begun to request written reports from me detailing my impressions, observations, and concerns about some of the boys when they were to appear before the court for their cases to be adjudicated. I didn't pull any punches. If I thought a young man deserved to be sent away to a state training school facility, I said so. By the same token, if I felt that a young man should be released and given another chance, I also said so.

A few months later, I was promoted to detention supervisor/counselor. I supervised six detention officers, but I still maintained a hands-on approach in working with the hard core older group of boys. All of my staff were college graduates or in the process of completing their degree programs. Each of them was a dedicated, caring professional and each of them possessed very valuable assets for the job not taught in school: intuitiveness and "street" smarts. My staff had that the ability to anticipate the unexpected and to discern subtle and unusual behavioral patterns exhibited by the boys which could be indicators that some very serious trouble was brewing.

During the next two years, all of my staff, except for one, had either graduated from college and moved on to other types of employment or had been promoted to positions in other departments. The one that remained was Kevin Bishop. He was white and had all of the tools for the job, including a passion for the martial arts. He was my back up. We worked well together, and in tense situations could even anticipate how the other was going to respond.

Two bad things happened. First, the five guys I received as replacement staff were all from privileged backgrounds and still had their silver spoons hanging out of their mouths. Four whites and one black. All were matriculating at various colleges in the area, working on degrees in psychology or sociology. They seemed to view the job as a social practicum that would allow them to apply the principles of what they had learned from studying Sigmund Freud and Carl Jung. They were going to use psychology to show the poor, misguided kids the errors of their ways before they became career criminals. It also didn't help matters when the black guy, who swished from side to side when he walked and held his wrist limply, proclaimed to the staff that he was gay. The majority of the kids we had to work with were young psychologists in their own right and they were sure to quickly spot and exploit the new staff members' lack of "street" sense. BY ANY MEANS NECESSARY!

The second problem was drugs. The usage of cocaine and other hallucinatory drugs by the kids we were getting had become more prevalent and more alarming. Statistics on violent crimes committed by teenagers was skyrocketing. On one occasion, the court committed two young men to us who had been charged with armed robbery and assault on a number of people, mostly the elderly. They would rob them and mercilessly pistol-whip them. Both were black, seventeen year old country boys from Alabama, and needless to say, dangerous. Robert was 6'4," 190 pounds with a muscular build and mentally slow. He came across as a dullard, but his lopsided smile and the spark of insanity in his eyes belied a strong, mother-wit intelligence. His partner, James, was 5'10," also of muscular build. He was an affable, fun kind of kid with a sense of humor. It was very clear that Robert was the leader of this wrecking crew and James was the classic follower. I told the staff to always watch Robert closely.

One morning while reading the night shift supervisor's activity report, I saw an entry detailing a physical attack by Robert upon James. Robert was angry because he found out that James testified against him. James had fingered him as the perpetrator and aggressor in the physical attacks on their unsuspecting victims. I talked with James concerning the attack and he told me, "Mr. Coleman, I was watching television with some of the other guys and Robert came up behind me and hit me over the head with a chair and knocked me to the floor. Then he started stomping on me. It weren't no fair fight; he jumped me from behind."

James had been taken to hospital to get numerous stitches for injuries. Fearing for their own safety, the other kids were giving Robert a wide berth. I could further see that the fear extended to all of my social work oriented staff, except for Kevin. For most of the day, I could intuitively feel an oppressive tension building. Kevin and I were in my office discussing the matter when we heard a loud commotion taking place in the day room.

When we entered the day room, two boys were standing face to face, screaming at each other and on the verge of mortal combat. All of the other boys had backed off and formed a circle around the combatants. My five staff members were standing outside of the circle immobilized by fear as the situation escalated. Kevin and I looked at one another and knew what we had to do. Something about the confrontation taking place didn't ring true. The two combatants were not the kind of boys who would engage each other in that fashion or that vehemently. Kevin moved quietly outside the circle behind the two boys while I moved behind Robert as he stood on the periphery watching. I saw him reach slowly beside him and wrap his hands around a chair and snatch it up over his head. Just as he turned to hit one of my staff over the head with it, I yelled in his ear from behind, "Boy, if you swing that chair I will break your damn neck!"

He dropped the chair and turned to me wide eyed and stammered, "I won't do'in nuthin!"

I took control and immediately called for a lockdown of all detainees. I then had a meeting with all of my staff. I explained to them that the two boys who were about to fight had no intention of fighting. Robert had intimidated them and he had made them fake a fight. And, during the ensuing commotion which would erupt, Robert planned to hit a staff member over the head with a chair. He would then grab that staff member's keys and try to escape. Except for Kevin, I could tell that the revelation I had just imparted to them had never crossed their minds.

One morning when I arrived at work everyone seemed to be in a heightened state of anxiety. I asked the night supervisor, whom I was relieving, what was going on. He told me that the FBI had come into our facility at four o'clock in the morning to bring us the most wanted teenager in the world. His name was Billy Isaac. He was seventeen years old and he had been on the run, eluding law enforcement officials for a couple of weeks. He had been serving a sentence at a juvenile correctional institution that I believed was in Ohio. His older brother, Carl, a cousin, and a black guy, named Dungee, had escaped from a prison in Georgia where they were serving hard time for some very serious crimes. The three of them were able to make it to Ohio and boldly broke Billy out of the facility where he was serving time. The specifics are a little hazy to me now, but if I remember correctly, they killed a couple of people as they stole cars, money, etc. while making their way back to

Georgia. Once they reached rural South Georgia, they went to a farmhouse where they found two women alone. One was an older woman, named Mrs. Alday; the other was younger and her last name was also Alday. They were mother-in-law and daughter-in-law and their husbands, along with a brother-in-law, were farmers out in the fields working the land. The four escapees made themselves at home and took sexual liberties with the women, and then with guns they found in the house, blew the women's brains out as they begged for mercy. Hours later when the men returned home, they were executed one by one as they entered the house. Their brains, too, were blown out.

Police agencies throughout the country were scouring the earth in their efforts to bring these vicious, deadly killers to justice, preferably with a bullet, being synonymous with justice. The television and radio stations saturated the airwaves with updated information on the search for them. Eventually, the group split up and went in different directions; one by one, they were captured. And as always, the ringleader, Carl, was the last one to be captured.

The boys we had in detention were aware that there was a notorious individual in their presence and that fact unnerved me. I met with Mr. Johnson and two FBI agents and voiced my concerns about housing Billy. The awe effect that Billy had caused among our detainees was akin to having "Billy The Kid" on the premises. And it could start our detainees to thinking about rioting or escaping, so I suggested that Billy be moved to the city jail where the FBI would have easy access for questioning him, and it would keep the media away from my staff and me. Everyone agreed with me and Billy Isaac was sent to the city jail late that afternoon. During the long wait for Billy to be transferred, I talked with him and he repeatedly said that he didn't want to escape, but "the others" had made him do it. He also said he didn't participate in the killings. While talking with him, he looked just like any other scared seventeen-year-old kid. However, the possibility did exist that he was a murderer and a rapist.

Billy turned states witness against the other three. It's now twenty-six years later and Billy is serving a life sentence, which might be forever, and the other three are all on death row.

This tension-filled episode caused me to seriously think about looking for some other type of employment. The staff I had been given was not prepared or fit for the job expected of them. The kids we were now getting were more violent, aggressive, and addicted than before. I told Mr. Johnson I felt that these two factors were the equivalent of nitro and glycerin. We were sitting on a powder keg and something was going to blow sooner or later. Mr. Johnson sympathized with my plight, but told me his hands were tied due to budgetary restraints of the legislature. For me, the job started to become a tension-filled, pressurized vacuum. I couldn't wait for my shift to end so I could go and have a few stiff drinks to unwind.

I had been dating a wonderful lady named Monica for about a year and a half. She was two years my senior and was a fourth grade school teacher. We spent a lot of quality time together. After much soul searching, I decided it was time for me to settle down and stop sowing my wild oats. In January of 1975, we were married. Within a year, I used my GI Bill to purchase a beautiful new home in a suburb of Atlanta. My wife and I liked to travel, and between work and play we enjoyed the company of great friends. Everything was going great, but the pressure of the job was still an albatross around my neck. My drinking had increased, but I was a social drinker and could handle it.

On Christmas day of 1977, my wife and I were blessed with the birth of a beautiful baby girl. We named her Azure Michele. I remembered how awestruck I was when on a trip to the Bahamas I saw the beautiful, blue color of the ocean there. I was told that the fantastic hue of the ocean was called azure. The awe and natural beauty of that ocean and the awe and natural beauty of my new daughter moved me to name her Azure. I also gave her the name Michele in deference to my first cousin Michele. She is the older sister of my cousin Stephen, the one who gave me the scary car ride from the airport when I first returned from 'Nam.

Shortly after the birth of my daughter, my cousin, Cheryl, introduced me to a cousin of hers, Rose Davis. Rose was the director of a county agency that provided protective custody for abused, neglected, and abandoned children. Cheryl had told Rose about my present job situation and my qualifications. Rose was in the process of trying to fill a supervisory position in her office. She had a staff of five women that provided care for very young children up to age seventeen. Roses' facility was housed at a secret location for the protection of the children in her care. She was looking for someone, preferably a male, with a counseling background and supervisory experience who could handle the problems of the larger and older boys who sometimes became unmanageable. She suggested that I come by her office the following week to apply for the position. I did.

A week later, Rose offered me the position, but I declined it at first. My reason for declining was because I perceived that Rose was having some problems with her all female staff. After doing some checking around, my suspicions were confirmed. Rose at one time had been a staff member and had worked her way up to her present position. The people she was director of had, at one time, been her co-workers and friends. They complained that she never did her work and this had caused them to do extra work. It was further alleged that she had hooked and crooked her way up the promotional ladder.

Rose told me if I took the position she would include administrative duties in my job description. I rationalized that having these skills on my resume could help me in seeking future employment, and the position would allow me to leave the pressures of my present job. So, I decided to take the job Rose had offered, and I informed Mr. Johnson that I would be resigning to take a lateral transfer of job assignments. He wished me well. I took pride in the fact that during the five years I worked at the court, none of my staff were ever attacked and we never had an escape on my shift.

CHAPTER ELEVEN

Fire and Ice

On the first day of my new job, I reported to Rose's office for a quick briefing, and she then took me to meet my staff. I met Jan, who would be my assistant and would work with the older children; Mrs. Brooks and Mrs. Nellons; two older ladies who were aides and would work with the younger children and babies; Joyce and Carol, two college students who were doing their internships and would divide their time between the older and younger groups of kids; and Mrs. Simons, the cook. All of the women were African-American except for Carol and Mrs. Simons. I gave my staff a pep talk and made sure they understood that I believed in an open door policy. If they encountered any problems or had any concerns or issues, which needed to be addressed, they were to feel free to bring them to my attention.

Within the first week I could detect some resentment from Jan. I discussed the matter with Rose and she informed me that Jan was probably uptight because she thought that she should have been given my position. I called Jan into my office and had a long heart-to-heart talk with her. During our discussion Jan made me aware that she was having some problems at home with her teenage daughter. She was also disconcerted because she had been dating the same guy for ten years and he didn't seem interested in marrying her and he had a gambling problem. I gave her some advice and offered my support, but I told her to make sure that she did not let her personal problems impact on her job performance or reflect negatively on the children we were responsible for. Our meeting laid the groundwork for us to develop an amicable working relationship.

Two weeks later, Rose called me into her office to talk. She informed me that Mrs. Brooks had been insubordinate to her earlier that morning. Rose had berated Mrs. Brooks about something she had forgotten to do. Mrs. Brooks was upset because Rose had embarrassed her in front of the other staff members and she let Rose know that she didn't appreciate what she had done. Rose then became angry because Mrs. Brooks "talked back to her."

Rose then told me, "I want you to write her up for being insubordinate to me and then I want you to suspend her for three days."

"Wait a minute Rose." I said. "The incident that happened between you and Mrs. Brooks has nothing to do with me. Any adverse actions taken against her should come from you, not me."

"Part of the reason that I hired you was to handle situations like this. If you can't do what I tell you to do, then I don't need you." She stated.

"Rose, I don't have any problems when it comes to following your instructions or orders, but when you ask me do something which is against the department's policies and procedures I have to draw the line." I replied.

Rose took a moment to think about what I had just said. "You're right," she told me. "I guess I was just upset with her, but you better talk to her and tell her it better not happen again."

Before talking with Mrs. Brooks, I reviewed her personnel file and found that she had an unblemished record and nineteen years of service. I also noticed that her birthday was April 8th, two days before mine. She was an Aries too! Now I knew why I liked her and why we got along so well. She was always helpful and made me aware of small things in the day to day operations that she thought I needed to know. This recent incident with Rose wasn't the first time that I had observed Rose singling Mrs. Brooks out for some type of verbal abuse. When I sat down to talk to Mrs. Brooks about the matter she enthusiastically said, "Mr. Coleman, I want to thank you for standing up for me. That awful woman has been treating me like a stepchild for years and what makes it so bad is I'm almost old enough to be her mama." I told Mrs. Brooks I would do what I could to try to shield her from Rose's wrath.

I completed my six-month probationary period for my new position and was given a favorable evaluation by Rose. Successfully passing the probationary period established me as a permanent status employee of the County Government system. There were times when I didn't know if I was going to successfully pass my probationary period because Rose and I had butted heads a couple of times. There were a few instances when she became downright disrespectful and vulgar to my staff and me. On each of those occasions I let her know that I didn't appreciate her actions and that I was not going to tolerate it. I could tell that she wasn't used to being challenged and it pissed her off, but I stood my ground and she apologized. She exhibited other types of aberrant behavior, which caused me to wonder if she had some type of emotional problem. I told my cousin Cheryl about some of Rose's antics and asked about her mental stability. Cheryl informed me that it was rumored among some of the family members that Rose had been dismissed from the military due to some type of nervous disorder. This revelation put me on notice to not take Rose lightly. A few weeks later, I used some of my business contacts to acquire a grant, which would provide our operation with $1,500.00 a month for one year. The grant stipulated that the money was to be used expressly for children's activities such as picnics, parties, and field trips to the zoo and the circus. When I made Rose aware of what I had accomplished she was excited and wanted to know how I had managed to do it. I wasn't about to reveal my sources to her, so I told her in a joking manner that I had connections. When the first check arrived at the agency I saw to it that the funds were used as intended. But, when the second monthly check arrived Rose informed me that as Director, she should handle the disbursement of the funds. I was suspicious of her motives, but she was the boss and I acquiesced. Two months later, I discovered that Rose had disbursed only $300.00 for each of the previous two months. One day I entered her office when she wasn't in it and I searched the financial records to see if I could determine what was happening to the money. I found information, which confirmed that Rose was spending the unused portion of the grant money every month to pay a contractor for renovations and additions to her home. When

Rose returned to her office later that day I confronted her with a few questions.

"Rose, how much money do we have left for the kid's activities this month?" I inquired.

Rose responded, "Oh! I don't know right offhand. Each month I send the check to my Director, Sandra Miller, over at the headquarters office and she disburses the money back to me and I give you and the other two shift supervisors equal amounts. I don't have the figures right now, but I will let you know how much we have later this week."

When Rose was giving me this information she became nervous and edgy and I knew without a doubt that she was lying and she knew that I knew she was lying. My attitude was that if she wanted to take money illegally and it didn't involve me, then it was none of my business. If she got caught it would be her problem.

One Wednesday afternoon Rose told me that she was having a birthday party for herself the following Saturday night and wanted me to come. When I got to her house the driveway and street was full of cars. When I entered her house the party was in full swing and both music and booze were flowing. I also noticed a section of the house, which looked as if it was still under renovation by the contractor. I was the only person from our office that had been invited, but I knew many of the other guests so I fixed me a drink and joined the party. Rose was the "Belle of the Ball" as she moved among her guest and socialized. A couple of hours later the party was still going strong and Rose approached me and took my hand as she whispered in my ear for me to come with her for a minute. I followed as she led me down a hallway and entered her bedroom where she closed the door behind us. She turned to face me and slid her arms around my waist as she looked up at me and said, "You sure look good. I've wanted to hold you like this all evening." I could smell the alcohol on her breath as she slurred her words and I could tell that she was more than a little tipsy. I also felt the heat from her body as she pushed closer to me. I tried placating her as I replied, "Rose, you look good this evening too, but I don't think we need to be doing this."

"Can't you see this is what I want to be doing?" She asked as she leaned forward to kiss me. "I just wanted you to know that I want you to hang around and stay here with me after everybody else leaves."

Rose was a nice looking woman, but she was my boss and I was a married man and to top it off. Rose was a very unstable person as far as I was concerned. I felt uncomfortable with her and my instincts were yelling at me to remove myself from the present situation. I tried to disengage myself as I told her, "Rose, you know that I'm a married man. And we both know that this isn't right, so I'd better be going."

"Screw that bitch! Screw your ass too! Get the hell out of my house!" Rose screamed at me. When I looked into her eyes I saw raw hatred and a glimpse of what insanity might look like. While the window of opportunity was presenting itself to me I took advantage of it and got out of there. On my way home I kept replaying the mental tape I had just recorded and thought to myself, "I've got a fool for a boss and I hope I don't live to regret the day I took the job."

On Monday when Rose got to work she came in all chipper and smiling telling everyone about the great party she had over the weekend.

Later she pulled me aside and told me, "I want to apologize for my behavior on Saturday night. I really should give up drinking, because sometimes I get so high that I can't remember things the next day. I hope I didn't say or do anything to upset you too bad the other night."

"Naw." I told her. "*You* didn't say anything too bad, but I did have some concerns about the way you went off on me. You've apologized and that's good enough for me."

"Are we still friends?" She inquired.

"Yes. Of course," was my response.

I thought our conversation had eliminated any further problems concerning the matter, but I was wrong. Rose had begun to call my home on the weekends, late in the evening to ask me some inane question relative to the job which could very easily have waited until Monday morning. Most times I could hear the now familiar slur in her speech which indicated to me that she was drinking. She would proceed to tell me that she was all stretched out in her big, beautiful bathtub enjoying a sensuous bubble bath, or that she was relaxing in her king sized bed on her beautiful satin sheets all alone. One day, I had a heart-to-heart talk with her and I asked her not to call me during my off time unless it was pertinent to the job. I was fed up with her antics and I went on to tell her, "Rose, I am not interested in you and I prefer to keep our working relationship on a professional level."

She angrily replied, "We'll see about that."

From that point on, working with her became hell. She became the proverbial "scorned woman." She began to question my decisions about job related matters and would harass me about things she would forget to do.

One morning in January I woke up to find that eight inches of snow had fallen during the night. It rarely snows in Atlanta, so the city was literally paralyzed. I called Rose at home to tell her I was snowed in. My home sat atop a steep hill and the driveway was covered with a sheet of ice and I wasn't about to attempt driving my car on it. Also, there was no public transportation available in my area of the county. Rose informed me that she had the same problem and had called her superiors. She told me that they were going to have a police patrol car to come and pick her up and transport her to the office. She told me not to try and make it on my own, but to stay put and when she got to the office she would send the officer's to pick me up. At ten o'clock a.m., I called the office and Rose answered the phone and told me to just wait, that the officers were on the way. I called her every hour on the hour until two o'clock p.m. to tell her I was still waiting for the officer's to arrive. Each time I called her she told me to wait, the officer's should be arriving soon. My regular work hours were from seven thirty a.m. until four o'clock p.m.; so at two o'clock p.m. I decided there was no reason for me to bother with trying to get to work.

The next day when I arrived at work, Rose docked me for a day's pay and gave me a written reprimand for not coming to work! I exploded on her. "What the hell do you mean by this? You told me to wait until the police that you were sending came to get me!"

She looked at me as if she didn't know what I was talking about and calmly said, "During inclement weather it is your responsibility to make alternate arrangements to get to work." I could see that I would be wasting my time trying to rationalize with her, so I sent an appeal request to her superiors. Three days later I received a decision from them upholding Rose's actions against me. Not only was I having problems on the job, but also I was having problems at home. My wife had maxed out all of the credit cards on clothing for herself and had not bothered to consult me about her planned purchases. This was not the first time that I had seen signs of her frivolous spending habits. But, I had made the mistake of letting it slide in order to avoid the arguing and fussing it would provoke. I was going through more than enough turmoil and chaos on the job and I didn't want to have to come home to the same hell. But, I was and I just didn't know it yet. She wanted to buy a new car and I finally agreed to the purchase of the car after she agreed to curb her abuse of the credit cards. It seemed that once she got the car, she developed credit card amnesia. Besides having the credit card bills, I had other rather steep bills and a heavy mortgage to contend with. I reached a point of hating to go to the mailbox. When I confronted my wife about her spending habits, we ended up arguing about the issue for a couple of days. Years later I came to realize how that particular argument was the beginning of an irreparable schism within the marriage.

The pressure was becoming overwhelming. I began to feel like a vice was closing in on me. I started having feelings not unlike the ones I had when I was back in 'Nam. These feelings were talking to me and they were saying that something very bad was coming. These feelings were so strong they would cause the hair on my neck to rise up. I felt that something bad was coming and I knew it. I began to think about some of the things Talley had told me concerning synchronicity. Maybe these feelings were preparing me for whatever was coming...be it good, bad or indifferent. I tried to relax and go with the flow, but anxiety was a strong emotion to contend with. During the ensuing weeks, I had a lot of difficulty sleeping due to my recurring dreams about death, destruction, and war. I would wake up shivering, bathed in a cold sweat and terrified. During the day, I was sometimes bothered by flashbacks about 'Nam. These flashbacks were usually precipitated by something I saw, touched, or smelled that reminded me of 'Nam. Sometimes noises like a car backfiring or the loud roar of a motorcycle would set me off. I needed something to knock the edge off, so I started drinking...heavily. I knew that the alcohol wouldn't make the nightmares and flashbacks go away, but I knew that as long as I drank the alcohol it would stave off and protect me from the excruciating intrusive thoughts whirling around in my head. The alcohol didn't solve my problems, but it allowed me to step out of the line of fire for periods of time.

One morning I was getting ready for work when I heard Monica emit a loud, piercing scream from downstairs in the kitchen. I rushed into the kitchen and immediately saw that the walls and cabinets above the stove were engulfed in flames. Monica was standing in the middle of the floor with a dazed expression on her face watching the fire claim anything in its path in order to fuel its vicious and voracious appetite. When I looked into her eyes I could see the dangerous, licking flames reflected in them. I yelled to her, "Get the baby and get out of here! Call the fire department from the neighbors! Move!"

I then turned and knocked out the kitchen window and ran outside to grab the water hose. I threw the water hose through the opening where the window had been and turned the water on full blast. Once I was back inside, I had to feel around to find the water hose because of the billowing, black smoke, which had begun to fill up the kitchen. I concentrated the water on the wall area because I knew that once the flames got to the interior of the wall, the vacuum created there would suck the flames up to the second floor of the house. I had seen a similar situation like that happen in 'Nam when a guy was using a flamethrower. I was making some progress in controlling the fire, but I was starting to breathe in too much smoke. Suddenly, I felt someone grabbing and pulling me away from the kitchen. When I looked around I saw a fireman with a black oxygen mask over his face pointing and motioning for me to get out. I complied with his instructions.

When I got outside the paramedics began to give me oxygen from a mask and asked me how I was feeling. I indicated that I was all right and in a matter of minutes the firemen had put the fire out. The Fire Chief came over to me and said, "Son, you did a pretty good job of retarding the fire's spread, but what you did was mighty dangerous. You should have gotten out of there with your wife and baby and let us handle things."

"Chief, sometimes you just don't think rationally and you just do what you have to do," I told him as I coughed and wheezed. "How bad is the damage?

"Well, the flames didn't get sucked up through the walls, so there's no fire damage to the upstairs. But there is smoke damage to most of the downstairs and two rooms upstairs. The fire damage was limited to your kitchen cabinets and two of the walls. We're going to use those big fans over there to pull that smoke out and we're going to clean up all of that excess water. Your insurance company will have you fixed up in no time. You might want to stay at a relative's house for a couple of days to let things dry out and allow for some of the smoke smell to dissipate."

I followed the Fire Chief's advice and Monica, the baby and I went to my in-laws for a couple of days. I called Rose to tell her what had happened and she was very sympathetic as she asked, "Is there anything I can do?"

"No," I replied.

"Well, you just concentrate on getting your house straightened out and don't worry about the job. You have plenty of leave time. How many days do you think you will need?" She asked.

"I'll probably need to take about ten or eleven days to get everything back in shape," I told her. "That'll be fine just call me periodically to let me know how things are going," Rose told me.

"What did she say?" Monica inquired.

"She told me to take some of my leave time to get the house straight." I remembered thinking to myself, *maybe Rose isn't such a bad person.* After all, she did seem genuinely interested in my plight and had unhesitatingly given me the necessary time off to take care of my dilemma.

During the next week, the insurance company sent a contractor for every phase of the work that needed to be done. There was a contractor for the wallpaper, the cabinets, wall construction, carpeting, flooring, furniture, draperies, etc. There was even a cleaning contractor to launder and dry-clean all clothing. I was glad that I had taken the necessary time off from the job because even though all of the contractors were bonded, it was still incumbent upon me being present to oversee their work. The complete job took eleven days.

When I returned to work, everyone welcomed me back very enthusiastically including Rose. I soon found out from some of the staff that Rose had been giving Mrs. Brooks a difficult time again. Later, during the day Rose stopped me in the hallway and told me, "I can't put up with anymore of Mrs. Brooks' bull. I have been having more problems out of her and I want you to suspend her for two weeks."

"Rose, we have been over this before. If you have a problem with Mrs. Brooks it is your job to take actions against her."

Rose stepped up so close to me I could feel her breath as she uttered through clenched teeth, "If you don't do it, I'm going to fire you!"

At that moment Mrs. Brooks stepped around the corner from the adjoining hallway and said, "Mr. Coleman, I heard exactly what Rose said and if you need a witness I'll testify to anyone who will listen as to what she said."

Immediately, Rose turned pale and looked from Mrs. Brooks to me, then back to Mrs. Brooks and said, "Bitch!" She then ran to her office and gathered up a sheaf of papers, ran out the door, jumped into her car and sped off.

Mrs. Brooks said, "Mr. Coleman, I meant what I said. I appreciate you for standing up for me like that, but watch that woman 'cause she's dangerous." I thanked Mrs. Brooks and told her that we needed to get back to work.

An hour later, Rose entered the office accompanied by her director, a white woman named Sandra Miller, and her black assistant director, Ruby Wise. Rose told me that the director wanted to see me in the office. On my way to the office I was wondering what the hell this was all about. When I entered the office they both greeted me with big, imitation, pasted on smiles. Right away I knew what this pow-wow was about; they had come to fire me! I don't know how I knew. Synchronicity? Maybe. But, I knew.

"Mr. Coleman, Mrs. Davis has brought some matters of great concern to our attention and we have come here to discuss them with you. Would you please look over these documents and see if the information contained in them is correct?" The director asked from behind a smiling mask as she handed me three type written pages.

The first page addressed the three times that Rose had told me to suspend Mrs. Brooks. The documentation stated: "On the three dates listed herein Mr. Coleman is charged with insubordination. I gave Mr. Coleman specific job duties to perform and he flatly refused to perform the duties I had ordered him to carry out."

Rose made sure that she didn't say what those duties were because what she'd asked me to do violated agency policy. The next issue was the $1,500.00 grant I was able to secure for the children. Rose stated: "Mr. Coleman was able to get a special grant of $1,500.00 per month for one year. He didn't tell me he had gotten the grant and when I found out about it through some of my sources, I took control of it on behalf of the agency. It is my contention that Mr. Coleman didn't tell me about the grant because he intended to use the money for his own personal gain." I couldn't believe what I was reading! Part of my job responsibility was to develop alternative funding sources, and when I was successful in doing that, I immediately told Rose about it. Her brazen statement now made me wonder how much of a kick back Mrs. Miller and Mrs. Wise were getting.

The third statement read: "On January 14, 1979, the weather was inclement due to an accumulation of snow and ice. Mr. Coleman called the office to say he would be coming to work as soon as he was able to get his driveway cleared and get his car down the hill of his driveway. At the end of the day Mr. Coleman had not reported to work or called back. He was absent without leave. Subsequently, I docked him a day's pay and gave him a written reprimand." I explained to Mrs. Miller that Rose had told me to wait at home until the police came to pick me up.

Rose blurted out, "I never told him that. Mr. Coleman lives in a different county and Atlanta police don't go into other jurisdictions to pick up people."

I responded, "My wife can verify that Rose told me to wait for the police to pick me up. I had my wife to listen on a second phone when Rose gave me those instructions because I was suspicious of her motives and I knew that police didn't usually come from one jurisdiction to another to pick people up. Rose said that the officers that she was sending were personal friends of hers and it would be no problem for them to pick me up."

Mrs. Miller interjected, "Well, your wife isn't here to verify this information so we will move on."

"I can call her," I shot back.

"That won't be necessary," Mrs. Miller adamantly said.

"I find it very interesting that this matter should resurface after having already been ruled on when I took it through the appeals process," I retorted to the Director.

The final page stated: "Mr. Coleman had a fire at his home and requested eleven days of leave time to take care of the repairs. I granted him the leave time and told him that he must call in to the office every day, which he refused to do. Due to the disciplinary problems, lack of respect for authority and questionable ethics that Mr. Coleman has brought to the agency, I am recommending that he be terminated from his position effective immediately."

I sat there momentarily stunned, but I didn't want these women to know it. A red, hot anger started creeping through every fiber of my being and a roaring sound like a freight train started screaming in my head. A vision started to play before my eyes like a VCR on fast forward. In the vision, I could see myself exploding up from my chair and grabbing both the Director and her assistant by their necks and slamming their heads together repeatedly, until I could hear the bones of their skulls cracking, popping and shattering. As their splattered brains began to ooze out of their lifeless bodies, I let them drop to the floor and I turn to find Rose cowering in a comer of the room trying to hide behind a file cabinet. As I advance on her, she's crying, pleading and begging for me not to hurt her. Her arms are straight out in front of her, palms turned toward me off, her fingers splayed in supplication, the snot and tears running down her face glittering as they catch the reflected sunlight angling in through the window panes. I reach forward wrapping both of my hands around her throat and began to slowly squeeze with all of my strength. I can feel the cords in her neck harden as they try to resist, her mouth opens in a scream that can't get past my hands on her throat. She starts to turn red in the face as her eyes began to bulge out of their sockets. I continue to strangle her and her face begins to turn a purplish color. I look into her eyes, and see that the tiny blood vessels in the white portion are turning to a mean, blood red color and getting thicker. And, just as life is about to exit her body, I hear a distant voice saying, "Mr. Coleman! Mr. Coleman! Are you all right?"

When I gathered my thoughts and glanced around me, all three women were looking at me strangely as Mrs. Miller again said, "Mr. Coleman, are you all right?"

"Yes. Yes, I'm fine," I answered her.

"I was asking if you had any questions concerning your termination," Mrs. Miller supplied. "And, if you don't have any questions we are asking that you give us your keys to the building and leave the premises now."

As I handed her my keys I said, "No, I don't have any questions, but I do have something to say. I hope that each one of you witches bum in Hell!"

I was suddenly gripped by the recurring fear of being back in the jungles of 'Nam lost, and cut off from everyone and unable to find my way back. Desperately I search for a rope or a lifeline that's connected to something that I can remember. I've forgotten why I'm fighting. How did I get out here untethered, lost, and unable to remember?

I got into my car and started home and before getting on the highway I stopped at the nearest liquor store and purchased a fifth of Vodka, a small can of grapefruit juice and a cup. I sat there in the parking lot and watched my hands shaking as I poured my first drink of the day. I downed it quickly and poured another drink. I gulped it down and fought the gagging reaction that usually occurred whenever I drank too fast. My forehead broke out in a feverish sweat as I felt the warm, burning sensation that accompanied the alcohol as it coursed its way to my stomach. As I sat there I began to wonder why the vision of me violently beating the women had seemed so real. Then I realized it was probably due to the violence I had experienced in Vietnam and had kept repressed for many years. My military training had prepared me to go to a foreign land to kill the people there. During basic training when the drill instructor yelled, "WHAT IS THE SPIRIT OF THE BAYONET?" We would yell back in unison. "TO KILL! TO KILL!" Before we were sent to 'Nam we were programmed and trained how to kill. When it was time to leave 'Nam and return home we were bona fied killers. We were taken out of the jungles, put on a commercial jet, and flown home in less than twenty-four hours. But, the government neglected to do something very, very important They neglected to DEPROGRAM the killers they had trained. This self-knowledge and guilt sometimes made it difficult to interact comfortably with others. When the fire of the alcohol I was drinking met the fire of anger in my belly, I was able to let some of my rage dissipate. I continued sitting in my car waiting for the familiar, fuzzy, comforting, and euphoric, mind-numbing "high" which would make my major troubles seem minor, at least for a little while. I entered the highway and started home to break the news of my firing to Monica.

Above: My buddies–Hannah, William, and me.

Center: My brother Mike and me in Vietnam (1968) at Cam Rahn Bay

Below: The boys in Base Camp

My late father and grand-father (the actual chauffer portrayed in the movie *Driving Miss Daisy*)

My Parents, Leila and T.R. "Bootee" Coleman

Me after Basic Training in 1967

Track teammates at NCCU, Paul Wilson (deceased) and Oba Akiawole (Charles Copeland)

Me winning the 120-yard High Hurdles
event at the first Integrated High School
City Championships in Atlanta, GA (1964)

My friend Harvey
"Punchy" Jackson

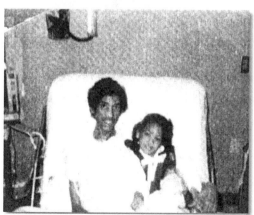

Me, hospitalized and weighing 89
pounds, sharing a few moments with my
daughter at Christmas (1982)

Spelman Nursery School 1949-50

L-R: James Neal; my wife, Paula; Jane Smith; me; Betty Graves; and Richard Hackney. In rear is James Neal's mother who was one of our teachers.

Paula and me at our wedding,
May 1992

My wife Paula, actor James Earl Jones, and me at the
Broadway Premier of *Driving Miss Daisy*

Mrs. Hunt, me, Governor Guy Hunt of North
Carolina, and my track coach Dr. Leroy Walker

Me and Native American Vietnam Veteran friends at the
Blackfeet Reservation, Browning, MT

CHAPTER TWELVE

The Grim Reaper Goes on Patrol

When I got home I told Monica what had transpired on the job and she was angry as hell for what Rose had done to me. During her tirade I also saw that she was angry with me for losing my job and was gripped by the fear of where we'd go from here, and angry with me because she knew I had been drinking. My having no job meant having no income and this realization added up to us facing very serious financial problems.

I tried to assure her that things would be all right. I explained to her that Rose and her superiors had capriciously orchestrated my firing and that I was going to file a formal grievance requesting a hearing before the Personnel Board. I assured her that when the board heard my side of the story and reviewed the evidence I would present before them, they won't have any trouble seeing that I had been terminated without cause. And then everything will be fine because they will have to reinstate me to my position. I knew without a doubt that I had been railroaded and I was going to fight with everything possible to prove it

The next day I went to the personnel board and filed all of the documents necessary to request a full hearing. Five days later, I received a letter advising me that a hearing date had been set to take place in two weeks and, if I was going to be represented by an attorney, it was necessary for me to submit that attorney's name prior to the hearing date. I went to see Attorney Thomas Jones to see if he would represent me. When I had completed telling him all of the particulars of my case, he agreed to represent me. Tom had been in private practice for four years had graduated tops in his law class, came highly recommended, and we had grown up as little boys together. We worked out the financial obligations and I felt confident having my friend Tom represent me.

Tom and I spent a great deal of time together preparing my case. On the day of the hearing we entered the hearing room confident that we were ready to do battle and win! There were five Personnel Officers and a Chairman assigned to hear my case. My witnesses were present in the hall outside. We had gotten two women, the evening and midnight supervisors, who would testify that Rose had told them she was going to get rid of me because I didn't take adverse actions against Mrs. Brooks when she told me to; and because I wouldn't respond to her amorous advances or date her. Mrs. Brooks would testify about the many problems she had experienced from Rose and about the things Rose had said and done against me in an effort to fire me. There were three other ladies who worked for the agency and would serve as character witness on my behalf. I felt that Tom and I had done a good job in preparing an excellent rebuttal and defense for the written documents, which had been used to terminate me.

The Chairman representing the Personnel Board was black and I recognized him as also being a professor at Morehouse College. When he saw me walk in he said, "Hello Coleman, how are you?

"Fine, Sir," I told him.

He then looked at me and said, "How are your parents?"

"They're fine also," I replied a bit confused.

I was not aware that this gentleman knew my parents, but it was somewhat reassuring to know that I might have an ally over in the enemy camp. Things were definitely looking good for the home team! To my surprise, a black attorney named Satterfield represented the agency. He was a tall, dark complexioned guy in his mid-forties, had gray, closely cropped hair and he looked a little bit like Sidney Poitier. He was nattily attired in a blue serge suit and he put the "s" in the word suave. He was cool, but my attorney, Tom, was no lightweight either. To everyone's surprise the hearing took two days to complete. Much of the time was spent examining and cross-examining the many witnesses. Satterfield was very meticulous and detail oriented and he proved to be a very formidable attorney. He continuously attempted to portray me as a disgruntled employee merely upset because I had been terminated for not performing my job. Tom proved to be just as formidable as he represented me, and fought to get me my job back. All of my witnesses did an excellent job of stating the facts on my behalf, and maintaining their composure under cross-examination. All of them were very convincing as they told the hearing officers how I had been treated differently from the other supervisors and how I had been exposed to constant sexual harassment by Rose. A few even told how Rose blatantly flaunted her authority by telling them a month before my dismissal that she was going to fire me when the time was right. Tom's closing summation was very powerful and succinct. I was satisfied that during the two days of hearings we had proved beyond a doubt that my dismissal had been contrived, trumped-up, and predicated by vindictiveness. Before leaving the hearing, the Chairman told Tom and me that we would be notified within a week to ten days as to the decision of the Board's findings.

During the following week, there wasn't much I could do except sit around the house watching television and getting drunk while waiting on the Board's decision. On the eighth day following the hearing, the decision arrived by mail. I hurriedly tore open the ominous looking envelope, which held my future in the balance. It read: "Dear Mr. Coleman, The Personnel Board of Directors, has reviewed all of the relevant testimony, articles and facts in your case as you seek reinstatement to your position. After careful consideration, it is the finding of this Board to UPHOLD your termination based on the facts in evidence. If you disagree with the findings of this Board you have ten days to file an appeal." I was momentarily crushed, but not devastated by the bad news. The alcohol I had consumed before reading the decision was comforting as it whispered to me, "Don't worry; we're down, but not out. We've just begun to fight. We're now going to take this matter through the appeal process."

The loss of my hearing before the Board put even more strain on my marriage, but I had to deal with first things first. Securing reinstatement to my job was a priority. I discussed all of the issues up to that point with Monica and told her that I planned to appeal the Board's decision. I told her that it would be necessary for me to take money from our savings in order to mount a successful

145

appeal. She was hesitant about the idea and told me so, but I explained to her that I was innocent and I had to clear my name and get my job back. She suggested that I just leave the matter alone and go out and find another job. What I didn't tell her was that I had been seeking other employment with the county, state, and private sector, and all were to no avail. To my chagrin, it had become increasingly clear that I had been "blackballed." When potential employers checked my credentials through my last employer, the Personnel Board, the message was communicated cryptically that I would be a risk to any employer and that I was a person beset with personal problems. None of the many employers I had talked with wanted to take a chance on hiring me.

Not only was I adamant about getting my job back, I was obsessed. If I could get my job back, the barriers to other types of employment would be removed. I could then transfer to another department within the agency or choose another career path with other agencies or companies and not have to worry about being "blackballed." Monica eventually agreed to me using the funds from the savings account to launch my appeal. I began in earnest to search for an attorney with good credentials as a labor relations specialist, and a few days later I met with just such an individual. Her name was Marcia P. Hammer. She was a matronly looking white woman in her early sixties. She wore her gray hair in a bun at the nape of her neck, had a cherubic face framed with granny glasses, was a big boned woman and looked as if her name should be Gretchen. She exuded a very calm and caring charm, but my research on her had revealed that Marcia was a giant killer. She had litigated and won many civil rights cases, cases involving women's rights, and had even won lawsuits against some municipalities and labor unions as she beat them up in the process. We sat and discussed my case for about two hours. She told me she would take my case, but I needed to understand that my case might not be resolved through the Personnel Board. We would attempt to ascertain a favorable appeal ruling through them, but if that failed then we would have to file suit to a higher ruling judiciary body. I agreed to let her represent me and we worked out a financial agreement, which all but wiped out my savings account; I felt confident that "the ends would justify the means."

The appeal hearing was scheduled to take place in a month, so I had more spare time to contemplate and I filed for my unemployment benefits and was approved. The unemployment checks would continue for about twenty weeks, but I was hoping to be back at work before the benefits ran out. I supplemented my income by signing up with a temporary employment service which provided occasional work. They would call and tell me to report to a job site when work was available. Most of the work was for production or warehousing in large plants, and I usually averaged about twenty to twenty-five hours a week. When I would finish a job for the day, I would head straight for the liquor store to pick up a bottle. On days when I didn't receive a call to go to work, I would spend the time sitting around the house drinking. There were times when depression would try to slip into my consciousness, but I refused to let it have dominion over me. There was no room for depression; alcohol had filled up all of the rooms; it had dominion over me, but hadn't yet informed me.

Sometimes I would look at my beautiful little daughter and think about her future. I wanted to make sure that I would be able to provide for her down the road and in order for me to do that, I had to make sure that I won my case. It was great when I would hug, kiss, and play with her and see her happy smile and bright sparkling eyes. *So innocent*, I would think to myself. Those were the happy moments.

The day of the appeals hearing arrived and we were prepared. The hearing was more austere than the first hearing. There weren't as many witnesses and all of the business, which was conducted, was done very matter-of-factly and the hearing only lasted one day. When the hearing was over, Marcia and I met to discuss the issues.

Marcia said to me. "Morocco, we are going to try and negotiate a settlement with these people. We have presented a very good case to them and, hopefully, they will realize that it would be in their best interest to reinstate you to your job rather than face the possibility of a lawsuit. I will give the Board a couple of days to ponder their decision then I will make our demands. I will keep you posted as to what develops."

"Marcia, what happens if they don't want to negotiate?" I inquired.

"Then we will go through the EEOC (Equal Employment Opportunity Commission) on our way to the Justice Department to file a lawsuit." She replied.

A week later, Marcia called to tell me that the Board had stood firm on my dismissal and she was going to forward my case to EEOC. She advised me that I should hear something from them within a month. And I did. Three weeks later, I received a letter from the EEOC, issuing me a "Right to Sue Letter." I was instructed to complete some enclosed documents and return the completed package, which I did. I next received a letter from the Justice Department authorizing my right to bring suit against the Personnel Board and included was a list of thirty-five names; all were names of attorneys in my area of the state. I was to contact the attorneys on the list to see if any of them would handle my case on a contingency fee basis. It took me two weeks to contact all thirty-five attorneys and not one of them was willing to take my case on a contingency basis. I had exhausted all of my savings and I didn't have any money to pay an attorney or any way of securing the funds necessary to file suit. The hard, cold, facts were staring me straight in the face. I had reached the end of the road. The light I had seen at the other end of the tunnel had turned out to be the light from another train coming straight at me. The bottom had fallen out of my world.

The part-time work I was able to get was sporadic and the pay I got when I did work was very minimal. In fact, most of the time the pay was just enough to cover the expense of my liquor bills. Monica and I began to argue and bicker more and more frequently about my drinking and lack of employment. She began to spend most of her free time at her mother's house. On the weekends she'd take my daughter with her to her mother's and I was usually passed out in the den when they returned late at night. I found out that most of Monica's family, on her mother's side, would meet up at her mother's house on the weekends to barbecue, socialize and enjoy a nice family gathering. I was hurt and angry as hell when I found out that I was not asked to attend their family functions. I started to become very bitter towards my in-laws as I thought about how everyone used to come to my house for the cookouts and to have a good time. I would get up early on Saturday morning and start cooking and preparing food for everyone. I liked all of my wife's relatives and loved having them at our home. Later in the day I would go to the liquor store to make special purchases for them; Coors beer for my mother-in-law; twelve year old Cognac for Aunt Helen and Uncle Cal, and Chivas Regal Scotch, domestic beers and wine coolers for the rest of the family. We would eat, drink, play cards and have a grand time until early in the morning. But, when my financial situation drastically changed, I was no longer included in the family functions and I began to hate each and every one of Monica's relatives.

I started questioning myself as to why things had started going so badly for me. Before things had gotten bad, I took care of my family and did things to help people. I had served my country honorably and all I had wanted to do was pursue the American dream, which I had fought to preserve. I had always tried to treat people as I would want to be treated. Why was I catching so much hell? I knew that I had my faults, but it wasn't as if I had killed somebody. KILLED SOMEBODY??!! Killed somebody! 'Nam. Killed somebody? Was that what it was all about? The taking of a life 14,000 miles from home. But, it wasn't my fault. A man gave me a gun and told me to go and kill that little brown man. No, I didn't know him, but they told me to kill him. They said I would be doing it for God and country. I didn't disobey the order. They told me I did good and they gave me some medals and a paper that said I had served my country "Honorably."

For the next couple of weeks, the bad dreams about 'Nam seemed to increase in their frequency and intensity. I also began to notice that sometimes when my thoughts would drift, they would suddenly catapult me back into the jungles of Vietnam where the war vividly flashed in front of my mind's eye. When the sensations would pass, I would frantically look around me to make sure of where the hell I was. I didn't mention this to anybody for fear of making someone think that I was losing my mind. One day while watching television, I saw a public service announcement about free counseling services available to Vietnam veterans. The services were being offered at a storefront type building for 'Nam vets who were having readjustment problems in civilian life. I wrote the address down and contemplated whether I should go or not. The next day I did go, and when I walked in the door I immediately felt a reassuring calm sweep over me. A white guy with a ponytail greeted me. He was wearing a pair of scuffed up Army issue jungle boots just like the ones I was wearing. He greeted me, "What's happ'nin, bro? What can I do for ya?"

I told him, "I'm a Vietnam vet and I think I might need some help."

"OK, blood. I'm Eddie, and I'm a 'Nam vet too. I was in the "twilight zone" (Vietnam) during the TET Offensive of '68 with the 5th Special Forces around Con Thien. Here, let me get you to fill out these forms and then we'll let you talk to our therapist."

"What kind of therapist are we talking about?" I asked.

"We call him Doc, but his name is Harris. He does the evaluations around here to determine what kinds of services that you need. He's cool. He was in the bush with the 1st Calvary in '66."

"What do you do around here?" I inquired of Eddie.

"I'm the alcohol and drug counselor. Man, I used to ride my Harley motorcycle with the thirteen percenters, doing plenty of drugs after 'Nam: speed, hash, coke, beauties, uppers, downers you name 'em, I'll claim 'em. Finally, I got tired of 'em and I cleaned up my act and got this gig helping other brothers from the bush country to find their way back home. Everybody that works here is a 'Nam Veteran including the director. This operation is a Veterans Administration funded project of vets taking care of vets. So, the sooner you get those papers filled out, the sooner we can start dealing with whatever ails you."

I completed the forms and waited to see Doc. A door across the room from me opened and when a guy came out I got a quick glimpse of what looked like a group of guys sitting around in a circle having a rap session. There were also a couple of guys sitting around in the waiting area with me and we talked with each other until Eddie called my name and ushered me into an office to meet Doc. Doc turned out to be a brother about my age, tall and slim with a dark complexion. He wore homed rimmed glasses that gave him a bookish appearance. He had a quick smile and I felt at ease with him as he greeted me and offered me a seat. He looked over my paperwork and asked me a few questions.

An hour and a half later I walked out of Doc's office to make an appointment for the following week with Eddie. Doc had listened intently to my life story all the way up to the point of how I had ended up in his Vet Counseling Center. He gave me some positive encouragement and told me he wanted me to start attending Eddie's counseling group which consisted of eight other 'Nam vets with substance and alcohol cross addictions. On my way home I felt uplifted by my experience. The Vet Center was a place where everyone there understood what you were going through. I had felt comfortable sharing my experiences, thoughts, and fears with guys who had been there and knew what the hell you were talking about. They didn't seem to judge you; they just met you where they found you. Their philosophy was, "extend your hand to give a fellow vet a hand-up, not a handout."

When I got home I told Monica all about the Vet Center and that I intended to become involved with their therapy program. She responded very skeptically and with very little encouragement, even after I told her there was also a counseling group for wives and significant others of Vietnam vets. The counseling group was to help them cope, support and understand what Vietnam vets were going through and why they were going through it. Undaunted by Monica's lack of interest, I did start attending the counseling sessions twice a week. The sessions had a positive effect on me and I was able to cut down on the amount of alcohol I was consuming. I began to feel better and more positive.

Early one Sunday morning while still sleeping, I was awakened by the clock radio beside my bed. Being only half-awake, I didn't pay much attention as the news report was broadcasted, "...and it has been reported that six people were killed and more than sixty are injured. All eight-passenger cars of the Atlanta-to-Washington Southern Crescent train jumped the track Sunday, just outside of

Charlottesville, Virginia, and tumbled down a steep embankment. At the scene, snow mixed with rain was falling in near-freezing temperatures. Blood was smeared on windows that had been broken when passengers escaped..." and I drifted back off to sleep.

An hour later I was again awakened, this time by the jangling of the telephone. When I answered, my mother was calling and immediately I could tell that she was very upset.

"Have you been listening to the news?" She asked.

"No," I responded. "Why? What's going on?"

"There's been a train wreck in Virginia and people have been killed. It was the Southern Crescent!" Mom frantically told me.

It was then that I understood the reasons for her consternation. My father worked as a dining car waiter on the Southern Crescent. My father and his crew had left Atlanta on Friday morning and they worked in the dining car until they reached New Orleans, Louisiana, where they would have a layover until the next day. On Saturday night, they came back through Atlanta on their way to Washington, DC, and would arrive there on Sunday morning. I then remembered the news flash I had heard when I was half-awake earlier that morning. I jumped up and sat on the side of the bed as I asked my mother, "Have you been contacted by Dad? Have you heard from him or any of the rail road officials?"

"No. You're the first person I've talked to."

"OK. You sit tight and I'll be right over," I informed her.

I hung up and called my brother, Michael. When I started to explain to him what had happened, he told me he had just heard the news on the TV and he would meet me at mother's house. When I got there, Mike had already arrived and he handed me a piece of paper with three phone numbers written on it.

"What's this?" I asked him. "Those are the numbers for the three hospitals in Virginia that the emergency rescue crews have taken the survivors to. I have already called the first two hospitals on the list to see if dad was taken to either of them and they had no record of him being brought in. I saved the third number for you to call."

When I looked into Mike's eyes and saw the naked fear in them, I understood why he hadn't called the third number. He and my mother knew that if they called and my father was not in the third hospital as a survivor, then he would be found wherever the morgue had been set up. That was an eventuality they were not prepared to deal with.

Filled with trepidation I began to dial the number. As I waited for the phone to start ringing I recalled that my father had been with the railroad for thirty-nine years and only had about eight more months to go before he would be retiring. When the hospital switchboard receptionist answered on the other end, I gave her my father's name and asked if he had been brought there. She told me to hold on, that she was going to transfer me to the emergency room and I could enquire there. The call was answered immediately by a Doctor Robinson and in the background I could hear someone yelling at the doctor. "Let me go! Let me up from here!" I told Doctor Robinson who I was and asked him if my father had been brought there.

Doctor Robinson asked, "You want to know if Mr. Coleman is here? Son, who do you think that is raising all of that hell in the background? Yes. We have Mr. Coleman here and he's being stitched up. He has numerous cuts, contusions, and abrasions and he's been knocked around quite a bit. I've recommended that he be admitted for a day or two for observation, but he doesn't want to stay."

"Can I talk with him?" I asked.

After a few moments Doctor Robinson said, "Your father said to tell you that he's all right and that he is going to continue on to Washington when he leaves the hospital in a couple of hours. He will call you when he gets to your aunt's house in DC."

I thanked the Doctor and hung up the phone with a sigh of relief. When I told my mother and brother what had transpired during the conversation, we all rejoiced nervously. Soon after the phone began to ring incessantly as family and friends called to ask if my father had been on the train which had wrecked in Virginia. We told them we had heard from him and he had sustained some injuries, but should be home in a day. Three hours later I received a call from my father after he had arrived in Washington. I asked him if he had made it to my aunt's house and he replied, "No. Not yet. I've stopped in at local bar where most of our dining car crewmembers hang out, but I'll be going there soon and I'll call you when I get there." My father sounded a little strange to me, so I asked him if he was OK. "Yeah, son. I'm doing OK and I'll call you soon." I relayed that latest bit of new information to my mother and the numerous relatives and family friends who had gathered at the house to lend their support and prayers. The television was tuned to a channel which gave continuous updates about the crash and when I saw the film footage depicting the aftermath of the crash I said, "My God, how did anyone survive something that bad?" The first six cars of the train had jumped off of the tracks and skidded for nearly half a mile before tumbling down the side of a steep embankment. The six railroad cars looked like tin cans that had been shredded and ripped open by the Jolly Green Giant on a day when he was famished for the contents inside. In every direction of the crash site you could see mounds and mounds of twisted metal, debris, and bloodstains. When the cars had overturned, some of them had slammed into the others in telescope fashion. One car had flipped over onto another, and one of the locomotives was resting on its back.

Around six o'clock that evening, my father called back and told me he was calling from National Airport in Washington, and that he would be leaving shortly on Delta flight 963 for Atlanta. His flight would arrive in Atlanta at 8:30 p.m. and he wanted me to pick him up. As he spoke, I noticed that his words were slurred and I wondered if it was because he had been drinking or if he was on some type of medication or maybe both. I told him I would be there to pick him up and I asked again if he had been to my aunt's house. "Naw. I didn't have time to go by there. Just be sure to pick me up."

Mike and I were waiting at the gate as the passengers on my father's flight began to enter the terminal. When I saw my father enter the area, I was stunned by his appearance. He was wearing a plaid, woolen shirt that was too big for him; a pair of his black work pants which were cut and torn in various places; and a pair of black, size ten shoes with no socks on his eight and a half size feet. His hair was frizzled and standing up on his head as if he hadn't brushed it that day. He had cuts and bruises on his face and head and some of them were covered with bandages and blood was still seeping through them. His eyes were glassy and he looked disoriented. I pulled off my all weather coat and wrapped it around him as Mike and I supported him on both sides and started escorting him out of there. Needless to say, everyone was staring at us trying to figure out what the hell was going on. The temperature in Atlanta was thirty-four degrees and I knew that it was snowing in Virginia and Washington, and my father had no coat. He had been walking around exposed to the elements a long time.

During the drive home, my father told us how horrific the train crash had been. "I got to the dining car about 5:40 in the morning to start preparing for the breakfast crowd when suddenly the train started lurching, bumping and rocking, and I knew we were getting ready to go over and I prayed that we hadn't reached the big bridge that goes over the river. It turned out that the bridge was two miles up ahead. When the crash started happening, I looked behind me into the dining car and it seemed like every chair and table in there had become unbolted from the floor and was flying through the air straight in my direction. I backed quickly into the pantry area and one of my co-workers ran towards me trying to enter the pantry also, but the chairs and tables had become one big jumbled mass of metal and it caught him square in the back and flung him crashing into me. The force of his body weight caught me in the chest and slammed my back into the wall. All of that metal literally sealed up the pantry entrance and I couldn't get out. It took the rescuers about two hours to cut me out of there. Roy Smith, the guy that stepped in front of me, was killed instantly by the debris that sealed up the entrance. Afterwards everything was real quiet, except for the sounds of moans, crying, screams and the hissing of busted pressure hoses. Then I heard the cook yelling for help and I asked where he was. He said he was trapped in the kitchen and he was in bad shape. He said he had been standing by the large iron stove boiling three industrial size pots of water when the crash occurred. He said that the stove had fallen over on him, pinning his legs at the thighs and the boiling water had turned over on him burning him bad from his face to his waist. I could tell by his voice that he was in very bad shape and I kept talking to him trying to help him hold on until some help came. After an hour he stopped answering me. I'm afraid he may not have made it. When the rescuers got me out, all I could see was wreckage and bodies. They put me in an ambulance and got me to the hospital. The railroad officials wanted to put me up in a hotel in Washington, but I didn't want that so I went to the bar. I lost my wallet, clothes, and everything."

"How were you able to get a plane ticket?" I asked him.

"I don't know," he replied.

Mike looked through my father's pockets and found my father's VISA card, which he had somehow been able to hold onto after losing his wallet. Dad had purchased his plane ticket with it and had no idea that he had done so. When we arrived home everyone gathered around my father to greet him, and after a couple of minutes I took him to the bedroom and helped him get ready for a bath. As he got into the tub, I saw that he had cuts and bruises all over his body. I had to change his bath water twice because he was bleeding in it. I patched him up as best I could.

By the time I had gotten him in bed I was exhausted and prepared to go home, but I decided to stay for a while. Despite my recent moderate success at curbing my drinking problem, I decided that my nerves had been sufficiently tested that day and I was going to do some serious drinking. When I left to go home about ten p.m., I had had quite a few drinks, but I felt fully functional enough to drive home. Halfway home, a heavy rain began to fall across the city. I drove along deep in thought about how close my family and I had come to losing my father in the train wreck. I also became melancholy concerning the problems which were affecting my marriage and my home situation. As I looked out the windshield at the night traffic, it became a little difficult to see clearly; I didn't know whether it was because of the falling rain or the tears of frustration in my eyes. I shook my head to make sure that what I was seeing was not my imagination. As I was crossing through an intersection, I saw a car with its bright lights on coming straight at me in my lane. When I looked to my right, there was a car beside me, which negated any attempt to move over and avoid the eminent collision facing me. There was a tremendous crashing sound as the oncoming driver hit the front left side of my car. After the impact, I groggily exited my car to confront the other driver. When he and his passenger walked up to me I could tell that they were "higher" than I was. Both were longhaired rednecks and they looked as if they were high on "speed." I didn't bother trying to talk with them; I just asked a passerby to call the police. A white police officer arrived on the scene and he quickly determined that the other guy was at fault and wrote him up and sent him on his way. The officer told me that he detected the odor of alcohol on me, but because I hadn't been at fault in the accident and didn't appear to be impaired, he gave me a stern warning and let me go. I was very thankful that the officer didn't lock me up for DUI. However, at that time I didn't realize that when I lucked out and avoided my first potential DUI charge, it instilled a false sense of security within me. I probably began to postulate that I could drink and drive and get away with it as long as I didn't hurt anybody. My car was drivable and I continued home. When I got home Monica asked me questions about my father's ordeal and when I finished giving her all of the details I told her about my accident. When she had completed viewing the damage to the car, she went ballistic. Her anger and rage was all directed at me and my uncontrollable drinking habits and our arguing became quite volatile.

The next morning my mother called to inform me that my father wasn't doing very well. She said that all during the night he was complaining about severe pains in his chest and back. Mike and I rushed over to my father's house and took him to his doctor's office. The doctor made arrangements for my father to be admitted to the hospital immediately. On the fourth day of my father's hospitalization, the doctor's determined that his injuries were not life threatening, but they did qualify him for a seven-month early retirement from the railroad with full benefits. A week later my father was released from the hospital and began to recover his health.

I began to understand that my father possessed a very strong will and an indomitable spirit. And, I also understood that I had inherited these traits from him. But, the stress of my father's recent ordeal was almost unbearable for me. When the train wreck happened I didn't know if my father was dead or alive. When I found out he was alive I was stressed out wondering how bad was he injured. It was the same kind of unbearable stress that haunted you in 'Nam when you worried about your buddy who's been wounded and you don't know how badly he's hurt, or if he will live. Those kinds of reactions are called "flashbacks" and they cause a lot 'of mental pain. I had learned that drinking lots of liquor would make the pain go away.

A few days after my father had been released from the hospital, I was awakened during the night with a fever and an abdominal pain that was so bad it caused me ball up in the fetal position. The pain became so bad that I got up and drove myself to the VA Hospital. The emergency room doctors determined that I was suffering from an irritated and inflamed stomach lining; a condition known as gastritis. The doctor gave me medications that eventually stopped the pain and I started to feel better. Before I left the hospital the doctor gave me some prescriptions to be filled and some advice. The doctor said, "Mr. Coleman, I would advise you to stop drinking. The episode you have experienced is called gastritis and in your case drinking too much alcohol caused it. The alcohol has inflamed your stomach lining which provides a protective coating for the walls of your stomach. If you continue drinking like you're doing, you could end up with a very serious ulcer or some other more serious problems." I thanked the doctor for his advice and concern as I hurriedly gathered my belongings and got out of there.

For the next week I abstained from all alcohol and continued to take my medicine as instructed. I began to feel much better and I was no longer experiencing any stomach pains. I went back to my old neighborhood, and while visiting there I decided to go "up on the block" to hang out with some of my old friends. When I got to the main drag there were about twenty guys hanging around in the parking lot of the liquor store. I knew a few of them and I walked up and started talking with them. We conversed for a while and then decided to pool our money and buy some liquor. This sounded like a good idea to me. A couple of hours later, four of us had consumed two large bottles of liquor and I was a little "woozy." I started walking toward my mother's house, but then I decided to go around the corner to my buddy, Leon's house. Leon was a lifelong friend and we were like brothers. Leon and I had co-hosted a teen radio program when we were in high school. Our show was highly rated and carried by the number one Black radio station in Atlanta. Leon was a fun guy and noted for his gift of gab and great dancing abilities. When I got to his house he opened the door and said, "Damn, man! Whatever you're drinking it sure smells loud!" We both laughed at his remark and he invited me in. We sat down and caught up on what we each had been doing since we had last been together. Suddenly my stomach and side began to hurt. The pain became excruciating and Leon asked me what was wrong. I explained to him what was happening with me and I told him about my recent visit to the hospital. He asked if I wanted him to take me to the hospital and I told him emphatically, "No!" I didn't want to have to go back to the hospital. I asked Leon if I could spend the night at his house and he said, "Sure thing. You can use the spare bedroom."

I got in the bed and I was doubled up in the fetal position, wracked with pain when Leon brought me some blankets. I didn't sleep a wink all night. I just tossed and turned and moaned. The pain was worse than it had been the first time I had experienced it. The next morning I wasn't any better and Leon insisted that I let him take me to a hospital. I decided to acquiesce and let him take me to see a doctor named Ray Morris. Dr. Morris was black, about seven years my senior and my initial impression of him was that he didn't seem very sure of himself. I didn't dwell on my observation because of the terrible pain I was experiencing. Dr. Morris examined me thoroughly and asked me a lot of questions about my health and family history. When he finished the exam he gave me an injection which quickly caused the pain to subside and allowed me to finally get some blessed relief. I also noticed that the injection produced a beautiful, euphoric "high" that had me floating on cloud nine. He then told me that he was going to send me to a nearby hospital to be admitted right away.

I asked him, "Why is it necessary for me to be admitted to a hospital?"

"Mr. Coleman, I don't know what's causing your problems, but I do know that whatever it is could be very serious. You might have an ulcer that is hemorrhaging or maybe a pseudo cyst; I just don't know at this point. But, I do know that I want to get you into the hospital now in order to run some tests and monitor your condition."

Leon took me to the hospital, and before he departed I asked him to call my parents and Monica to inform them of where I was and what the doctor had told me. Shortly after Leon left, the painkiller I had been given began to wear off. I was on a stretcher in the emergency room contorted with pain when a nurse came to draw some of my blood for testing. The nurse became angry because each time she attempted to stick the vein in my arm I would toss and turn in reaction to the awful pain I was experiencing.

The nurse very sternly said, "Mr. Coleman, stop moving around so much; your pain can't possibly be that bad!" I wanted to choke her. She had no idea just how bad the pain was. She finally got the blood she needed and left me there on the stretcher to moan and clutch at my midsection. Sometime later I heard one of the nurse's say, "My God! No wonder Mr. Coleman's all doubled up in pain. His amylase count is three thousand five hundred! Send for Dr. Morris!"

Dr. Morris arrived and immediately began issuing instructions to the nurse's. An IV line was placed in my arm and a plastic bag containing a clear solution was suspended above me and began to slowly drip into my arm. Dr. Morris then told the nurse, "Give him 100 milligrams of Demerol, 'push'."

"Mr. Coleman, I'm about to insert an NG (nasal gastric) tube into your stomach and it will be a bit uncomfortable at first, but I'll go slowly," Doctor Morris informed me.

He produced a clear, plastic tube, about four feet long and coated one end of it with a clear gel and proceeded to push the coated end up through my left nostril. I felt like I was about to sneeze and then the sensation passed, as I next felt the tube start to descend down the back of my throat. I thought I would gag, but that sensation quickly passed as I felt the tube traverse my chest snaking its way to my stomach. "There." Said Dr. Morris, "Now, X-ray him to make sure the tube is placed where I want it." An X-ray camera was pulled across my chest and a picture was taken. When the doctor determined that the tube was properly placed, he taped my nose to hold the tube in place and attached a plastic bag to the end of the three-foot section of tube that extended from my nose. I began to feel like I was floating again and realized that the Demerol that had been pushed directly into my IV line was kicking in. And, oh what a wonderful feeling it was!

As Dr. Morris spoke to me, his voice seemed to filter through a haze as he said, "Mr. Coleman, we have tested your blood gases and found that your amylase count was 3500. In an adult male the count should be somewhere between 98 and 150. Most of your pain is being caused by such an exceedingly high amylase count."

"Doc, what's amylase?" I inquired.

"Amylase is an enzyme that helps change starch into sugar and is produced by the pancreas. The pancreas plays a major role in the breakdown of food for digestion. Pancreatic juice is produced by the pancreas and contains the enzymes Trypsin, Amylopsin, and Steapsin. Those enzymes are very powerful and all of them work to breakdown proteins and change starch into sugar for the body to burn. They break things down. Your pancreas is producing an excessive amount of these enzymes and due to your chronic use of alcohol and poor eating habits, the enzymes don't have much to digest. So, they're starting to digest you!"

"What are you going to do to get me well?" I asked the doctor.

"Well, the NG tube is going to continuously pull the pancreatic and gastric juices out of your stomach and deposit them into this bag tied below your bed and you will be given Demerol every four hours for the pain. You will not be allowed to eat or take anything by mouth for quite a while and all of your nutrients will be given intravenously. We are going to run many different tests to try to determine what's causing your pancreatic problems. Any other questions?"

"Yes," I replied. "Doc, what do you think might be causing my problems?"

"Mr. Coleman, at this point I can't really say. It could be a pseudo cyst blocking the duct opening to the pancreas, or a stricture in the bile duct, or any number of things. In the mean time, we are going to try to make you comfortable and pain free during the next three or four days of testing and hope that your pancreas will cool down, because right now it's what we call very 'hot.' I'm going to have you assigned to a room now and if you experience any problems ring for the nurse."

I thanked the doctor and then an orderly began to push my stretcher down a long corridor towards the elevator that would take me to my room.

My room was set up to accommodate only two patients and I noticed that the bed nearest the window on the other side of the room was already occupied by a middle aged guy who looked to be of Spanish or Mexican descent. I was placed comfortably into the bed along with all of the wires, tubes, and monitors that had been hooked up to me in the emergency room. The medications I had been given were making me very drowsy so I began to drift off. I was almost asleep when I heard a loud moaning sound coming from the man in the other bed. When I looked over at him, he was staring in my direction but his eyes seemed unfocused and oblivious to me being there as he continued to moan. I felt pity for him and turned away from him as I continued to try to get some sleep. Throughout the night I drifted in and out of sleep as the nurses came in and gave me more pain medication and assisted the moaning man in the other bed. About five o'clock in the morning I was awakened by loud and excited voices in my room. I looked around me and saw a group of doctors. They were feverishly working on the Spanish man. After working on him for about five minutes, the doctors covered his face with his sheet and pronounced him dead! Soon afterwards, two orderlies came in, put him on a stretcher, and rolled his body out of the room, taking him to the morgue. The thought occurred to me that death had quietly slipped into my room and taken the life of the Spanish man. IT had just as stealthily exited the room undetected and left the Spanish man's body as a calling card. And IT had known that I was there. IT had seen me in 'Nam, but I had been lucky enough to elude IT.

Was IT again stalking me like it had in 'Nam and was that the reason for me being in the hospital? The next day, Monica and my parents came to visit me and I could readily see in their eyes the concern and anguish that they were experiencing as they saw me lying there helpless. I was in pain and not feeling well, but I didn't want them to know it. They stayed about half an hour and we talked about what the doctors had told me; things that I wanted them to bring me on their next visit; personal affairs that needed to be taken care of; and then they prayed for me before leaving.

For the next two weeks Dr. Morris ran a battery of tests on me to determine the course of treatment I should have. By the third week he told me, "Mr. Coleman, at this point we have ruled out the possibility of an ulcer and a number of other stomach problems. I am still trying to determine if you have a pseudo cyst that we haven't found yet or a stricture of the common duct. But, your pancreas has cooled down somewhat and I will probably let you go home in about three days. You still can't have any food, but I will start you on a liquid solution called Pedialyte and you can begin to drink small amounts of it to see if your system can tolerate it."

My body was weak and I had lost about seven of my 170 pounds. I had developed a routine of walking about fifty feet down the corridor outside of my room to get some exercise. I would hold on to the stand, which supported my intravenous equipment and push it in front of me as I slowly made my trek. One day as I was about to reenter my room after my walk, I looked toward the end of the corridor and saw a woman standing in the doorway of a patient's room observing me. She had on a nightgown and housecoat and she looked vaguely familiar to me. When she saw that I had noticed her, she quickly ducked out of sight back into the room. Later that evening when the night nurse came on duty I asked her, "Who is that lady I saw earlier today in room 640?"

The nurse replied, "Oh, she's a new patient who was brought in last night. It seems like she's had some sort of nervous breakdown. She was ranting and raving when they brought her in and she had to be sedated. Why do you ask? Do you know her?"

"What's her name?" I asked.

"Rose Davis." She replied.

Rose Davis! My mind screamed. That's why she looked so familiar to me. It was the same Rose Davis who had been my boss and saw to it that I was terminated from my job. Later that evening, the nurse told me that Rose had a nervous breakdown after her superiors terminated her from her job when they found that she had been embezzling funds, mistreating and discriminating against other employees.

The next day Rose was gone. The nurse told me, "When Ms. Davis saw you yesterday, she became upset and called her doctor and told him to transfer her to another hospital."

It was good to know that Rose hadn't gotten away with the illegal acts she had been practicing on the job. And, I felt somewhat vindicated, but none of that changed the predicament I found myself in.

CHAPTER THIRTEEN

Is That You, God?

Dr. Morris, true to his word, released me on the third day to go home. He gave me five different medicines to take with me and instructions as to what I could and couldn't do. The only thing I was allowed to take by mouth was medicine, Pedialyte, and beef bouillon. I did pretty well during my first day at home, although I slept through most of it. But, about midnight on the second day the terrible abdominal pain once again reared its ugly head. I was in total agony and told Monica to call Dr. Morris immediately. Dr. Morris instructed her to get me back to the hospital right away.

When I arrived at the hospital I went through the same exhaustive procedures as I did on my first admission. After I had been assigned to a room, Dr. Morris came in to talk with me.

"How are you feeling?" He asked. "I'm a little more comfortable now that the pain medication is starting to take effect." I told him.

"Good. It seems as if your pancreas is very unstable and still not able to tolerate anything introduced to your digestive system. Let me ask you a question. You didn't try to drink any alcoholic beverages did you?"

I shot him an unbelieving look and said, "Are you kidding me?"

"Just making sure," he said. "We don't need any surprises. I think we are going to take things very slow and easy for a while and give your pancreas a long rest so it can cool down. We need to also run some more tests starting tomorrow. OK?"

I told him OK, and he left just as the medication began to edge me toward sleep.

Four months later, Dr. Morris was again briefing me, as he was about to release me from the hospital. During my continuous, four months of hospitalization I had been made to feel like I was a human guinea pig. I had received a plethora of tests and consultations from internists and other doctors interested in my case. Dr. Morgan told me that one of the tests had revealed damage to the pancreas, which had probably been exacerbated by alcohol abuse. I was discharged with a batch of new medicines and instructions.

One of the first things I did when I got home was to weigh myself to determine just how much weight I had lost. I was shocked when I saw the needle on the scales move no further than 120 pounds! For the next two weeks the only foods I would be allowed to eat were Jell-O, Pedialyte, and chicken or beef bouillon. I started out readjusting to being back home very slowly. After being home for a week I felt as if I was progressing fairly well until I was awakened at about ten o'clock p.m. by the now familiar abdominal pains that signaled the on-set of an attack of pancreatitis. Within thirty minutes the excruciating pain had me doubled up on the floor writhing. I didn't have any pain medication so I asked Monica if she had anything I could take. She said the only thing she had was some Valium and I told her to give them to me. Preoccupied with my pain, I mistakenly thought that the Valium, which is a sedative, was a pain medication. I quickly took two of the Valium in an effort to stop the pain because I wanted to avoid at all cost having to be readmitted to the hospital. Twenty minutes later, the pain had gotten worse instead of better and I had taken a total of seven Valium. After considering the lateness of the hour, and that my young daughter was sleeping, I told Monica that I was going to drive myself to the hospital. She tried to persuade me to let her take me, but I told her she need to stay with our daughter. Then she said that she would call for an ambulance. I told her that we would have to pay for an ambulance to transport me and that would be too expensive. I made my way to the car and struggled in behind the wheel. And just as I pulled out of the garage a heavy rain began to fall. When I got about four miles away from the hospital, the Valium coursing through me began to cause a deleterious effect on my system. I became disoriented, but as the rain continued to fall I knew that I had to make it to the hospital.

As I rounded a curve in the road, a blinding flash of lightning streaked across the sky and momentarily reflected off of the asphalt roadway. In the reflection I could see the black shimmer of the asphalt, the pelting rain and the small dots of the street lights cast on the pooling surfaces of water. Without warning, the curve quickly became a fork in the road with a large telephone pole separating the two distinct directions. I was confused, hurting and gripped by fear as my car headed straight for the telephone pole at a speed of 40 mph! In nano seconds I tried to determine which fork in the road I should take and just as I pulled the steering wheel to the left I heard a tremendous screech of metal as the front right headlight and fender impacted with the telephone post. My car was in the median with the right side door pinned against the telephone post and the front right tire blown out and steam rising from under the hood. When I got out of my car I staggered, not because the impact had shaken me up but because of the disorientation the Valium had caused. I opened the trunk of the car and struggled to get the spare tire out so I could change the tire and continue on to the hospital. I jacked the car up and removed the blown tire as the rain completely drenched me. I gritted my teeth against the terrible pain surging through my abdomen as I attempted to put the spare on. I heard a car approach and, when I looked up, I saw blue lights flashing atop a police cruiser. The officer got out and walked over to me and asked me what had happened. As I began explaining what had happened I noticed that my words were slurred and the officer quickly asked for my driver's license. As I reached for my pocket I realized that in my haste to get to the hospital, I had left my wallet at home. The officer pulled out his handcuffs and told me to turn around. And at that time, I doubled over as I tried to cope with the abdominal pains I was having. I quickly explained my dilemma to the officer and when I finished he put me in his car and proceeded to "blue light" me to the hospital. Once at the hospital, I was again processed in, given the NG tube, IV's, pain medications and assigned a room.

The next day I had the usual banter with Dr. Morris as he began to assign different tests for me to have in an attempt to figure out why I wasn't getting better. Later in the day, my parents came to visit with me and their worry and concern was very visible. When my father left to go down stairs for some cigarettes, my mother used his absence as an opportunity to talk privately with me.

"Son, your father and I have decided that we're going to pay your bills until you get well enough to handle things for yourself." I tried to issue a feeble protest, but my mother waved me off and continued on.

"We feel that part of the reason you're not making satisfactory progress with your health is because you're dealing with a lot of stress related to your bills and other responsibilities. So, some of these worries we can eliminate for you. We've already had your car towed to be repaired. Now, this is what we have decided to do and no further discussion is necessary and we're glad to do it because we love you."

"The second thing I want to tell you is, 'pray!' You were baptized and introduced to the church and the teachings of the Bible at early age, but when you became grown you started leaning (walking) into your own understanding. I think you are now beginning to understand that your leaning (walking) unto your own understanding is what has led you to this hospital room. God is greater than all understanding and you must learn to believe and trust in him. Always keep your hands in the hands of THE MAN upstairs. Promise me that you will work on renewing your faith."

I promised my mother what she asked and soon after my father returned and they departed for home. After they had gone, I sat for a long time thinking about my situation and what my mother had said to me.

Two months later I was still in the hospital and my weight had now dwindled down to eighty-nine pounds. I was still not allowed to ingest anything by mouth except ice chips. The IV's were continued and the NG tube was still in place. I didn't realize it at the time, but I had become addicted to the Demerol. For nearly seven months, I had been receiving injections of the powerful painkiller. Every four hours in a twenty-four hour day I received 100 milligrams of Demerol. My addiction was so strong that I could tell when it was time for my next injection by the cravings I experienced. After receiving my injection I usually "nodded out" for a while and when I awoke I was like a zombie until my next injection. Much of my hospitalization was a euphoric blur. There was a nurse, named Mrs. Winston, who on two separate occasions refused to give me my injection when it was time for me to have it. She explained that I was becoming too dependent on the Demerol and that I should learn to tolerate some of the pain that I was experiencing. I became irate and contacted Dr. Morris and he berated Mrs. Winston for not following his orders and instructed all of the nurses to not withhold my medications. Needless to say, Mrs. Winston detested me as much as I detested her. And after that incident we didn't speak to one another unless it was utterly necessary.

On one particular night about eight o'clock, I was lying in my bed and the only light on in my room was the light cast from the television. I was in a rather somber mood and for some strange reason hadn't requested any pain medication for over eight hours so my thoughts were very lucid. Without warning, from the direction of the television I saw a small, round, white-hot light began to grow rapidly and fill up my room. Suddenly the light became all-encompassing and filled my room completely. Its white luminous energy penetrated my very being and when I tried to look into its essence I had to turn my eyes away because I couldn't look into it. Then, I felt a presence in the room and a voice with clarity spoke saying, "Look into the light!" When I looked up the light had rolled back to reveal something akin to a vision depicting an ugly, scary place that looked like the lair of all that is evil and malevolent. There was a trail at the entrance to the ugly place and I felt it more than saw it. The trail led to a place in a terrible jungle where the dark one takes your soul and the torment welcomes you. Your psyche is torn in half and the worms began to slither into your eyes, nose, mouth and every orifice and you scream but no one hears you because there is no sound. I was gripped by a fear so profound that I thought I would lose my mind in the next instant. Then, the voice spoke again, "This road is the one you are traveling!" Immediately the blinding light usurped the ugly place and bathed me in its glow and I felt love and heard musical chanting like monks in a monastery. And with majesty and power the voice said, "This light is the road I offer you! Which do you choose?" Then, I heard a "whooshing" sound and it all had disappeared—vanished! I was afraid to move and asked myself aloud, "What did I just witness? What happened to me?" As I asked myself these things, I felt my conscious or inner voice speaking to me armed with knowledge and wisdom "You have a serious medical problem. Your pancreas is badly damaged and your life force is being pumped from your body daily through your NG tube. You are not getting any better and eventually the medicines you are getting will become toxic to your system. You weigh eighty-nine pounds and your body is wasting away and soon your biological and organic systems are going to begin shutting down. If all of these things are true, you are dying! It's just a matter of time."

"Here son, take these." I looked beside my bed and Mrs. Winston was standing there tenderly patting my hand and handing me some tissues. The look on her face was one of care and concern. But, why was she handing me tissues? It was then that I realized water was pouring from my eyes. I wasn't weeping or crying, but water was flowing freely from my eyes and I couldn't explain why. Mrs. Winston continued to pat my hand and she reassuringly told me, "Son, it's going to be all right."

The realization of what my inner voice had revealed caused me to frantically ask her, "Mrs. Winston, can you find me a Bible?"

"Sure son. I'll be right back." I sat there terrified as I awaited her return. When she returned she gave me a new Bible, which was probably given to the hospital for the patients. "Here. This is yours to keep." I thanked her and as she departed she again told me, "Everything will be all right."

I didn't know where to start reading, but I remembered what my grandmother used to tell me when I was a child. She would say, "Honey, when you need an answer just open the Bible and start reading, the answer will be there." I opened the book and where my eyes fell upon the page I began to read: "For verily I say unto you, if ye have faith as a grain of mustard seed, ye shall say unto this mountain, Remove hence to yonder place; and it shall remove; and nothing shall be impossible to you. Matt. 17:20."

Amazing! I thought to myself. I was seeking spiritual help and seeking truth, and I did have some faith even if it was just the size of a mustard seed. As I continued reading a calm came over me and the fear began to subside. I read for a couple of hours and some of what I read I understood, and some of it completely baffled me, but I didn't let that stop me. Finally, I drifted off into a peaceful sleep.

When I awoke the next morning Dr. Morris was sitting near my bed reading my medical chart. When he realized I was awake he asked me the same rhetorical question as he did every morning. "How are you feeling today Mr. Coleman?" I usually began by listing the problems and pains I had experienced during the night, but this time I looked at him and said, "Dr. Morris, I had a restful night and believe it or not I feel kinda good." He looked at me and with a smile on his face he said, "Yes. I know."

"What do you mean by, 'Yes I know'?" I asked quizzically.

"Well, I was just looking over the reports that the night nurses entered on your medical chart when they monitored you during the night. And the reports indicate that sometime during the night all of your vital signs started to change for the better. I think you are starting to come out of the woods," Dr. Morris stated with pride.

"What caused this change in my condition?" I asked him. "Mr. Coleman, I can't really say specifically what caused your condition to change. There are just some things in medical science that we don't have answers to and this is one of them. I'm going to make my other rounds now, but I will be back later and we can start to discuss a new course of treatment for you."

After Dr. Morris was gone I began to think about what he had said; "There are just some things in medical science that we don't have answers to." I began to wonder if the metaphysical or spiritual experience, or whatever it was that I had witnessed during the night, had anything to do with my getting better. I did know that I had prayed about my condition and my condition had changed radically. After some serious thought, I knew that I was afraid to believe anything other than the fact that God had answered my prayers. And I held to that because "There are just some things in medical science that there are no answers to."

I spent the rest of the morning thinking about the months and months of hospitalization and treatments that I had been going through. And it became clear to me that Dr. Morris was a pretty good doctor, as far as being a general practitioner. And it was true that he had consulted with a couple of internists about my illness, but I felt that I now needed to be under the care of a doctor who specialized in internal medicine. I concluded that Dr. Morris was really experimenting with me, whether intentionally or unintentionally, by ordering expensive tests and trying various methods of treatment. I had started to have questions about them being necessary. My medical bills were astronomical, but they were fully covered by Monica's family plan insurance program from her job with the Board of Education. Later that day when Monica and my parents came to visit me, I told them the good news about my condition improving and of my decision to seek a doctor who had experience in treating patients with pancreatic conditions. They were in agreement that it was my decision to make and they supported me. I told them what I wanted them to do in helping me make the necessary arrangements and they complied.

When Dr. Morris returned in the afternoon I told him of my desire to be transferred to another' hospital and another doctor that specialized in internal medicine. Dr. Morris wanted to know why I had made such a decision and I didn't hesitate in telling him of my concerns with my present treatment and methods. At that point, Dr. Morris began to tell me how much better I had gotten in the last twenty-four hours due to his medical expertise and hands on treatment of my condition. He told me about the extensive research that he had involved himself in to better equip him in treating my condition. He further explained how that research was now starting to payoff and how I could now see the results of it by my improved condition. While he was telling me all of this, my mind flashed back to his statement earlier that morning, "There are some things that we just can't explain."

I refused to budge from my position of being released by him to seek other medical treatment. For a brief moment when I looked into his eyes, I saw a flicker of his greed and the potential monetary loss of the insurance claims that he was milking. In that flicker of the moment, I saw his true nakedness without the mask and I knew I had made the right decision.

"I see that you have made up your mind about this." He stated. "So I will make arrangements for you to be released in a couple of days."

"No! I want you to release me within the next few hours. I have already made arrangements for me to be transported by ambulance to the Veterans Administration Hospital across town." I defiantly told him.

Dr. Morris was very upset with my decision, but he acquiesced to my wishes and processed all of the paperwork that was required for me to leave the hospital. I was transported by ambulance to the emergency room of the VA hospital where I was processed in and assigned to a room on the eleventh floor. An hour later I was visited by Dr. Carl Royster. Dr. Royster was middle aged, sandy haired and looked younger than he was. He was about medium height, had the physique of a running back, and looked like he did a lot of weight lifting. He exuded an air of confidence and competence, was very precise in his mannerisms and speech, and impressed me as being a no non-sense type of person. After introducing himself, he looked over my chart and said matter-of-factly, "Mr. Coleman, you have been suffering with this condition for a long time. Nine months ago you were seen here and told what types of problems you were experiencing and what could possibly happen to you. And it has happened. Your illness has been going on far too long and it's now time to do something about it. We have developed a new surgical procedure for patients like you who have chronic pancreatitis. This procedure is still in the experimental stages, but so far, we've had a pretty good rate of success with our patients. If you want it, I can offer you the surgery. Take some time to think about it. Do you have any questions?"

"Yes. I do. If I decide that I want the surgery, how soon would it be before I would have the operation?"

"I would probably perform the surgery within two days after you have made a decision. But, you have a little time to decide because for the next three weeks I intend to put you on a special program designed to build your system up enough to tolerate a surgery. Think it over for a couple of days and let me know what you decide."

I took three days to assess my situation and the options available to me and decided that I wanted Dr. Royster to perform my surgery.

During the three weeks of preparation for my surgery, I had become friendly with all of the nursing staff and they encouraged me and lifted my spirits. I also became friends with a beautiful, black respiratory therapist named Angie and Mr. Harris, a gentleman who was the dietetic food specialist who saw to it that I got my special diet ordered by Dr. Royster. I was allowed to eat for the first time in nine months! My meals consisted of Jell-O, custards, or broth and it was like tearing into a T-bone steak. Angie was married, raising a child, working at the hospital and attending a local college where she had been elected as class queen. She came by my room to see me every day and always had a sunny disposition. I later found out that Mr. Harris was an old school friend of my father. Their daily visits meant a lot to me.

On the morning of my surgery before the orderlies came to get me, I said a prayer and read my Bible. I turned my fate over to God and a peace calmed my jangled nerves. The nurse gave me a pre-surgery injection, which put me on cloud nine and had me "tripping." The orderlies came with the stretcher to roll me to surgery and there to see me off were my parents, Monica, Angie and Mr. Harris. They all gave me words of encouragement as I was rolled out of the room and I looked back and told them, "I'll see y'all in a little while!" Then, an ominous thought crept into my thinking, *I wonder if this is the last time I will ever see them?* I quickly fought to push such a debilitating thought from my mind; I had already prayed on the matter and it was a done deal. I would return. When I arrived in the operating room it was freezing in there and I looked around and marveled at all of the strange looking equipment. After I had been placed on the operating table, Dr. Royster leaned over and spoke reassuringly to me through his surgical mask. He also explained that I was about to receive an injection of Sodium Pentothal which would put me to sleep and he wanted me to count backwards starting with the number one hundred. I felt mischievous and decided that I was mentally stronger than the drug so I was going to fake everybody out by counting backwards all the way to zero. Dr. Royster said, "OK. Start counting."

I began counting. One hundred. Then I felt a stinging in my hand where the Sodium Pentothal was being injected and one hundred was the only number I heard from my mouth before darkness swallowed me up.

Twelve hours later, I awoke in a post-op intensive care unit where they monitor you after surgery. When I had oriented myself I immediately began hitting the buzzer to summon a nurse because my complete abdomen was on fire! I was in tremendous pain and it made me feel like my midsection had been saturated with gasoline and set on fire. The nurse came and quickly gave me an injection of morphine, which knocked me out.

When I awoke again, I was back in my room and soon after a nurse came in and gave me some pillows to hold across my abdomen and instructed me to cough. I asked her why that was necessary and she replied, "You need to clutch the pillows close to your abdomen and execute a series of deep coughs in order clear your lungs of fluids. This procedure is to keep you from contracting pneumonia." Then she showed me how to do it and left the room. From a psychological standpoint I did not want to cough and upset the eight hours of surgical slicing and dicing Dr. Royster had performed on me, fearing that I might break something. But, I didn't want pneumonia either, so I began coughing and to my horror when I pulled the pillows away from my stomach they were covered with blood. I had broken something and I began buzzing and calling out loud for the nurse. When she saw what had happened she put out a call over the intercom paging Dr. Royster. He arrived quickly and assessed my situation and instructed the nurse as to what he was going to need and she ran to get it. He frantically climbed up on my bed and straddled both his legs over mine and began pulling off the big, white bandage covering my abdomen. When the bandage was off I nearly fainted when I looked down and saw the angry ten inch, crescent scar that crossed my solar plexus from left to right and was held together by fifteen oversized staples! Dr. Royster continued to work frantically, but he was cool as he injected an area of the incision with Novocain to deaden it He next took an instrument that looked like pliers and began removing some of the staples and opened up the wound and began to dig into the open area as I turned my head away to avoid seeing what I didn't want to see. Dr. Royster spoke calmly and deliberately as he said, "Ah ha! There it is. You've got a bleeder here that wasn't tied off." He tied off the bleeder and re-clamped the staples and told me everything was fine now. The nurse gave me an injection to calm my nerves and before long I drifted off to sleep. The rest of my recovery was uneventful and I made steady progress daily. Six days later Dr. Royster released me to go home and told me before I left, "Mr. Coleman, you are a very lucky man. Your pancreatitis was slowly killing you and you were literally on borrowed time. Personally, I'm surprised that you made it as long as you did before you came to us. Most patients don't survive as long as you did under the same circumstances. You must have some great angels protecting you." He briefed me on the medications I was to take and explained the type of bland diet I was to practice and forbade me to touch any type of alcohol. I sincerely thanked Dr. Royster, all of my nurses, Angie and Mr. Harris for all they had done for me. I hugged each of them and got into the car with Monica and headed home to start my recovery and get my life back on track.

CHAPTER FOURTEEN

I Saw the Tether Line

The first six months of my recovery were a very trying and difficult time for me, but I was determined to gain back my self-esteem and overcome the many obstacles facing me. I made sure that I followed Dr. Royster's medical instructions and kept all of my follow-up appointments at the hospital. I was also attending two meetings a week at the Vietnam Vet Counseling Center. One of the meetings was group counseling for veterans like me that were suffering from the traumas of war, and the other meeting was for one-on-one counseling with a therapist. My new therapist was named Willie Chappell and he was one of the best in the business for helping veterans. He was ex-military and possessed a plethora of therapeutic and medical knowledge, but he also had the common man's touch when it came to helping veterans with their problems. He explained to me that I was experiencing and suffering from PTSD, a phenomenon that was showing up in many Vietnam vets. He explained that PTSD stood for Post Traumatic Stress Disorder. "Continuous exposure to a particular traumatic experience or experiences causes stress and every one deals with stress differently'" Willie told me. "I think some Vietnam vets believe they don't have a right to be happy. Loss of friends has left some veterans with enduring sadness lingering far beyond the war's end. Unresolved grief, loss, and death are important counseling issues facing many combat veterans. The guys who experienced the most human destruction for the longest time are usually the least able to let their sadness surface. Some veterans unconsciously think that here-and-now happiness would detract meaning from the death and memory of a best friend or buddy. Keeping memories alive, though often depressing, may become an abject way of honoring dead buddies or other fallen warriors."

"Not showing vulnerability drives some combat vets inside themselves too. Vulnerability means showing sadness and admitting fear and some combat vets are reluctant to relax their guard. Some guys think that if they ever feel their emotions— sadness, anger, and fear—they will never be able to have control again. So, it is common for some combat vets to maintain emotional detachment to protect themselves from further loss and grief. And when the vet perceives some of his old personal thoughts beginning to try and sneak up to haunt him, survival mechanisms kick in and he's got to be in control. Of course, being too much in control can mean loss of control for some veterans and they don't realize that they are setting themselves up for failure. They find themselves alone, depressed, and feeling out of control. When this happens the vet will resort to drugs, alcohol, aggression and myriad other coping skills and defense mechanisms."

As I listened to Willie he asked me, "Did you see yourself in any of this stuff I just told you about?"

"Yeah," I replied. "I know that I have a problem with being in control of my surroundings. I don't mean that I try to force my military training and views on others, but I don't like having to deal with people who don't have a clue as to what's going on around them. For instance, if I go into a club or bar, something like that, I immediately survey my surroundings to check people out; locate the back door or exits; and I make sure to sit with my back to a wall so no one can ease up behind me."

Willie responded by asking, "Do you know why you do that? Before you answer, I'll tell you why. Because many of you combat vets are reluctant to give up your hardness and callousness. Increased vulnerability brought on by lowered defenses scares some of you and you fear the loss of your ability to survive and believe that once a crack in the emotional armor occurs, you may lose all control. Some vets think counselors and therapist are trying to take something away from them that has maintained their survival over the years. However, they need to know they have a Ph.D. in survival and it cannot ever be taken away from them. We're just trying to add to their strengths. While in Vietnam, you learned that taking risk was not free, so you move cautiously today.

The reality in Vietnam was that people sometimes got killed taking risk." I was very impressed by Willie's honesty and straightforward approach and over a period of time we even became friends. Two months later, Dr. Levenberg, the Vet Center psychologist submitted a medical report about me to the Veterans Administration Rating and Compensation Board attesting to "substantial symptomatology associated with Post Traumatic Stress Syndrome." Eventually, I was contacted by the Veterans Administration and instructed to report to the VA Hospital for a psychological evaluation to determine if I was entitled to receive compensation for PTSD as a service connected disability. When I reported to the hospital I was evaluated by a Dr. Fulton, who was the Chief of Psychiatry. He looked just like the old, bald curmudgeon on the Muppets television show that sat up in the balcony box at the theater with another old geezer and shouted insults at poor "Fonzie Bear" as he tried to perform on stage. My two-hour evaluation with Dr. Fulton was very adversarial and he pushed a lot of my buttons. It was very easy to discern that he held veterans in very low regard. A week later I received the rating decision based upon Dr. Fulton's report which read: "There is no doubt that the patient was involved in combat and suffered the trauma of that exposure as is common with all combat veterans. But, I seriously doubt the finding of PTSD in this patient." DIAGNOSIS: (all things considered) are as follows:

❖ Alcoholism–chronic, severe
❖ PTSD–alleged by patient
❖ Personality Disorder, Paranoid Type–severe

I was devastated by Dr. Fulton's report! Not only could I not justify what Vietnam had and was doing to me, but also now I had to contend with a medical evaluation which certified me as being Looney Tunes! After conferring with Dr. Levenberg and Willie, they told me not to let it get me down because Dr. Fulton was notorious for disqualifying a lot of veterans for entitlements and he was being investigated. That was great to know, but it didn't change my circumstances. They advised me to immediately file an appeal to the Appeals Board in Washington, DC. Months later the Appeals Board decision arrived and it upheld Dr. Fulton's decision.

The next day I spent job hunting all over town and I had a few interviews, but nothing seemed promising. I arrived home after dark and thought it rather strange when I didn't see any lights on. But then I rationalized that Monica and my daughter were probably visiting at her mother's house. Instantly, my sixth sense kicked in when I walked into the darkness of the house and I knew something was very wrong! I steeled myself to be ready for anything as I reached for the light switch. When the light flooded the foyer and the living room near where I stood, I was shocked to see that all of the furniture was gone. I rushed through the house checking first the dining room, then the family room and the four bedrooms upstairs. All rooms were completely devoid of all furniture except one bedroom and the kitchen, which was still occupied by a breakfast table. I checked all of the closets and saw that all of Monica and my daughters clothing was gone. The facts facing me were so profound that I tried momentarily to delude myself into believing that a band of thieves had broken in and robbed my house. But, reality would have no part of my flight of fantasy and I went back down stairs where I found a long white envelope lying on the floor. I opened the envelope; its contents marked only the second time in my life I had received devastating news by mail. The first was my "Greetings" from Uncle Sam and the second, which I held in my hands, was from an attorney notifying me that Monica was petitioning me for a divorce. Strobe lights started flashing in my head and a terrible pain was behind my eyes as I walked out the front door.

I went to the nearest liquor store and bought a large bottle of Vodka and some chaser and went back home. I sat down at the kitchen table and poured a big stiff drink and contemplated what I was about to do. It had been almost a year and a half since I had taken a drink and I thought about what it had done to me before; the months spent in hospitals; the pain and that strange and special "light" which visited my room. Then, I thought about some of my sessions with Willie and his words of wisdom, "Too many veterans are merely surviving; unconsciously cutting themselves off from social interaction and meaningful relationships. Life is passing them by. Some do not recognize how they are setting themselves up.

They manage their existence, but many find themselves alone, depressed and feeling out of control!" I looked into the glass full of alcohol and understood that I was—and things were out of and beyond my control. I tilted the glass up to my lips and drank. When it was empty I refilled it. As I sipped on my third drink I called Monica's mother and asked her if Monica and my daughter were there. She replied that she hadn't seen them and had no idea where they were. I knew without a doubt that she was lying and I hung up the phone. Sometime later I passed out drunk.

The next day my father called and said he wanted me to come over to his house to discuss some business. When I got there I thought he knew about and wanted to discuss Monica's leaving but he never mentioned it. What he told me was a friend of his had died and the wife of the man wanted to offer my father the first opportunity to buy his car. Dad said the woman didn't want much for the seven-year-old Pontiac and he knew I needed a car since Monica refused to let me drive hers. He said he knew that I would need to get around town for job interviews and he would buy the car for me if I wanted it. I told him I wanted it and we went to look at it. The car was a big, four-door model in need of a paint job and a new vinyl roof. But, it had a big engine, which ran good, so I got it.

Now that I had a car I would get up in the mornings and go job hunting until eleven thirty in the a.m. Then, I would go to the liquor store near my old neighborhood and hang out in its parking lot with the many alcoholics who were there. Many of them I knew from high school as having been star athletes in football, basketball, and track. Most of them lived in abandoned houses, but some of them were lucky enough to have menial jobs and they lived in rooming houses. A good many of them had teeth missing and scars on their faces from fights or from getting drunk and falling out and banging their heads on the concrete. Some were also 'Nam vets with PTSD so bad they were delusional. A number of this merry band of street people were outsiders who had migrated to Atlanta from cities all across the country. Cocaine, heroin, and eventually crack, were used by some due to the fact that they were cross-addicted. The order of the day or night in this environment was survival—pure and simple—at any cost. Your survival depended on you being on "point" at all times, and to not do so could result in you being knocked in the head with a pipe or brick, slashed by a razor, stabbed by a knife, shot, or killed. It was easy for me to gain quick acceptance by the "dudes on the block" because some of them had known me when we were kids or before their lives started the downward spiral. Of course there was a feeling out process where they tried to figure out why I was hanging out with them. After all, I was educated and at one time had a good job and some modicum of status. But they had been down and out on the fringe of society for so long that they had forgotten that many of them had, at one time, similar backgrounds. What I wasn't able to see on my side of the fringe was that I was at the threshold of becoming one of them.

In order to support our craving for alcohol, guys in a clique would pool their change to ante up enough to buy a bottle of wine or liquor. If we came up short we would approach a patron of means who was going into or coming out the store and ask them for some change and in short order we would have what we needed.

The first time I had my "point" challenged was by a guy I didn't know but had seen hanging around with the guys in one of the other cliques. I was sitting on one of the guard rails surrounding the parking lot and sipping on a drink when he walked up to me and said, "Hey man! Give me some change." I immediately knew that he was attempting to intimidate me and to impress his cohorts by exhibiting a "gangsta attitude."

I looked at him and replied evenly, "My man, I don't have anything to give you."

To which he replied, "I bet if I kicked your ass you'd give me some money."

Again, I replied evenly as I said, "I don't believe you want to even think about doing something like that to me."

"You're right. I think I'd rather cut your throat," he yelled as he quickly pulled a knife out of his pocket and popped the blade open.

Using the element of surprise I reached my hand down to the top of my jungle boot and extracted a sharpened bayonet I kept hidden there and jumped forward grabbing his collar and pulling him towards me. As he stumbled forward I brought the blade of my bayonet up to rest securely across his throat. Speed and surprise could have cost him his life as I asked him, "Now what was it that you wanted me to give you?"

"Nothing man! Nothing!" he stammered. "I didn't mean no harm."

"You make sure that you never step into my space again," I informed him as I pushed him away from me.

One day a guy I knew from the block told me he wanted to discuss something with me so we talked. He explained that he and two other guys were doing some hustling to make some quick money and wanted to know if I were interested and I asked him what was the scam? He said they were adept at stealing meat products out of grocery stores and had a buyer that would pay them for all they could bring him. I asked him how did I fit into all of this?

"Well, we have become known in all of the stores on this side of town, so the managers watch us like a hawk when we walk in the doors. What we need to do is go into other areas of the city where the store managers don't know us, but we don't have any way to get to the other areas. You've got a car. And if you would take us and wait for us to get the merchandise and get us out of the area, we are willing to make a split of the profits with you." Considering that I had no source of income and no one seemed interested in hiring me, I agreed to throw in with them. I took the three guys to a large supermarket out in the suburbs and when they went into the store all of them were about the size of Barney Fife, Andy Griffin's deputy from Mayberry. When the guys came out of the store they looked like they were the size of Fat Albert. They had slabs of ribs, steaks, hams, pork roast and an assortment of all types of meats stuck down in their pants and under the coats they were wearing. I couldn't believe what I was seeing! We hit about five stores in a matter of hours. I then drove them to a house where a numbers banker had his operation set up. They introduced me to "Slim" the numbers man and then we sat down to negotiate the price for the merchandise we had brought. Since I was the one with the car, the license, and the most to lose if we got busted, I demanded and got the larger split. When I counted up my portion I had $300.00! I considered that not too bad for half a day's work.

I visited my parents and found out Monica had told them she had filed for a divorce and that we were no longer together. I told my parents I was going to have to sell my house because I could no longer make the mortgage payments. I told them when the house was sold I was going to take some of the equity money and setup a trust account for my daughter. I asked them if I could stay with them for a while until I could get back on my feet and they said yes. Monica began making phone contact with me at my parents home and discussing unresolved business matters. I told her I would pay off her outstanding bills and put a portion of the equity money aside for my daughter. I meant what I told her and at the same time I was hoping that she could see a change in my attitude and that we could possibly try to work out our problems. She refused to tell me where she was living, but she did act as if she was interested in us trying to talk about our problems. She told me she didn't want me to pay off her bills and that I should take the equity from the sale of the house and get my life back on track. She told me, "The house is yours. You purchased it with your VA guaranteed home loan and you are the one who fought and bled for it and paid on the mortgage, so I don't want to take that away from you."

I continued drinking, hanging on the block, hustling the grocery stores and looking for a job. I felt that if I could get a decent job I would maybe have a chance at getting my family back together. I went to the closing sale of the house and while sitting there with the family that was purchasing it, their attorney and the brokers, I looked up and Monica walked in. I thought she had come for sentimental reasons. After the sale was consummated I was to receive $20,000.00 in equity, but before I was given the check the attorney announced that he had been contacted by Monica's attorney and told of our pending divorce. He had been instructed to place the money into an escrow account until the divorce was finalized, at which time the money would be divided equally between us. The attorney then said, "Since we're only two weeks away from the Christmas holidays, if Mr. and Mrs. Coleman are willing, I will issue each of them a check for $1,000.00 and place the remaining monies into the escrow account."

I turned to Monica and said, "I thought you didn't want anything."

She replied tartly, "You must be out of your mind."

Because of the fact I needed every dime I could get, I reluctantly agreed to the stipulation and accepted the $1,000.00 surprise Christmas bonus.

Within a matter of days I moved in at my parent's home and reclaimed my old bedroom. The first week or so, I stayed pretty close to home because it was the holiday season, I missed my family, and I was depressed. During this troubling period, I had a couple of the old familiar nightmares and had begun to have occasional "flashbacks." I would treat these unwanted symptoms with large doses of alcohol and it usually worked just fine. One night, I was feeling sorry for myself and had been drinking rather heavily when my father walked into the den where I was sitting. I had the television turned on and the sound turned off. At the same time, I was listening to a record album I was playing on the stereo by Aretha Franklin. Aretha was singing a very melancholy, thought-provoking rendition of "God Bless the Child That's Got His Own." My father had been drinking earlier and he interrupted my soul searching mood by bellowing, "Why do you have my television on with no sound on and my stereo playing at the same time? You're not even watching the television so all you're doing is running my electricity bill up. And might I remind you that you haven't paid any electricity bills around here!" My father had no idea as to how much emotional pain I was going through and his outburst was the last thing in the world that I needed at that moment. So, I got up and turned both the TV and stereo off and walked back to my room and lay down across my bed. My father then stood in the doorway to my room and said, "Come and sit here in the living room. We need to have a talk." His tone of voice and demeanor immediately caused me to recall how we used to play out this same scene when I was a teenager and he wanted to set me straight on a few things by lecturing to me. Respectfully, I complied with his request and when I got to the living room my mother came in and told my father that this wasn't the time to sit down and discuss business with me because he had been drinking. I think my mother understood my emotional state at the time and was trying to intercede on my behalf, but my father was adamant about talking with me so my mother left the room. My dad started his rambling soliloquy by telling me how terribly I had messed my life up by losing my job, my family, and almost my life. As my father continued to berate and castigate me, I knew that what he was saying was the truth, but I didn't want to hear it. And when I told him so, the tension built and we began to argue vehemently. We became so confrontational that my father recited to me the mantra of all parents in a similar situation, "I brought you in this world and I'll take you out!" In a fit of anger I shouted to him, "You don't know enough to take me out!" He then hurriedly went to his bedroom and when he returned he was clutching his nine millimeter P-38 pistol. He pointed the gun at my head as he told me, "Don't tell me I can't take you out. Do you see who's got the winning hand here?" He sat back down on the sofa and placed the gun directly in front of him on the coffee table.

I was livid but I kept my temper under control as he continued his haranguing of me. I told him that it looked as if he had the upper hand and I was going to make myself comfortable and listen to his words of wisdom. I then proceeded to unlace and pull off my jungle boots. With lightning accuracy, as I pulled my boot off, I flung it towards the coffee table aiming for the gun. The boot landed on the table and skidded along its surface knocking over and breaking figurines and ashtrays on its collision path with the gun. My boot made contact with the gun and sent it flying off the end of the table where it thudded harmlessly onto the carpet as I jumped across the room and grabbed the gun before my father could reach it. I turned to my father where he sat with a dazed expression on his face and my anger exploded as I put the gun to his temple and yelled at him, "Who did you say you were going to take out of this world?! I fought in a jungle where they aimed weapons at your head and didn't threaten to pull the trigger...they did! I don't appreciate nobody pointing a loaded weapon at me."

The look I saw in my father's eyes was part anger, fear, hurt, pity, guilt, and shame. I saw myself in my father's eyes. I took the magazine out of the gun, cleared the chamber; put the safety on and placed the gun back down on the table and went back to my room and closed the door. I sat down and recapitulated the events, which had just transpired and regretted all of it. I came to the conclusion that my father was probably acting out his pain and anguish at not being able to wave a magic wand and make his son's problems disappear and his life take on a more meaningful direction. I really felt bad about my actions.

Ten minutes later I heard the doorbell ring and someone enter the house. My bedroom door opened and standing in the doorway was a young, black policeman who asked me to stand up. Perplexed, I did as he had asked. He next asked me if I had any weapons on me. After I told him no, he patted my pockets and told me that I would have to leave the premises at my father's request. My father had called the police and wanted me out of his house. I got my coat and hat and started towards the door. I tried to reason and apologize to my father but he would have none of it. The policeman grabbed me by the back of my shirt and roughly pushed me through the front door telling me, "Your father wants you out of here, so move it!" When I turned to extricate myself from his grasp he said, "Because you beat up an old man don't think you can do it to me!" Then he pushed me towards the steps and I told him, "Officer it's not necessary for you to get physical with me." He didn't answer he just whipped out his handcuffs and cuffed me saying, "You're under arrest for not obeying my instructions to vacate the premises and resisting arrest!" He threw me in the police car and off to jail I went for my first visit. After I had been booked into the jail holding area, I called my mother asking her to reason with my father and tell him to come and bond me out. She was upset and told me that my father refused to even discuss my situation with her. There was nothing she could do. Anger again began to well up within me. I decided to call Sandra, an old girl friend of mine that I hadn't seen in years to see if she would help in getting me out of jail. She was surprised to hear from me and when I told her of my predicament, she said she would help me. Five hours later, I was released on bond and Sandra took me to my parent's home to get my car. When she found out I was going through a divorce, she told me give her a call sometime and preferably not when I was in jail. I drove to the liquor store parking lot and joined the after dinner, late night drinkers; for the first time I slept in my car. That day was truly a day of many firsts' for me. That night, I had a dream in which I saw myself trapped in a forest or jungle full of thorns and choking vines. I couldn't find a way out and there was a feeling of fear all around; I could feel it and the sky was purple with ugly, ominous, orange clouds. A thought kept flashing through my mind, but I couldn't grasp it. Instinctively, I knew that the elusive thought held the answers that I needed to find my way out of that place. Suddenly, I felt the presence of something above me and when I looked up I saw a black line. When I got a better look, it appeared more like a tightrope or tethered line that stretched straight across the horizon with no end points. It just reached into forever and was suspended about fifty feet up in the air. I was able to grasp a piece of the fleeting thought as it passed just out of my minds reach. It revealed that I could get out of there if I could hook onto the tethered line, but it was too high up in the air. The thought also revealed that I could escape by reaching the safety of the tethered line but only if I could remember what had led me there. Then, the fear became over powering and I heard loud screaming. I found myself sweating and staring into the darkness and realized the screams were my own.

For the next two months I either slept in my car or hung out in the streets all night with the "night people." I was now homeless. Homelessness is a condition of dire consequences. You find that your condition is in very bad shape, because your anchor has been taken away from you. You are akin to a rudderless ship twisting in the wind and you're lost. I was operating in full jungle mode just like back in the bush of Vietnam. To ensure that I kept money in my pocket, I continued to drive the guys to the super markets so they could do their "grab and run" number. But, after a while I began to have second thoughts about that kind of activity. I started getting "that feeling" again; the one that always seemed to warn me when something bad was coming. I felt as if the warning was telling me that it was only a matter of time before I ended up in jail or something worse if I continued what I was doing. So, I quit.

One day I noticed a new brown Corvette pulling into the liquor store parking lot. It was driven by my brother, Mike. He came over to where I was standing and we warmly greeted each other. He told me he had heard about the run-in I had with dad. After I had given him my version of the story, I asked him how he could afford a Corvette.

He informed me, "After I got back from 'Nam I started working in the warehouse of a picture frame manufacturing plant and eventually I met the owner and we developed a rapport and became friends. The owner's name is Carl and he promoted me to the position of sales manager. We travel all over the country to shows and conventions and I'm the company's number one salesman, so financially I've been quite successful."

"Yeah, well I'm glad to hear that you're doing good," I told him.

Mike continued, "The reason I stopped by here to talk to you is because you know and I know that you need to get off of this corner and to stop hanging out with these folks who can't do anything for you." He raised his hand and waved off the protestations I was about to raise. "Hold on. Let me finish. My secretary's uncle is the personnel manager at a warehouse on Fulton Industrial Boulevard and they supply all of the food products needed for McDonald's franchises throughout the Southeastern States. They load the products on trucks and ship them out. I told my secretary you needed a job so she spoke to her uncle about you and he wants you to come and see him tomorrow morning at nine o'clock. Here's the address and his name." For a moment I didn't know what to say, then I grabbed Mike and gave him a bear hug and thanked him. "If you show up in the morning the job is yours," he said.

I reported at eight thirty the next morning to the address Mike had given me. At nine o'clock I was introduced to Tony Madison, the guy I was there to see. Tony welcomed me into his office and immediately began telling me about the job as he handed me an application for me to fill out as we talked. Tony was a tall, slim, white guy about my age and he exhibited a kind of devil-may-care attitude. He impressed me as a rather sharp, knowledgeable person who didn't believe in a lot of rigidity in the work place. In fact he said, "Once you learn the job, just do your job and there won't be any problems." I felt rather giddy when I opened the application and found the W-2 withholding tax forms. This indicated to me that I was being hired on the spot. Tony explained that there was a conveyor belt, which ran the length of a portion of the warehouse, and a team of four men walked the line pulling items from the bins beside it. The materials to be pulled were called out by a team leader; the materials were put on the belt and transported to the cargo area of a tractor-trailer truck, which was backed up to the dock doors. Two rotating team members took the materials off of the belt and packed them into the truck. The materials were syrups for sodas, boxes of meat patties, boxes of McMuffins, all the products needed to operate a McDonald's store for a week. You could usually load the merchandise for four or five stores to each tractor-trailer. Tony told me my starting salary would be $7.80 an hour to start! Fantastic! In 1982, $7.80 an hour was a decent starting wage and I almost couldn't believe my good fortune. Suddenly, I had visions of how I was going to get my life straightened out. I would buy a new car, new clothes, get an apartment and work on getting Monica and my daughter back. I even thought about going back to school to finish the year and a half I needed for my degree in psychology. To flirt with thoughts of plans and dreams that could become a reality was a luxury I hadn't experienced in a long time. When I had completed all of the paperwork, Tony told me I was hired and to report for my shift the next day at three o'clock p.m. I was elated, but what Tony didn't tell me was that it was hard work and you earned every penny you were paid. I knew I could handle it.

By the end of my first week of work I was sore from head to toe. The work was very demanding but I took solace in the fact that it was helping me to rebuild my body. The recovery from my surgery was a long and arduous process and I now weighed 150 pounds, still below my normal weight of 170.

I went to the bank to open a new account and cash my first check. When I came out of the bank I bumped into my long, lost compadre Punchy.

"Hey Rock!" Punchy exclaimed. "You're looking pretty good man. I heard about you almost dying. I wanted to get by the hospital to see you, but you know how it is."

I thought to myself, *Yeah I know how it is.* If the tables had been turned I probably would not have gone to see him either. 'Nam does that to you. If I heard that he was laid up dying I wouldn't want to go and see him. It has something to do with surviving a war and all the death and then coming home and dying. Hard to cope.

"What are you doing now?" I asked him.

"Aw man! I just got divorced. I got married and had a kid and was doing good, but my lady and me couldn't make it. So, I'm starting over. Getting ready now to go look for an apartment."

"I'm going down the road you just traveled. I'm in the process of a divorce and I'm looking for somewhere to live too." I told him.

"Well. Hell," Punchy boomed. "Why don't we go find a place and be roomies again like the old days?"

"Why not?" I said.

Before the day was over we had secured a two bedroom apartment, that had a large living room, a fireplace, and wet-bar. It was located in a suburb just outside of Atlanta near the airport. Things were beginning to look up.

I had been talking by phone with Monica quite a bit in an attempt to rekindle our marriage. Sometimes she would talk as if we might get back together and on other occasions she would become angrier and angrier as she brought up bad memories from the past. I began to feel like a yo-yo on a string and after nearly three weeks of trying to work things out to no avail I started to become angry. I began to rationalize that she had no intent of us getting back together and was just stringing me along simply because she could and wanted me to truly suffer. I concluded that she had gone on with her life and now it was time for me to get on with mine. I demanded that she stop playing games with me and to proceed with her divorce intentions. We argued violently and the next day I went and retained an attorney and the "War of the Roses" was on. A week later, Monica and her attorney met with me and my attorney at my attorney's office. Attempting to work out an equitable settlement was a very ugly event. She wanted everything and when I say everything, I mean just that. She had taken nearly everything when she had left me. We finally worked out an agreement that we could both accept including the child support. The final business to be conducted was the division of the $18,000.00 equity from the sale of the house. The attorneys Monica had used against me to freeze the assets had absconded with the bulk of the money! The account contained only $3,000.00, which was divided equally between us, and I received $1,500.00! She had prolonged the divorce by pretending that she was seriously considering us getting back together, but in reality she wanted to make sure that I became a broken and implicitly useless human being, good for nothing and good for no one. She didn't want me back and wanted to make sure that no one else would have any use for me either. She had played me like a violin and I detested her. But, there was one positive fact that rose above all of the anger and bitterness; from this broken marriage the Lord had blessed me with a beautiful daughter.

Punchy and I began meeting a lot of the single women in our apartment complex and through them, we met other single women. I began dating a number of them and attending a lot of parties and social functions. Many of the new people I was hanging out with and meeting were into fashionably smoking marijuana. In order to not be perceived as the odd-man-out, I also participated for a while. But, I didn't hang with it long because it was too much of a hallucinogenic for me. It made me paranoid, and the high that the marijuana induced made me feel as if it was in charge of me, and it was. I felt as if I was giving up too much control to the drug. Powdered cocaine didn't really do anything for me, nor did "popping" pills. I guess the reason was because I had such a high tolerance level working against them due to the massive amount of

Demerol and morphine I had been given during my long hospitalization. It was sort of strange—my body wouldn't allow me to become a junkie, but reserved the exclusive right to allow me to become an alcoholic. Oh well! Women were always stopping by our apartment to visit and just hang out. Punchy and I were known for having some great parties at our place and I was starting to enjoy the bachelor life.

CHAPTER FIFTEEN

I Killed the Water Heater

Some situations became rather trying on my job after working there for four months. I stayed pretty much to myself during breaks and I didn't talk a lot of shoptalk with the boys during the lunch break. I usually sat off in a corner and read a book. I worked with seven white guys and all of them were rednecks from South Georgia. They were thick as thieves in their friendship with each other. While working, they would converse among themselves and their conversations would contain veiled racial comments and statements laced with double entendres in an attempt to shoot the message over my head. Then they would laugh thinking I didn't know what they were doing. I kept my cool on these occasions, and didn't let on to them that I knew what they were doing. There were two other black guys on my shift and I didn't associate with them either. They were usually the butt of openly racist jokes or comments by the rednecks and they would "shuck and jive" and laugh right along with them. I resented these so-called "brothers" and considered them to be "Uncle Toms." They probably picked up on my vibes and knew I didn't care for, nor respect them. At the same time, they resented me and the reason was probably because of the shame and self-loathing they felt at knowing that I knew what they truly were "handkerchief headed Uncle Toms!" Judging by their ages it seemed a bit unusual, but none of that crew, black or white, had ever been in the military. I think my military background may have also intimidated all of them. Instead of wearing work boots like them, I wore jungle boots; instead of T-shirts, I wore army fatigue shirts with the sleeves ripped off. Everyone wore a personal pocketknife in a leather case on their belts, which was used to cut the ropes and plastic wrappings off boxes of products to be shipped. I wore my bayonet on my belt in a sheath.

One day Tony, the guy who hired me, called me into the office and told me that he had been observing the actions of the white guys towards me and felt it would be best if I changed over to the third shift. I told Tony I appreciated his concern, but I could handle the situation and I wasn't worried about them hurting me.

"I'm worried about the opposite," Tony told me.

"What do you mean?" I asked him.

"Rock. I'm a pretty good judge of character and I think if these guys keep on messing with you, you might hurt one of them. I've got a brother-in-law that went to that war over there and I've seen what he's done to some folks when they got on his bad side. Let's just avoid the potential for a bad situation and move you to the midnight shift."

I liked Tony and I didn't want to cause anybody, including myself, unnecessary grief so I agreed to change shifts.

My grandfather, Will Coleman, my father's father, called me the next day, which was my off day. He told me that he would like for me to drive him to take care of some errands and asked if I was available. I told him I was available and would be glad to do it. When I got to my grandfather's house he gave me the keys and said, "Let's go in my car." Ever since I was a little kid I called my grandfather "Son." I don't know why, but I always called him Son. The funny thing was, I called my grandfather Son, and he was 97 years old. He did his own cooking and cleaning and drove himself all over town. He even had a nice "little old" lady friend. He told me that he needed to pick up some newspapers from different people's houses. Son had been retired for ten years and to keep active he would go by his friend's houses and pick up all of their accumulated newspapers, put them in the trunk of his car and take them to the paper recycling plant. At the recycling plant he would pull the car up on the scales for the papers to be weighed and then the foreman would pay him. Son's car was a vintage 1964 Cadillac and it was in excellent shape with a beautiful, shiny paint job which he kept simonized. Son bought the car dirt-cheap from his boss, but she didn't know that she had sold it to him. It's a bit confusing, so let me explain.

In 1948, when I was two years old, Son was offered a job as a chauffeur for a wealthy, Jewish widow who lived in an exclusive section of Atlanta with her daughter and husband and two grandchildren, a boy and a girl. The widow's name was Mrs. Fox and her son-in-law was named Ralph Uhry. Mr. Uhry was an entrepreneur and owned some furniture stores around the city. Many of the other chauffeurs who knew Son tried to persuade him not to take the job because Mrs. Fox was, "a tough little old lady and she's feisty." But, Son didn't let their concerns cause him to fret. He needed the job and he reasoned that working for Mrs. Fox couldn't be as bad as they all said. But, Son was in for a big surprise. Mrs. Fox gave Son the blues, but he was the kind of person who loved everybody and, after much trial and tribulation, Mrs. Fox finally accepted Son as her chauffeur. She reached a point where she didn't want anyone to drive her but Will, as she called him.

Mr. Uhry was an excellent artist who painted and produced drawings using many mediums such as oil, pastels, charcoal and pencil. When I was about four years old I liked to draw and sketch. So one day Son took some of my little kiddy sketches for Mr. Uhry to see. Mr. Uhry had Son to bring me some drawings, which he had placed, on semi transparent onion skin paper for me to trace on paper and send back to him. These exercises became a ritual and as I became a little older he would send me drawings or sketches to reproduce. By the time I was a teenager I was pretty good at sculpting, painting, drawing, and sketching. There have been times in my life when I have been far from home and in need money and I have been able to fall back on my artistic abilities to earn some income.

Over the years, whenever Mrs. Fox sent Son to trade in her old car and pick up her new one, he would work out a deal with the salesman to purchase her old car. Son was the only one who ever drove the old car, so he knew it was in excellent condition. And, because the salesman knew Will always bought from him, he always gave him a good deal on the car. So it was almost like buying it from Mrs. Fox, that is until she found out what Son was doing. He would park his car around the corner from the house to keep Mrs.

Fox from seeing it. He reasoned that if she realized he could afford to buy the car, she'd feel he didn't need a pay raise. Eventually, someone saw the car and told Mrs. Fox what was going on and she confronted Will. When she found out it was true she told him, "Well, you stop parking it on the street and start parking it in the garage!"

Mr. Uhry's young son, Alfred, grew up to become a writer and he's pretty good at it too. He wrote a story that became a play and was so well received and acclaimed that it garnered the coveted Pulitzer Prize! The play then became a movie, which was so well received and acclaimed that it garnered the coveted Oscar Award from the Academy of Motion Pictures Arts and Sciences! The story extols the agape (God's love) relationship which develops between two elderly people from vastly divergent backgrounds and holds it up to the prism of all of God's creation for us to discern that we are all God's children.

The story was about Alfred's grandmother and my grandfather. And, he entitled this true story "Driving Miss Daisy." But, I'm getting ahead of myself. Anyway, as Son and I drove around on a beautiful, crisp, sunny day picking up the newspapers, I told him, "Son, this is my off day and I hope you don't mind, but I'm going to stop at the next liquor store I see and get me a little something to sip on. OK?"

"If that's what you want to do, it's fine with me. I just 'preciate you takin' the time to take me around like this," he told me.

When I pulled into the parking lot of the liquor store and was about to exit the car Son said to me, "Rocky. How 'bout getting me a little somethin?" I was shocked. I had never, ever seen or heard of Son drinking anything alcoholic.

"Son. You don't drink." I retorted. "Naw, I don't, but it's just such a pretty day and I think I'd like to taste a little wine." I went inside the store and purchased my usual and I picked out a nice Zinfandel wine and a cup of ice for Son.

The remainder of the afternoon we spent taking the paper to the recycling plant, picking up his watch from the jeweler's where he had it cleaned, and picking up some grocery items at the supermarket. Ironically, the supermarket was one of the one's I had taken the Fat Albert gang to a number of times to steal meat. Son patronized only the exclusive stores in the affluent section of town where the Uhry's home was located and all of the merchants knew him. Mrs. Fox had died many years before, as had Ralph Uhry. Mrs. Uhry, Alfred's mother, still lived in the house and Son would go by there three times a week to check on her, take the mail in, and tend the garden that he and Mrs. Fox had planted together. This was an agreement he and Mrs. Fox had made before she passed.

As we rode along Son and I discussed many things. He told me about his mother who had been born into slavery, was part Indian, and was 116 years old when she died. I had seen "Mama Deilia," my great grandmother only two times in my life. And, both times were during the last year of her life. She lived in South Carolina, a place called Waterloo, where Son was born. She was a small, dark woman with white hair that she wore in two long braids. She was a wiry, tough little lady with a quick wit and good memory for her age. She told me a lot about my heritage and about the interracial relationships which were a part of my family tree. This explained my light complexion. It was also mind-blowing to hear my great-grand mother telling her son, my ninety-something-year-old grandfather, "Baby hand me this," or "Baby hand me that." *Unbelievable*, I thought to myself; at his age he's still her baby. Son told me about his uncle named Bro Jim, who decided that he no longer wanted to be a slave. One day Bro Jim was seen walking, his back ramrod straight, across the fields towards the wooded tree line in the distance and once there he disappeared. Poof! Gone. Bro Jim was different from the others. He didn't march to a different drum, he marched to a different band. The overseers and the dogs were dispatched to bring Bro Jim back, but after four days of searching they returned without finding him. Many months later it was presumed that Bro Jim had died out in the wilds because he was never seen or found. For the next few years landowners and farmers complained about a crafty thief that was stealing their chickens and taking meat out of their smokehouses. On these occasions the dogs were loosed and search parties dispatched, but the dogs always lost the scent of the perpetrator. A few days after slavery had been abolished and slaves became freedmen, a lone figure was seen emerging from the wooded tree line on the horizon. And, as the figure became discernible as that of a man, the people suddenly began to jump and shout for joy. It was Bro Jim! His clothing was ragged and torn and he wore a long beard and his hair was so long it was down to his shoulders and he resembled Frederick Douglas. Everyone wanted to know how Bro Jim managed to survive during the two or three years he had been on the run. He told them he had been the one stealing the chickens and the meats from the smokehouses and he had also learned to survive off of the land. He said he slept in hollow logs as protection against the elements. Whenever the dogs would pick up his scent he would tie tree bark under his feet to confuse the dogs and throw them off of his scent. I immediately knew that this ancestor of mine was one I would love to have known. I could identify with a lot of the character of Bro Jim, plus we had something else in common—the art of stealing meat for survival.

Son asked me some questions about how my life was going and what I was planning on doing with myself. I honestly told him what was going on with me and how I was trying to "get it together." He asked me, "Did that war over there do this to you?" I knew that he was saying "over there" because he probably couldn't pronounce Vietnam, but I understood. I told him yes and explained some of it to him. When we got back to his house I felt elated that I had been able to spend some quality time with him. Before I left he said to me, "Rocky. The family has been telling me things about you that are not too good. And I've watched you grow since you were a baby, so I had to see for myself if the things they were saying were true. You've got some problems, but you're strong and you got a good head on yo' shoulders. When you were a little boy you knew how to do things other kids had a hard time figgerin' out. You're smart. Stay smart and just make the right decisions and you'll figger' out where you suppose' to be going and what you suppose' to do. You gonna be jes fine."

I successfully completed my six-month probationary period on the job and received a pay raise and a cost of living increase. I was now making a whopping $8.90 per hour! The new crew I worked with was much better than the other group. The crew consisted of three white guys and two other black guys. One of the black guys was about seven or eight years my senior and he was retired from the military and his name was George Gilchrist. He was a short, dark complexioned guy who had his hair cut in a military style and wore a spit shine on his work boots. He was introduced as my new supervisor. I was told that he was a Vietnam vet, but either it wasn't true or if he did go across to the big pond he didn't see any action. There just wasn't any *esprit de corps* between him and me. He was very hyper acting and he let little things get under his skin and he was always yelling and screaming at someone. Behind his back, some of the guys used the term "bitchy" to describe him. In an effort to avoid problems in the future, I told George that if I did something wrong on the job and he needed to correct me on it he wouldn't need to yell at me. I let him know that I had no problems with being corrected or accepting constructive criticism, but I did have a problem when it came to someone yelling at me. George said, "No problem."

A month later, Punchy couldn't pay his portion of the rent and it was the second month that this had happened. He decided to move back home with his folks because he had neglected some of his other financial responsibilities and had over extended himself. I had to move into a more affordable apartment in another apartment complex. It took me three days to move all of my stuff by myself and I was exhausted. Plus I had been working overtime all week. Monica and I had a big argument over her refusal to let my daughter visit with me for the weekend. My nightmares about Vietnam were increasing, so I had been drinking more and had even gotten my first DUI. When I went to work that night I was angry, tired and upset. I got on the forklift and began moving some of the heavier stock to the front of the warehouse to make it easier to get. Fifteen minutes later George ran up to the forklift I was on and began yelling, and berating me. "I've found five large boxes of materials that you've damaged with the blades on this forklift! Syrup is running all over the floor from one of the containers you busted. What the hell do you think you're doing?" I heard a roaring sound in my head and I felt my blood run cold and in a flash I had jumped off the forklift and was staring into George's wild looking eyes.

"Who do you think you're cursing at?" I yelled in his face.

"I'm cursing at you for damaging goods!" He yelled back. Then it dawned on me what had happened. The guys I had been having problems with on the earlier shift had hung around after their shift was over. I remembered seeing them. They had sabotaged the materials George was talking about and left it to look as if I had done it.

"And, get out of my face!" George screamed at me, as his right hand started to inch calculatingly towards the knife on his right side. I saw the move and quickly wrapped my left fist around the handle of my bayonet and readied myself to pull it out of its sheath if necessary.

"George, if you pull that knife off of your hip this will be the day that your wife becomes a widow," I told him. And, I meant every word. I was angry and hurting and I had no compunctions at that moment about making someone else hurt too!

George backed down and removed his hand from where it had been and told me to go on back to work. I started walking back towards the forklift and I was trembling with rage and knew that I had to leave right then! I told George I needed to leave and that I was going to take eight hours of sick leave. He "OK'd" it and I went home.

The next morning I received a phone call from Tony asking me what had happened last night. He had received a phone call from George and had heard his version and wanted to know my side. I told Tony my side of the story including my suspicions of who had damaged the products. Tony told me that George didn't want me back on his shift because he was afraid of me. Tony then told me, "Rock, you're a good worker and I like you, but George is the supervisor and I have to respect his wishes if he doesn't want you on his shift. You and I both know why I moved you off of the other shift and I definitely can't move you to the day shift, because we've got worker's with seniority who have been waiting a long time to get on the day shift. I'm going to give you George's home phone number and you give him a call and see if the two of you can work it out. If he's willing to take you back on his shift, it will be fine by me. But, if he won't let you come back, I'll have to let you go. I'm sorry, but that's the way it is. Nothing personal."

I called George at home and talked with him. He said, "Man, you scared me and then you threatened me. I just can't work with somebody like you. Man, you're crazy. There's something seriously wrong with you." I used coercion, sympathy, and sincerity in trying to get George to change his mind but he refused to relent. George controlled his crew through intimidation; that's why he always yelled and screamed at them and I had exposed his Achilles heel in front of them. Yeah, he was afraid of me and he had a right to be. He was a power and control freak, and when he realized that he couldn't intimidate me, it made him feel impotent and powerless. Be that as it may, I was out of a good paying job. I sat down and did some soul searching and as I looked back on my life all that I saw was one failure after another.

The following day, my mother called and asked if I would come by to see her. She and my father wanted to talk with me. When I arrived they told me that they wanted to try and work through the problems that had occurred between us. I was told that we could start by me apologizing for what I had done. "What I had done! I was the one who had the gun put to his head," I thought to myself. But, in spite of everything I offered a sincere apology and was sanctioned back into the family. My mother then offered me dinner. While I was having dinner my parents told me they were going out and would be gone four to six hours and I was to make sure I locked up the house if I left before their return. When they left I went to the liquor store and got me a bottle of Brandy and went back to the house. I consumed almost the whole bottle and I was feeling no pain. Depression started to set in and then I began thinking about the circumstances, which led to me to losing my job. Then I became angry again. I didn't know which way to turn. I had been able to get back into the work force and then the rug was pulled out from under me again. By this time I was drunk and out of control. I thought about the three guys from the second shift I had seen hanging around the night I had the run-in with George and who had caused me to be terminated. I decided I wasn't going to let them get away with it and I didn't have anything to lose. I decided that I was going to make them pay. I had lost everything and now they were going to lose everything. I decided that I was going to go and kill them! I went into my father's bedroom and got his P-38 and took it out to the back yard. I put three coke bottles up on the fence and test fired the pistol to make sure that it was zeroed in like they taught me in the military. When I zeroed the pistol in, I was able to put a bullet through each of the three bottles from fifty feet away. I went into the kitchen and sat down to plan my strategy. I would go out to the job site after dark and wait until the three-crew members came outside to take a smoke break. And then I would open fire on them point blank within a fifty foot firing radius. If I could get close enough, I would go for head shots and, if that weren't possible, I would go for body mass and aim for their chests. I had an hour and a half before they took their break and while waiting I would clean the pistol. As I sat at the table I took the magazine out of the gun and pulled back the slide to eject the live round that was still in the chamber, but it was jammed in and wouldn't eject. I put the safety on and made sure I didn't have my hand on the trigger and popped the slide back again to eject the shell and still nothing. On the third attempt there was a deafening explosion as the gun fired the uncooperative bullet across the room. When the shock of the explosion had passed, I could smell the heavy odor of cordite permeating the kitchen and then I noticed water shooting through the air! The water was coming from the hot water heater across the room in the corner. The errant bullet had struck the hot water heater dead center! There was a bullet hole of equal distance from the top of the water heater to the bottom and of equal distance from one side to the other side. Dead center! Arcing through the air and shooting across the room was scalding, hot water. I tried to get to the hot water heater to stop the flow of hot water that was starting to flood the kitchen, but the steaming water was so hot that I couldn't get to it. The only thing I could do was wait until the level of the hot water fell below the puncture hole caused by the bullet. When that finally happened, I had to bail, push, and sweep water out of the kitchen. I called the nearest Sears store and told them to come out immediately and bring a new hot water heater. By the time I had gotten all of the water out of the kitchen, and by the time the repairman had finished installing the replacement heater, I had sobered up completely! My thoughts of contemplating murder had vanished. And I wondered what had possessed me to plan and think about carrying out such an act? There had to be a God out there somewhere. It was as if God were saying to me..."My son, before I let you go into the streets to commit three murders which you will regret for the rest of your life, I will cause you to kill a water heater instead. And, the time you will spend cleaning up the mess you have made will be sufficient to sober you up and let you review what the devil almost got you to do for him."

The bill for the replacement water heater came to $218.97. The total amount of money in my checking account was $220.00.

CHAPTER SIXTEEN

Spiritual Happenings

One day I happened to see an old high school friend of mine as he came out of the door to the liquor store I was about to enter. His name was Harvey Woods, but during our high school years we had given him the nickname "Har-Boom." Harvey was tall, boyishly handsome guy with hazel eyes and he always looked like he had a golden suntan. He was a "life of the party" kind of guy who always had a funny joke to tell and would have everyone rolling on the floor with laughter. Harvey didn't go to 'Nam, in fact he was never in the military, but he did share something in common with a few Vietnam vets: he was crazy as hell! This fact had a lot to do with him acquiring the moniker "Har-Boom." During our junior year of high school Harvey had been working on the DCR (Diversified Career Training) Program. This program allowed some students to attend school half day and work the other half of the day learning a life skill with employers approved by the school board. With the money he earned, Harvey bought a real nice second hand '55 Chevy. On a cold winter weekend night during the Christmas holidays I was riding with Harvey and two of his cousins to a party we had heard about. The party was in a section of the city that was considered enemy territory because it was the neighborhood of the high school which was our archrival, Turner High School. But, we knew that Turner High had a lot of pretty girls who would be in attendance at the party, so we were willing to take our chances and try to blend in with the crowd once we got there. We arrived at the party and knocked on the door hoping to be admitted. The door was opened by a beautiful girl I didn't know, but had seen on numerous occasions at some of the football games. She smiled and stepped back to allow us in, when suddenly one of the football players for Turner High yelled out,

"Hey y'all it's some fools from Watt'n'ton (Washington) High!"
"Let's get' em!" The four of us made a hasty retreat at full gallop
back to Harvey's car and got the hell out of the area as fast the '55
would carry us. When we realized that we weren't being followed,
we continued to cruise for a while until Harvey spoke up saying,
"Man, I don't like the idea of those dudes running us off like that.
We ought to go back and crash the party like we started to do." I
had determined that Harvey had lost his mind and told him so.
But, Harvey is a very stubborn kind of guy so back to the party we
went. When we got out the car and approached the door for the
second time that night, I noticed that Harvey had gotten something
from under his front seat as he exited the car and had put it under
his trench coat. As we stood in front of the door about to knock,
Harvey produced a sawed-off shot gun from under his coat and
aimed a blast from the gun at the door handle. BOOM! The sound
shattered the night. The door had a big, splintered hole in it where
the lock and handle had previously been. Smoke and the acrid
smell of gunpowder wafted precipitously in the doorway and on
the night air. The blast had also shredded the arm off of a sofa
positioned just inside the door and when I looked into the room I
could see balls of cotton, dust, and feathers floating in the air. And
through this gauzy haze I could see the shocked expressions on
everyone's faces including the football players. Everyone's eyes
were round like saucers and I felt that was an appropriate time to
"get out of Dodge" before their shock wore off. Afterwards, we
rode around for a few hours laughing off the tension of Harvey's
unexpected act of lunacy. We joked about how Harvey just walked
up to the door and went BOOM! Thus, "Har-Boom!"

Harvey and I stood outside the liquor store and reminisced
about the old days. He told me that he was working as an
independent contractor preparing apartments for new move-ins.
Harvey explained that he spray painted the apartments, shampooed
the carpets, and performed minor repairs. He needed someone to
help him and he offered me the opportunity to work with him and
learn the job. I began working with him as his helper shampooing
carpets and doing trim paint work. My pay was $35.00 per
apartment and we usually finished three or four per day. We started

about six o'clock in the morning and would finish about eight o'clock p.m. We took regular breaks during the day to drink as we worked, and because we had no one to report to, we encountered no problems. The managers of the apartment complexes just wanted the work completed on time and we were known for doing very good work.

Often after work I'd go home and get cleaned up and meet Harvey at a club we frequented regularly. One night when I got to the club Harvey was sitting at a table talking with two attractive women and when he saw me he motioned for me to join them. I was introduced first to Brandy, a beautiful statuesque, twenty-six year old, and Karen, a Midwestern transplant from Kansas who had been in Atlanta for eight years. Through conversation I learned that Brandy had moved to Atlanta from New Jersey and was working locally as a stripper. Karen was a registered nurse, two years my senior, and worked at a local hospital. She told me she was divorced and had two adult daughters and a son. Karen possessed a subtle beauty, which hinted at a touch of her Native American ancestry. She was five foot four inches in height and was buxom. She had a warm and engaging personality and I liked her right off. Karen didn't approve of Brandy's line of work, but realized that she was capable of making her life choices, so she played the role of big sister by giving her advice when she deemed it necessary. We all sat, talked, drank, and danced for a few hours and then left for my apartment. At my apartment we continued talking, drinking, and having a great time until around three a.m. when Karen said it was time for them to leave. As they were leaving I asked Karen for her phone number, but she refused to give it to me. I told her that I would like to see her again. And, again she refused saying, "I'd rather not give you my number, because I don't have time for any type of relationship. I have family obligations, which make it impossible for me to see anyone." I was determined to get her number and finally she relinquished and gave it to me.

The next day I called Karen and we talked for a while, but when I asked her to go out with me, she adamantly refused, again stating her family commitments as the reason. For four days I called and spoke with her and on each occasion I asked her out and I received the same negative response. Finally, on the afternoon of the fifth day when I asked again she stated, "All right. I coming to pick you up and I'm going to show you why I don't have time for you." An hour later she came by and told me, "Let's go."

"Where are we going?" I inquired.

"You'll see," was her reply.

We rode along talking for about ten minutes and then she turned into the driveway of a modest bungalow home and said, "This is where I live. Come on in." When we walked into the living room I was introduced to a heavy set, very pretty girl about Brandy's age named Pamela and she was Karen's oldest daughter. She was watching the television and when she looked up to acknowledge me her eyes were so sad. I saw something in her eyes that caused me to have a flash back to 'Nam .... I saw something that I had seen many times in the eyes of some soldiers. No will to live. Pamela's eyes said to me that she had given up on the will to live. So, I thought this is what Karen had brought me to see. Wrong. She then led me into a bedroom where a nurse dressed in white was writing on a chart the temperature reading she had just taken of the patient in the room. The patient was a little boy, five years old and he was strapped into a padded, specially built medical high chair. The child was a beautiful, robust little fellow with a head full of tight curls of red hair. The child sat motionless, and the only movement I observed was the involuntary movement of his tongue through his partially opened mouth. His eyes were open, fixated, staring blankly into space, and oblivious to all around him. When I looked at Karen with a question mark on my countenance she responded, "Ibis is Pam's son and my grandson. We call him "DJ," short for Derrick James. He's in a coma and knows nothing. If you rate a coma on a scale of one to five with five being the worst, he would be a four. His eyes close and he sleeps for a few hours. He is fed baby foods into his mouth and his tongue involuntarily moves the food into his throat to start the digestive process. He has a plastic tube which has been surgically placed to protrude from his abdomen and that's how we give him his medicines and fluids."

"How did he end up like this?" I asked.

"When he was two years old, the nursery that cared for him called Pam at work and told her that her son was sick and she should come and get him. When she got there to pick him up he was running a very high fever and was very listless. So, she immediately took him to the emergency room of the nearest hospital, Thompson General. The doctors determined that DJ had the flu and after working on him for a few hours, they weren't having much success in getting his high temperature lowered. So they arranged for him to be airlifted by a helicopter Life Flyte to the Mitchell Children's Medical Center north of the city. Five minutes into the flight DJ died. Eventually, the emergency flight crew was able to revive him, but the oxygen deprivation to DJ's brain caused him to lapse into this coma that you now see him in. The doctors have said that his condition is irreversible and that he would probably live for another year in this vegetative state and then die. So far, he's defied the odds and has survived two years longer than the doctors predicted. "

"Isn't it odd for a child to die from the early symptoms of the flu?" I asked.

Karen regarded me cryptically as she replied, "That's what I've been saying to anyone that will listen. What happened was that the doctor's misdiagnosed DJ's symptoms. He didn't have the flu, he had contracted spinal meningitis! And, if the doctor's had properly diagnosed the symptoms as spinal meningitis they would have known better than to send DJ up in that helicopter. The combination of the de-compression which took place in the confines of the helicopter as it ascended into the thinner atmosphere profoundly impacted upon the spinal fluids and the cranial pressure exacted by the spinal meningitis. I contend that the doctors were negligent in their diagnosis and are therefore liable for DJ's comatose condition. He has three shifts of nurses that are here around the clock. I have taken on the responsibility of being his nurse from midnight to seven o'clock in the morning. When I met you the other night it was my scheduled off day. So, as you can see I don't have time for any involvements outside of my family."

I looked again at little DJ and thought to myself, "How cruel, deadly and evil the ruler of the darkness is to visit such a dastardly act upon such an innocent little boy." As that thought moved through my mind I unconsciously reached out with my hand and placed my palm caressingly against the side of DJ's cherubic little face. The moment my hand made contact with his face I felt a surge of electrical or kinetic power, something I had never before experienced. It was a pure, unconvoluted, ancient, bonding and overpowering feeling. Suddenly, DJ threw both his arms up into the air, looked around at me fully focused and emitted a loud sound from deep within him. "HIIIIEEEEEEI!" In that instant I felt him in my consciousness as he said to me without speaking, "I am here!"

I heard another scream behind me and, as I turned to look, the nurse that had been in the room hurriedly ran past me toward the front door. It was then that I noticed I was the only one in the house except for DJ. I went to the front door and peered out into the yard and all three of the women were standing there huddled together, looking at me strangely with wide-eyed expressions on their faces. As I stepped toward them I detected a precipitous movement of withdrawal from each of them. "What's going on?" I asked of Karen. "Why did you all run out?"

Karen walked over to me and looked into my eyes intently and asked, "Who are you?"

"What do you mean? You know who I am," was my reply. "Karen, will you please tell me what's going on here?"

She answered by saying, "My grandson has been like a virtual vegetable since the day we brought him home from the hospital three years ago. He has not responded to anyone or any anything. No response to any outside stimuli. And, you, a perfect stranger walk into his room and touch his face and he lifts his arms up into the air, tries to talk and looks directly at you—right at you. He's never done any of those things since he's been ill. So, needless to say all of this spooked us. But, again Mr. Coleman, I ask, who are you?"

I realized that Karen had a lot of personal family issues that made it difficult for us to date seriously, so I became a friend who called her occasionally to see how she was doing. I began to casually date a number of women whom I found interesting. Invariably, each of them began to discuss my drinking problem with me and they each wanted to help me stop drinking. Two women I dated Doris and Sharon, each wanted me to attend church with them and at various times I did attend, because I felt a spiritual void in my life. Doris and I had dated for a short time after my return from Vietnam, but now she was very active in the church and was practicing celibacy, while she waited on the Lord to send her a husband. After attending church with her for two months I decided to "join" the church. The minister usually delivered a pretty good sermon and I felt fairly comfortable among the congregation's members. One Sunday morning I had decided that I was going to walk forward and "join" church. But, near the end of the service when the minister announced, "Those of you here who are interested in becoming members of our congregation please come forward now," I got cold feet and didn't go forward. I hadn't told Doris or anyone of my decision to step forward that day. No one. Suddenly a little old lady I had never seen before in my life walked up the aisle to where I was sitting and took my hand and asked me, "Weren't you going to do something for the Lord today?" Momentarily confused by her insight, I looked into her eyes and I saw an all knowing kind of wisdom that frightened me. I stammered to her, "Yes Ma'am. I was." The little old lady turned and motioned to the minister to hold on a minute and then she led me down front to "join" church. I looked beside me and saw three other people who had come forward to accept Christ into their lives. When the minister ended the services, the four of us were taken to the church office to fill out the required forms acknowledging us as new members. The office quickly filled up with choir members who came in to hang up their robes as I frantically looked around trying to spot the little old lady. I saw her on the other side of the room standing against the wall, behind a group of people engaged in conversation. She was a small, grandmotherly looking woman and appeared to be in her late eighties. She was wearing a pink suit, a matching pill box hat with a veil on it, and she held her purse in front of her bosom with both hands clutching the carry strap as if she was holding a steering wheel. When I made eye contact with her she smiled at me and made a perceptible nod of her head. I remember thinking, *Her smile is mysterious like that of the Mona Lisa.* I hurried to complete the forms I was filling out so I could rush over to her and find out how she could have possibly known of my intentions to join church that morning. As I handed the completed forms to the church secretary I looked over at the little old lady and she was gone! That quick. In the twinkling of an eye she was gone! I looked all around the room trying to find her, but she had just disappeared. I turned back to the church secretary and asked her, "Did you see which way the older woman in pink went?"

"A woman in pink? Where was she standing?" The secretary inquired.

I was starting to think that maybe I was losing my mind. Maybe I was the only one who had seen the woman. And if that was the case I might be in need of a sanity check. "She was standing over there, across the room near the wall." I replied.

"Oh. Yes, I did see her, but I didn't see her leave." The secretary's statement confirmed for me, that I really had seen the woman.

"Who is she? Do you know her?" I asked.

"No. I don't know her. In fact I've never seen her here before."

I continued going to the Sunday services for about three months before I stopped going altogether. The reason was because Doris had started to become rather possessive of our friendship. She seemed to feel that her efforts in helping me with my spiritual needs required that our relationship should become a more committed one. I didn't feel that I was the potential husband that the Lord had chosen for her to "wait on." I never went back to that church and to this day I have never again seen the little old lady in pink. I still sometimes ask myself what or who she was. Some months later I was attending a "Word" church with Sharon on a fairly consistent basis. A "Word" church emphasizes the methodology of teaching and studying the Bible in an effort to seek accurate knowledge of the scriptures. During my association with the "Word" church I felt that I truly had become enlightened as my knowledge and understanding of the scriptures grew. I decided to become a member of that congregation and one Sunday morning I went forward. I stood with six other converts before the minister for acceptance. When the minister completed the acceptance ritual he told us to turn around to be viewed and accepted by the congregation. When I turned around to face the church members my eyes fell upon a very heavyset woman sitting on the front row. She looked at me and the moment we made eye contact a look of contrition came over her countenance. She jumped straight up from her seat, let loose with a piercing scream and fainted at my feet! I felt like I was experiencing deja vu. Eventually, Sharon determined that I wasn't interested in being involved in a committed relationship at that time, so much like Doris, we kept our friendship platonic.

Months later, through a chance encounter I ran into Karen again and we talked at length, catching up on what each of us had been doing. She told me that her family situation had changed somewhat. She and her daughter had filed a medical malpractice lawsuit on behalf of DJ and had won. The daughter and DJ had moved into a new home equipped with a swimming pool, Jacuzzi and physical therapy room. A nursing service provided DJ with nurse's twenty-four hours a day and the daughter had purchased a specially equipped van to transport DJ. The judge who heard the case mandated that DJ would have all of these things to make his life as comfortable as possible. And there was a monetary settlement, which was more than two million dollars. Karen had started working at a local hospital again and she informed me that she now had time to go out with me if I was still interested. I told her I was still interested and we began dating.

Within the first year of our relationship, we were living together. We had a lot of fun and did a lot of things together. My drinking continued and by now my drink of choice had become Brandy or Cognac, which was some pretty heavy stuff. Karen didn't drink nearly as much as I did, but she did regularly drink with me. One Sunday afternoon I had been watching the football playoffs and drinking quite heavily when Karen asked me to go with her to the grocery store. She had to go to work at the hospital in two hours and she wanted to pick up some items before she had to leave. When we got to the car, she told me that she would drive because I had probably been drinking too much. As we were returning from the store and only one block from home, the front right tire on the car blew out. I told Karen to walk the short distance home and call her co-worker who lived nearby and ask her to pick her up on the way to work. I would stay and change the tire and take the car home. I had almost completed putting the spare tire on when a police cruiser pulled up and a black officer got out and came over to me. As he walked up I saw him observing the skid marks made on the pavement when the tire had blown.

"Is this your car?" He asked.

"Yes, it is officer." I replied.

Then he said, "Let me see your license." I complied with his request and continued working on the tire as he went back to his car to check me out over his radio. I knew that my license was clean and that I had paid the fine on my first DUI more than a year and a half before. I then noticed that a black female officer had arrived on the scene and she came over to me and told me to put my hands behind my back. When I asked her why, she told me not to give her a hard time; then the first officer came back over to me.

I asked him, "Why do you want to put cuffs on me?"

He replied, "Just do as she told you."

When I refused to let the female officer put her handcuffs on me, the male officer grabbed me and held my hands behind my back while the female cuffed me. As I was being taken to the police cruiser I continued to ask why I was being arrested. Finally the male officer said, "We'll think of something by the time we get you to the jail."

When I got to the jail I was booked on a charge of DUI! I had to post a $300.00 bond to get out of jail and $75.00 to get the car out of the impound. When I went to court, I explained to the judge that at no time did the officers observe me driving the vehicle. And, I further explained that Karen had been driving the car. The judge didn't want to hear my explanation. He let the charge of DUI stand; he fined me and suspended my license for thirty days.

Pamela, Karen's daughter, spent some of her newfound wealth on the purchase of time-share condominiums and she loved to travel. She took her mother and me with her on trips to San Juan, Puerto Rico, Hilton Head Island, South Carolina, Virginia Beach, Virginia and the Island of Antigua. I began to notice that when we would get to these vacation spots, we were literally at the mercy of Pamela. She would pay for the entire trip and all accommodations. She would then become tyrannical as to what we could do, when we could do it, and how we should do it. She had recently become very involved with a religious cult whose teachings forbade almost everything except giving them all of your worldly possessions and all of your money. When we were in Antigua, Pamela told me that she no longer wanted me to smoke, or drink alcohol, or read any more of those satanic Stephen King novels while we were on our trip. I told her to go to hell. And, when we returned home I told her that I would never, ever, travel anywhere with her again. She also began to tell her mother what she could and couldn't do. The docile young girl with the sad eyes had become someone I didn't know, or care to know. With her new wealth she had become like my old boss, George, at the warehouse, a power and control freak. She began loaning money to her brothers and sisters in the religious cult and they elevated her to Sainthood. Everyone wanted to be her friend. She didn't date nor have a boyfriend; her new found religion supplied all her needs and she adopted all of her new brothers and sisters as her new family. Karen was heartbroken when her daughter told her that she could no longer consider her as her mother unless she too joined the cult. Otherwise, she would regard her mother as just another lost soul out in the pagan world. I would have nothing more to do with Pamela and this began to cause a lot of problems between Karen and me.

During the following summer Karen and I were married in a simple ceremony by a Justice of the Peace. I felt that our marriage would solidify our relationship and give us the nucleus for the stability and strength necessary to deal with the family dilemma and myriad other problems

I discovered that Karen had come from a large, dysfunctional family and that her childhood had been a nightmare. Her father and mother had both been alcoholics and physical and mental abuse was a constant occurrence within the household. Her father would get drunk and terrorize the entire family. Karen got married early in order to escape the living hell she was trapped in. The marriage produced three children, but it didn't last because she married a man who was as abusive as her father. Her youngest daughter was twenty years old, pregnant, crack cocaine addicted, and living from place to place with her friends. Her son was cross-addicted to marijuana, alcohol, and crack cocaine. Karen had made the mistake of not disciplining her children when they were younger; instead, she made the mistake of trying to be their friend. When Karen would allow them to visit us, I began to notice that after they left, jewelry, money, and other personal items would turn up missing. A serious rift developed between Karen and me when I told her that her children were no longer welcome at our house. Karen began to develop a drinking problem, and because of all of the family chaos, she and I started having serious arguments. I told her kids that I wouldn't tolerate them coming to our house when they were under the influence of drugs. My contention was: I didn't know where they had been; who they may have ripped-off; who they might owe money to; or who might be after them. Under anyone of these scenarios, they could lead some trouble right to my front door. I further explained to them the police might see them when they purchased some drugs. The police would follow them to our house, and pull a raid on the house. Everybody in the house would be arrested, even those who don't use drugs. This problem created a great dilemma for Karen as she tried to find ways to support my position and at the same time (behind my back) find ways to continue providing support for her children who were, by all standards, adults. I was attempting to help them with "tough love," but she wouldn't or couldn't support me in my efforts. Karen, from a young age had always taken care of her younger siblings, cousins and other relatives. It seemed as if everyone, young and old, came to her with their pains and their problems. As a young girl and then as a young woman, she was not emotionally, physically, or spiritually equipped to handle all that was put upon her, but she persevered and did the best she could. Being unprepared for many of the problems she encountered, she had to resort to trial and error methods. And unfortunately, there were many more failures in her efforts than successes.

Based on these learned experiences over the years, she developed a martyr complex. She would involve herself in the burdens of others and try to help them overcome whatever obstacles they were facing. This is perhaps one of the many reasons that influenced her to choose nursing as her profession. She would take upon herself the suffering of others, but there was never anyone she could take her troubles to. These factors caused her to believe that her life was destined to be bereft of true happiness and peace of mind. In dating or marital relationships she subconsciously looked for reasons or ways to make the relationship fail because she didn't believe that she deserved to be happy. Chaos in her personal life was familiar to her; peace and harmony were abstracts.

I began to notice that Karen and her daughter, Pamela, had started communicating again. When I questioned Karen about it she admitted to me that she had been attending services of the religious cult of which her daughter was a member. She began to tell me how enlightening the services were and how friendly and welcoming the members were to her. She then pleaded with me to go with her to the next service to see for myself. I felt that old familiar "weird feeling" come over me which was usually a signal to me that something is amiss and I very calmly told her I would think about it. I took a couple of days to think about going and I decided to go and see for myself what was really going on.

We attended a Friday night service and I was impressed at how nicely everyone was attired; men in conservative business suits and women in Sunday dresses. As I was introduced to various men who were leaders of the group, I couldn't help but notice that when I shook each of their hands they all gave me a weak handshake and they didn't make much eye contact. To me, the eyes are the windows to the soul, and the kind of handshake I receive from a person tells me a lot about their character. I wasn't impressed. When the services began everyone had a Bible that was somewhat different from the King James Bible I was familiar with. As the leader began teaching and reading from various scriptures I began to notice that certain passages seemed to be slanted to accommodate a particular thought. I found myself reading the paragraph before and the paragraph after the passage in order to get a more complete understanding of the passage. A pattern began to develop in my mind's eye as the leader continued to extrapolate selective passages to fit the logic he was proselytizing. Some of his teachings did not fit well with me as being of "accurate knowledge." Certain things he spoke of didn't feel right...like walking to the edge of the jungle in 'Nam and not wanting to go any further cause "it don't feel right." When we left that night I felt very uncomfortable. I went back four more times and tried to keep an open mind to make sure that I was not biased in my opinions based on preconceived ideologies. I left there even more strongly convinced that the members were like lambs being led to the slaughter.

One day while contemplating this situation it became clear to me what was happening. Karen wanted to reestablish her mother-daughter relationship with Pamela, so she had agreed to attend the cult services. The leaders of the cult had come to realize the importance of having Karen become a convert. So, in all probability, they began working on Pamela to get her mother involved. The reason for this was based on Pamela's newly acquired wealth. If Pamela happened to meet an untimely death, her mother would be the beneficiary of Pamela's estate and the executor for DJ's welfare. Pamela had already made a sizable contribution for an additional wing to be added to the cult's present facility and had personally paid to have central air-conditioning installed in order for DJ to be comfortable (due to his condition) when she took him to the services. If the cult could maintain a form of mind control over both mother and daughter, they would eventually control the money. When I shared this information with Karen, she was in denial and we argued constantly. This dilemma, coupled with my drinking and the many other problems, caused us to have some very violent arguments. During some of these confrontations, she called the police and had me evicted from the premises. And on other occasions she would tell the police she wanted to leave and she would go and stay with her daughter. These separations would last three days to maybe a week and we would get back together.

On one occasion the arguing started to heat up and in a fit of anger I left the house and went to hang out with my old crowd back on the block. The regulars were glad to see me and I began drinking heavily in an attempt to pacify the rage that had built up inside me. The parking lot was crowded that Friday evening; it was payday. I was standing near the side of a building when a guy I had never seen before walked by and bumped into me intentionally. When I turned towards him to see what was going on, I caught a peripheral glimpse of a second guy to my left as he swung a fist towards my face. I couldn't avoid the punch and it caught me on the right temple breaking the dark glasses I was wearing and causing a cut on the bridge of my nose. Blood spurted from the cut on my nose, got into my eyes and clouded my vision. I frantically wiped my eyes with my sleeve as I jumped into a defensive fighting stance as the two guys advanced on me. I started swinging punches and all hell broke loose in the parking lot as everybody started fighting everybody. As I was dealing with the two dudes in front of me, I realized that a woman was coming up on my side with what looked like a wooden plank. She swung the plank towards my back, but being occupied to my front by her cohorts I just tightened up my back muscles as she swung and kept on fighting. The plank broke when in made contact with my back but I didn't feel it at the time. Then, the wail of police sirens could be heard in the distance and everybody started disengaging and getting the hell out of Dodge. A guy I knew grabbed my arm as he ran by and pulled me along with him through an alley that led over to the next street. When we were a safe distance away Doug, the guy who had grabbed me by the arm, looked at my cut and said that it wasn't too bad but would leave a scar.

"Doug, who in the hell were those dudes and that chick that came up on me?" I asked.

Doug said, "Man, and I ain't never seen them fools around here before. Maybe they thought 'cause it was payday they could come around here and try to rob somebody. Come on with me. My woman don't stay too far from here. We can go by her place and she can patch up that cut on your face."

For the next week I asked around trying to find out who the people were who caused me the grief in the parking lot, but nobody knew anything about them. Also during that week Karen and I had another big fight, and in anger, I again left the house. I drove to the nearest liquor store and bought a little half-pint of Brandy, which I drank quickly on my way back home. It was at night and I almost missed my turn and at the last second I hit my signal light and swung over in the turning lane and made my turn. All at once, two police cars pulled in behind me with their blue lights flashing, signaling me to pull over. One of the officers walked up to the car and asked me for my license and when I reached for my wallet, I realized that in my haste to leave the house, I had left it behind. The officer smelled the alcohol on me and told me that I was under arrest for DUI. It was my third arrest for DUI. Karen came to bail me out of jail and my irresponsible actions provided additional fodder for more arguing.

CHAPTER SEVENTEEN

Heads or Tails, Life or Death

The job I had working with "Har-Boom" was starting to become a bit sporadic, and considering that I was going to need additional money to take care of my third charge for DUI, I decided go and look for a job. I walked through downtown Atlanta for hours and found a few businesses that were accepting applications for employment for various positions. I submitted an application to a couple of them. While walking along I noticed a sign for the State Employment Service and went in to see what might be available. At the information counter I was given an application to fill out. When I returned the application to the lady at the counter she looked it over and said, "Oh. I see here that you are a veteran. Hold on just a minute and I will arrange for you to talk with one of our Veterans Representatives."

I asked her, "What do Veterans Representatives do?"

"The Veterans Representatives provide many types of services to all veterans including employment referral." She stated.

A few minutes later a black gentleman came to the counter and called my name. When I answered and walked up to him, he shook my hand and told me that his name was Leroy Spriggs and to come over to his desk and have a seat. Mr. Spriggs was about four years my senior, a bit overweight, and a very friendly and humorous guy. He told me that he was a disabled Vietnam Veteran and had been retired from the Air Force for two years after serving for twenty years. We discussed what kind of work I might be interested in doing and what type of work I had done in the past. Mr. Spriggs suggested that I might try a few of the positions he had which were in sales. I told him I was interested and he called the companies to set up appointments for me. Before I left he told me if the referrals didn't work out that I should come back to see him. When I left his office I felt rather elated. Mr. Spriggs seemed to be a great guy and it had been good to talk with a fellow 'Nam vet who could relate to what I was going through. Mr. Spriggs had treated me with dignity and respect and made me feel like I was "somebody." It was also great to see a Vietnam vet in such a responsible position.

I returned to see Mr. Spriggs a week later after I found out that I was not selected for the positions he had referred me to. Mr. Spriggs looked over my application again and said, "I want you to apply for a position like the one I have."

"You must be kidding me." I told him.

"No. I'm serious. Your major in college was psychology; your past work history reflects that you have a background in counseling and you have supervisory experience. You also have a 10 percent disability from the military, which is a mandatory requirement. There is a position open in this office because we just had a vet to retire," he told me.

Mr. Spriggs gave me a State Application to take with me and fill out and told me to bring it back to him as quickly as possible. I took the application back to him the next day and he told me that he would forward it to where it needed to go next.

Two weeks later, I reported to a designated location to take the State test for the position of Veterans Representative. The official job title was DVOP, which was a Disabled Veterans Outreach Program Specialist. After taking the three-hour exam I felt that I had done fairly well. And this was confirmed a week later when I received my results through the mail. I hurriedly tore open the envelope and let loose with a primal yell when I saw that my raw score was 97, and as a disabled veteran, when my ten points were added my score topped out at 100! I immediately called Mr. Spriggs and told him of my good news. He sounded like he was genuinely happy for me and told me that I would probably be contacted soon for an interview. Three days later I went to interview for the position.

I arrived for the interview a half-hour early, and at the appointed time the office manager and the assistant manager interviewed me. The interview lasted approximately forty minutes and my interviewers were very cordial, but were rather poker faced, making it difficult to judge how I was fairing. On the way home I felt that the interview had gone well, but I was a little apprehensive. A week later, I received the much-anticipated letter from the State Personnel Office. I sat down and tentatively opened the envelope and began reading until I got to the part that read "...we want to thank you for your interest in the position of Veterans Representative (DVOP), but we have selected another applicant who..." I was devastated. I began to berate myself for being stupid enough to think I had a chance. I had made the mistake of starting to believe that fate was going to allow me to pick myself up and get back in the race. I decided to hell with playing by the rules I was going to go back to the streets and start hustling again to make some money, which I did for two weeks. And, then I received another letter from the State Personnel Office similar to the first one I had received requesting that I come back to the same office for an interview. I didn't plan on going again, because they were probably just sending me the letter as a part of their protocol since my score was at the top of the list.

But, on the morning of the interview I changed my mind at the last minute and cleaned myself up, put on a three-piece suit and went for the interview. The manager who had interviewed me the first time had retired and the assistant manager had been transferred to another office in South Georgia due to family reasons. A new manager and assistant manager had replaced the other two. The interview lasted close to an hour and I thought it was probably one of the best interviews I'd ever had. It was very relaxed and informal as I sat there like a salesman selling them my product. I felt that I had done a good job, because I knew my product intimately: I was the product. When I walked out of the interview, I felt euphoric; like I was walking on a cloud, but I remained guardedly optimistic.

As I crossed the street and headed towards the entrance to the subway, a woman stepped up next to me and asked if I would give her some change so she could get something to eat. Something about the woman seemed familiar to me and suddenly it hit me. She was the woman in the parking lot that day who had hit me across the back with the two by four! She evidently didn't recognize me because I had recently shaved off my beard and gotten a haircut. A thought flashed through my mind: *She can lead me to those two guys who jumped me.*

"What's your name baby?" I asked her. "My name's Crystal, honey. What's yours and where you from?"

"My name's Roger and I'm visiting here from New York," I lied to her.

"You kinda good looking honey. You get high?"

"Yeah," I lied again.

"Well, look. If you buying, I know a place where we can go cop some good cocaine. OK?" She cooed.

"Yeah. That sounds good to me. Where do we have to go?" She then informed me that we would have to take the train to the south side of town and that I would have to pay her fare for the train. I agreed to do it. I was going to the south side anyway because that's the community I lived in. When we got to the house, it was only about five blocks from where she and her friends had ambushed me. She knocked on the door and a guy let us in and we went down a narrow hallway and entered a small room where four guys were sitting at a card table playing poker. I told Crystal to tell the dope man what she wanted; she did and he went out of the room to get it. The two guys I was looking for were sitting at the table deeply engrossed in their poker game. When I saw the opportunity, I grabbed a nearby chair and crashed it upside the head of the guy who had hit me in the parking lot. He screamed and fell over sideways as a spray of blood erupted from his head. When his partner jumped up, I swung the chair at his neck and heard him gurgle as the legs of the chair broke his windpipe and he crumpled to the floor. Other people ran into the room and everybody started fighting and trying to get to the door. I had my back turned to the hallway as I fought, backing up toward the door. Crystal tried to claw at my face and I had no pity for her as I laid her out with one punch. I got to the door and, as I backed out of it, I felt someone grab me from behind in a bear hug. I struggled to look behind me and when I did I saw that I was being held by an Atlanta policeman as five others rushed into the house. The police had been keeping the drug house under surveillance and I had walked into the trap at the wrong time. The police confiscated drugs, drug paraphernalia, and weapons from the house. All of us that had been in the house were put into the paddy wagon except for the two guys on whom I had exacted my revenge. They were both placed into an ambulance and transported to the hospital. As I was being transported to jail, I realized that no judge was going to believe that I didn't use drugs and that I was not in that house for that purpose. I was going to be facing some serious jail time. Then, I thought about how well my interview had gone that morning, and how confident I had felt that I just might get that job. Well, that was all lost now, because I was going to jail. But, suddenly a smile creased my face as I thought, *Well, I did pay those suckers back for ambushing me.*

When we got to the jail the officers lined the twelve of us up in the hall and started processing us in one by one. As I looked through the glass window into the booking office, I saw an officer I knew personally. He was the shift commander and when we made eye contact he had a female officer to come and move me to the end of the line. After everyone in front of me had been processed upstairs and locked up, the female officer told me that the commander wanted to see me in the booking office. Commander Lyles was six years my senior and he had known me as a youngster. Our parents were good friends. When I finished telling him why I had been in the drug house and what had happened there, he cursed me out and threatened me profusely. He then told the female officer to throw me out the back door and that's literally what she did. She took me to a rear area of the building that was under construction and had a four-foot drop off and she kicked me in my butt sending me flying out of the back door.

Three days later, I received a phone call from the manager that interviewed me at the Employment Office and he asked me, "Mr. Coleman, can you report day after tomorrow at the State Employment Office to begin orientation for your new job position as a Veterans Representative?"

"Yes! Yes! Yes!" I shouted into the phone.

I began working in my new position October 1, 1985. Mr. Spriggs welcomed me and introduced me to my new co-workers. There was Alex, who had served with the 5th Marine Division in Vietnam two years after my tour in '68; Stan, a retired Army vet who had served in Korea and Vietnam; Eugene, a retired Navy vet; and Jim, a medically retired Vietnam era vet and the only white guy in the group. They all greeted me warmly and welcomed me as a new member of their team.

Mr. Spriggs told me to call him Leroy and over the next few weeks he became a mentor to me. He was always willing to help me learn the intricacies of the job, as were all the other guys. Sometimes after work we would go around the corner to a local bar and have drinks. After I had been on the job for about three months we started getting together on the weekends to play bid-whist, a serious card game. An important aspect of the job was to be well versed on the federal laws governing the myriad services which we were to provide to all veterans when they came into our office. I worked hard at learning everything I would need to know, and at the end of my probationary period of six months I received an excellent evaluation and was given permanent employee status. At the end of my first year I was presented the DVOP of The Year award for placing the most veterans into gainful employment and rendering outstanding services to veterans. Through the efforts of my co-workers we also won the honors for Best Veterans Unit in the State of Georgia. We all worked well together and were dedicated to making sure that we took good care of our fellow veterans who were in need of assistance and services.

I loved my job and I was determined that I was going to do everything within my power to help every veteran that came through our doors. I began doing outreach on my own time by going to speak to groups of veterans in prisons, at homeless shelters, soup kitchens, on skid row, and any where I could find veterans in need of help. Because of my work ethic I began to gain a reputation as a veteran's advocate and an authority on veteran's issues. I had begun to realize that many veterans didn't know how to access many of the benefits they so desperately needed and had earned such as: housing, medical assistance, burial benefits, education, vocational rehabilitation, counseling, and employment training. So, I started networking with officials at the Department of Veterans Affairs, the VA Hospitals, Veterans Service Organizations and the Vietnam Veterans Counseling Centers. These efforts strengthened my abilities to provide a comprehensive continuum of services to veterans.

At the beginning of my second year on the job, our unit received a new supervisor named Tom Rice, who had been transferred from another office. On the morning he showed up I received a phone call from a Roy Sumlin, a friend and a fellow Vet Rep I knew whom Tom had supervised at the other office. He was calling to warn me about him. He said, "Rock, he's a closet racist and he's very smooth at hiding his racism. He claims to be a Vietnam vet with a disability, but I haven't been able to find proof of either claim. I noticed that he didn't seem to exhibit the same type of camaraderie we, as 'Nam vets, shared with one another so I became suspicious and had him checked out. I did find out that he was in the Air Force during the Vietnam War, but he never went to 'Nam. So, not only is he a racist, but he's also a liar. Be careful and watch him, buddy."

I did watch Tom and found that everything Roy had told me was true. The office I worked in was the largest in the state and located in the heart of the black community. Our Veterans Unit provided services to more black veterans than any other office. Tom began changing the way we did things and constantly wanting to try new techniques, which everyone could clearly see, weren't going to work. We all complained among ourselves, but we gave Tom's ideas a try. We had a total of fifty-two offices throughout the state, and within two months we had gone from first place to number thirty-six. Tom then started requiring us to perform services for non-veterans. This was a blatant violation of the federal laws governing what we could and could not do. When I refused to circumvent the law, he gave me a written reprimand and I filed a grievance against him. The grievance went through the proper channels to be ruled on. The personnel director and three of the department commissioners ruled that my issue was non-grievable! I had researched the law and knew beyond a shadow of doubt that my issue was grievable, but management had stacked the deck against me. The bad thing was that I had been the only one in the unit who had challenged the system and drawn attention to myself as a troublemaker...even if I was right. In ruling that my issue was non-grievable, management was firing a warning shot across my ship's bow. I interpreted this as "back off or we will deal with you."

The job had helped to ease some of the tension at home with Karen, but the same old problems were lying dormant under the surface. Her son had gotten married to a woman fourteen years his senior and she invited the whole family to go home with her to Cincinnati, Ohio for her family reunion. We agreed, and she rented a large van and arranged hotel accommodations for everyone. The van comfortably seated all eight of us and we left Atlanta on a Thursday night headed for Ohio. I had been bothered by some minor stomach pains earlier that week. I attributed them to excessive drinking. The stress I had been dealing with concerning Tom had been causing me to experience some of my old nightmares again, so I had been drinking rather heavily to get through the nights. I had brought along a bottle of Brandy on the trip and I had only one stiff drink on the way to Ohio and stopped because the pain got worse. We arrived in Cincinnati early Friday morning and checked into our hotel. Because of the pain I was experiencing, I stayed in the bed all day while everyone else went to participate in the family reunion activities. The next day I wasn't feeling any better, but I went to the family picnic for a few hours until my discomfort caused me to return to my hotel room. On Sunday morning as we were preparing to return to Atlanta, I realized that I needed to go to a hospital. Karen's family took me to the nearest VA Hospital emergency room. The emergency room doctors determined that I was suffering from a serious attack of pancreatitis and they told Karen they were admitting me to the hospital. Arrangements were made for Karen to stay with friends in Cincinnati while the rest of the family returned to Atlanta. The doctors followed the same procedures as the doctor's had in Atlanta: placing an NG tube in my nose; starting an IV line in my arm; and administering 100 milligrams of Demerol for pain. Then I was assigned to a room on one of the wards. Later that night when I was resting comfortably, Karen went home with her friends to get some rest and said she would return in the morning. After she left I drifted off to sleep. When I woke up I looked at the curtains hanging in front of the window and saw that the colors on them were brown, black, and white, arranged in abstract patterns. Then, to my amazement the colors began to look as if they were beginning to shape shift and starting to change into some type of holographic picture. Suddenly, the curtains turned into a picture of a village in Vietnam and I saw a squad of American soldiers engaged in a fierce and deadly firefight with the Viet Cong. I felt as if I was in that village and I had to escape.

I didn't realize at the time what was happening to me, but I later found out that what I experienced was an episode of delirium tremens better known as the "DTs." "DTs" can develop in a person after unusually prolonged or heavy drinking of alcohol and causes visual illusions and hallucinations that are brief but terrifying. The condition may last three to ten days and sometimes death can result, often because of pneumonia or heart failure.

Feeling as if I had to escape, I vaguely remember pulling the NG tube out of my nose, taking the IV needle out of my arm, and removing the heart monitoring equipment from my chest. I got out of the bed and started walking down the corridor of the hospital looking for a door that would allow me to escape. A nurse came toward me and tried to escort me back to my bed. I pushed her to the floor. A second nurse attempted to grab my arm. I pushed her into the wall as I began sprinting down the corridor looking for an escape route. People stared at me wide eyed as I rushed past them. In my mind, I was back in the jungles of Vietnam and I had to escape! I turned down another corridor and came face to face with three hospital security officers who were blocking my escape. One of them was wearing captain's bars on his collar indicating his rank and he said to me, "Mr. Coleman, please lay down on this stretcher so we can take you back to your room."

"I can't do that," I replied. "I will fight all of you if I have to, but I can't allow you to capture me." The uniforms they were wearing made me think that I was facing soldiers of the North Vietnamese Army.

"Mr. Coleman, we're not going to hurt you. Please lay down on the stretcher; we don't want to use force," the captain implored of me.

Realizing that I was in a no win situation, I relied on my military training which dictated that I should not resist and allow them to capture me. But, after my capture I would stay vigilant and look for another opportunity to escape. I laid my head down on the stretcher and that was the last thing I remembered before passing out.

When I awoke I was very disoriented and I looked around trying to determine where I was. I saw that I was in a large room surrounded by six beds with other patients in them and that when I tried to get up I couldn't. I looked down at my body and saw that my legs were spread apart and that I had leather restraints on both of my ankles; both of my wrists were secured by my sides in the same fashion. Further examination revealed that I was being restrained on a wooden foundation that was inclined at a forty-five degree angle and I was completely naked. There were IV lines protruding from both my arms and all types of wires and cords hooked to my body and attached to a monitor. At that moment, I saw Karen walk past me.

In a raspy voice I asked her, "You're not going to speak to me?" She froze in her tracks and slowly, cautiously turned towards me. In an inquiring tone she said, "Morocco? Is that you? Is that really you?" "Of course it's me. What's wrong with you?" I said. She immediately called a doctor over to where we were.

"Mr. Coleman, how are you feeling?" The doctor asked me.

I told him I felt fine, but I was hungry. He looked at Karen and they both began laughing as the doctor said, "I think he's back with us." The doctor then instructed a nurse to remove my restraints and give me a hospital gown to put on. When the nurse had finished carrying out the doctor's instructions, she brought me a bowl of oatmeal, which I began to ravenously devour. As I ate, Karen proceeded to explain what had happened to me.

When the doctors had determined that I was experiencing the "DTs," they immediately put me into the intensive care unit where I now was. I was having hallucinations, which were so profound that the doctors had started giving me massive doses of tranquilizers in an attempt to sedate me. The sedation didn't seem to have any effect on me and I had been constantly ranting and raving about Vietnam the whole time.

Karen told me, "Your hallucinations have been about Vietnam and they have been constant ever since you were brought into the intensive care unit. You have been reliving your experiences from the war up until a few hours ago when the tranquilizers finally started to take affect and you went to sleep.

"How long have I been here in intensive care?" I questioned.

"You been here ranting and raving for four days!"

"Four days!" I exclaimed. "I've been here like this for four days?" I couldn't believe it. Four days of my life had gone by and I knew nothing about it. Unbelievable, I thought to myself.

Later that day, my primary doctor determined that my condition had stabilized and improved to the extent that I could leave the intensive care unit and be moved to a private room. On the second day, the doctor told me that I had recovered surprisingly well and he was going to release me to go home to Atlanta. He gave me some prescriptions and told me to go to see the doctors at the VA Hospital when I got home to let them do a follow-up on me. The doctor also gave me some sage advice: "Mr. Coleman, many people don't survive what you have been through. You have had pancreatic surgery as a result of your excessive drinking and you were at death's door at that time. This recent bout of pancreatitis coupled with the delirium tremens almost took your life. You must stop drinking completely. And, if you don't you will soon die. I could tell that the doctor was serious—dead serious.

A short time later I was walking through the corridor of the hospital on my way to the business office to be discharged. My parents had gotten seats for Karen and me on a flight to Atlanta and the hospital had arranged to get us to the airport. While walking, I saw a black guy about my age, dressed in business attire coming toward me and I asked him for directions to the business office. After he gave them to me I thanked him and resumed walking a few steps until I heard somebody call my name. "Morocco!" When I turned to see who had called me it was the same guy that had given me directions. He said, "I don't know your last name, but I know that your first name is Morocco. Are you about to check out of the hospital? I don't believe it!"

"Why?" I asked him. "Who are you?"

"Come with me." He said.

"What's this about?" I asked as I began to follow him.

"Here. Let's go in here," he said as he entered a door with a sign on it that read CHAPLAIN. He walked over to a large desk and sat down behind it as he gestured for me to have a seat. Again he said, "I don't believe it. You're really getting ready to check out of here?"

"Yes." I replied. "Who are you and why are you so concerned?"

"My name is Wilton Blake and I'm the hospital's chaplain. And, less than forty-eight hours ago I was summoned at three o'clock in the morning to come to the hospital to give you last rites. You were in intensive care and your heart suddenly went into ventricular tachycardia, which then brought on cardio-fibrillation and you were about to die. Your heart was threatening to burst out of your chest. There were two principalities vying for your soul...the principality of the *light* and the principality of the *darkness*. Your life was hanging in the balance between God and the Satan. And, when I leaned over you to deliver the last rites you opened your eyes and looked at me, and I'll never forget that look in your eyes as you began yelling and cursing at me. Then, to my amazement, you broke free of the leather restraint on your wrist and reached for me. When that happened, please excuse my French but, I got the hell out of there."

"My brother, if the Lord has seen fit to raise you up from a death bed like the one I saw you on, then he wants me to tell you to get ready because he's got some powerful works that he wants you to carryout for him. God has lifted you up from a very dark place, down where the dry bones are resting, and you can give witness to the things you have seen. Now you must speak on them."

Reverend Blake and I talked for a few more minutes and he gave me his phone number and told me to stay in touch with him. Karen and I then departed for the airport.

CHAPTER EIGHTEEN

Lord, Give Me the Words to Speak

A few days after Karen and I returned to Atlanta, I went to the VA Hospital as instructed for my follow up exams. The doctor told me that I was progressing well and to continue my abstinence from alcohol.

I went back to work and all of the staff welcomed me with encouraging words of support. But, I soon found out that Tom Rice had become more dictatorial in supervising the Veterans Unit, alienating himself from the staff and causing the morale of the unit to plummet. Tom's unscrupulous behavior not only caused staff problems, but also caused the veterans that came to us for help and assistance to suffer. They were suffering because they weren't being provided the full array of services to which they were entitled and as mandated by Federal Law. Our job was to apply all of our knowledge, experience, training, and resources to uplift and empower our veteran clients, enabling them to become gainfully employed and able to take care of their families. Tom and I had another disagreement over a policy issue, which he wanted me to circumvent. And when I refused he again presented me with a written reprimand. He knew that he was wrong, but he also knew that his corrupt superiors would support him and that I had no one to turn to.

When I left work that day I wanted to stop at the liquor store, but I decided against it and went to see Dr. Carl Rosen. A friend had recommended Dr. Rosen to me and he was a psychiatrist in private practice that specialized in alcohol and substance abuse. I had made up my mind that I was going to do something about my alcohol problem. During my second counseling session with Dr. Rosen he wrote me a prescription for medication which would gradually curb my physiological urges for alcohol. The next thing I did was to fully involve myself in the group and individual counseling offered by the Vietnam Vet Center. I also thought about what Chaplain Blake had said to me, so I began to earnestly read and study my Bible. In my counseling groups we were told that we should ask for help in conquering our addictions by praying to our "Higher Power." People had different names for their "Higher Power," and this became somewhat confusing to me because the Bible says that he has only one true name. Every day I had to fight the urge to have just one little drink. And every day that I didn't drink made me a little stronger. So I took it one day at a time.

It seemed that the harder I worked at overcoming my demons and drinking problems, the harder negative forces were working against me. I was bombarded by traumatic events. My grandfather, Son Coleman, died in the hospital at the age of ninety-eight. He was laid to rest next to my grandmother who had preceded him in death by twenty-two years. At the time of Son's passing, my father was in the same hospital recovering from prostate cancer surgery; Karen and I were becoming less and less tolerant of one another and the marriage was failing; the problems at work between Tom and me had escalated; my service connected disability began to cause me additional physical problems and my nightmares and flashbacks had begun to get worse. But, throughout all of these trials and tribulations I was able abstain from taking a drink of alcohol.

Due to the worsening condition of my service connected disability I had filed a claim the year before at the Department of Veterans Affairs, seeking an increase in my percentage rating. A few months later my request was denied and I immediately filed an appeal of the rating board's decision. My appeal was also denied, so I forwarded my claim to the Board of Veterans Appeals in Washington, DC. The Board of Veterans Appeals denied my claim and I appealed their decision.

My personal problems became overwhelming and I turned to the Bible for solace. I decided to turn my problems over to God. I prayed and told God I was giving him the problems that I could no longer handle and I believed by faith that he would handle them. A couple of days later I received a letter from the Board of Veterans Appeals. The letter informed me that BVA had decided to award me a rating increase of 30 percent bringing my total rating up to 40 percent! I was further informed that I would soon receive a check for the increase, which would be retroactive for twenty-four months. Shortly after receiving the check I was again contacted by the BVA advising me that I was entitled to more money for my dependents, Karen and my daughter. That money would also be retroactive for twenty-four months, but in order to get it I would have to submit proof that I had legitimate dependents. I would have to submit a copy of my daughter's birth certificate, a copy of my divorce decree from Monica, and proof of my marriage to Karen. I also had to submit a copy of Karen's divorce decree from a prior marriage, which took place in Kansas. I had secured all of the necessary documents except for a copy of Karen's divorce decree, which she was unable to locate. She contacted her relatives in Kansas and none of them could find copies or assist her in getting one. Finally, after much frustration, I contacted the Office of Vital Statistics in Kansas to see if I could get a copy of the document. I was informed that Karen had never gotten a legal divorce from her husband! She was still married to him! I had wanted to leave Karen for quite a while, but I kept hanging on to the marriage in an attempt to make sure that I had done everything I could to make it work. The revelation that Karen was a bigamist and that we weren't legally married proved beyond a shadow of doubt to me that prayers are answered. I left Karen that same day, moving temporarily back to my parents' home. A week later Karen had me served with divorce papers seeking alimony and other types of support. I talked with a number of attorneys in an attempt to have my marriage to Karen annulled, but they all told me that I would have to seek a divorce from her. I asked why it was necessary for me to get a divorce from a woman to whom I had never legally been married. I was told that because there was a marriage license between Karen and me registered and recorded with the State of Georgia, it would necessitate my having to expunge the record through a divorce. If I filed for divorce it was going to cost me eight to twelve hundred dollars. When I examined my options I determined that I had legal problems on two fronts: the federal laws (which governed my job) which I was being told by my superiors to violate; and the specter of having to suffer a divorce from someone I wasn't legally married to. I decided to further my legal training, so I enrolled in a six month paralegal course at a downtown law school. I used my two legal problems as assigned projects, which were required research necessary to complete the course and receive my paralegal certification. Halfway through the course I found what I had been looking for concerning my impending divorce. I found case law, which literally stated that if Karen was married to someone else at the time she married me, then she could not contract to marry me. It constituted a void at inception, a void now and a void forever more. I contacted a lifelong friend of mine, Don Hillsman, an excellent attorney who happened to be a Vietnam combat vet. He got us an audience with a judge of the court who annulled my marriage to Karen in a matter of minutes. I paid fifty dollars for the court cost and one hundred dollars to Don for his services. I completed the requirements for my paralegal course and received my certification. I continued to file grievances against my superiors in an effort to bring attention to the complete disregard of the laws, which affected the lives of many veterans. I received a phone call one day from a veteran friend of mine and he told me about a black guy named Ron Armstead that was coming to town from Washington, DC. Mr. Armstead was a Vietnam veteran and he was going to be speaking at one of the hotels downtown about the plight of minority veterans. I went to hear what Mr. Armstead had to say. He turned out to be an excellent speaker and he touched on almost every issue that minority veterans were facing as they struggled to assimilate back into the work force and society after suffering the traumas associated with the Vietnam experience. Ron was a proud black man who wore his hair in long dreadlocks. After he finished speaking we met one another and talked at length about the problems facing black veterans.

· I shared with him the problems I was encountering on my job and he said to me in very serious tones, "You need to come to

Washington and tell your story to the congressmen on the Committee of Veterans' Affairs. It seems as if your superiors are trying to fire you and if you testify before the committee you have nothing to lose and much to gain."

"Ron, that's a noble thought but I don't know anybody on Capitol Hill that can help me to do what you're suggesting." I said to him.

Ron explained that he was working on the staff of Congressman Charlie Rangel (D-NY), and the Congressman was the chairman of the Congressional Black Caucus Veterans Brain trust. Ron told me if I wanted to come and testify he could arrange for me to receive correspondence from Congressman Rangel's office requesting my presence to testify before the Veterans Committee of the 102nd Congress. A few days after Ron had left Atlanta, Mr. Emile Milne, the legislative assistant to Congressman Rangel, contacted me. Emile explained the procedures that I needed to be made aware of before my testimony was to be given. It was required that I first submit a type written copy of my planned testimony to the committee and a transcript of my spoken testimony would be published after the hearings were completed. Emile informed me that he was sending me a formal letter signed by Congressman Rangel requesting that I come to Washington and participate in the Hearings before the House Subcommittee on Oversight and Investigations of the Committee on Veterans' Affairs.

On September 23, 1992, I gave my testimony before Congressman "Sonny" Montgomery (D-MS), Congressman Lane Evans (D-IL), Congressman Charles Rangel (D-NY), Congressman Joseph Kennedy (D-MA), Congresswoman Maxine Waters (D-CA) and others. The room was packed with veterans, veteran's advocates and interested citizens from all across the country. The media was there and it was a heady and awesome experience as I spoke from the heart about the obligations that this country owes to veterans. I told of the instances when I had been told by my superiors to circumvent the law governing the continuum of services to help veterans and how agencies like mine were accepting federal funds to provide priority services to veterans, but were in fact doing just the opposite. I spoke for approximately fifty minutes, and to my astonishment when I finished the audience in the hearing room erupted into cheers and applause. Afterwards, I left the hearing room and went out into the cavernous hallways of Congress and many of the people that had heard my testimony came over to shake my hand and to let me know that they appreciated what I had said. Some even told me that they were experiencing the same problems on their jobs, but were too afraid to come forward and speak out. Ron came over to me and told me that I had done a great job and I thanked him for giving me the opportunity to speak.

A few hours later, I was sitting in on another hearing as an observer. At the conclusion of the hearing, Ron stepped up to the podium and announced that it was time to elect National Chairpersons for the thirteen different Veterans Committees. I was appointed as National Co-Chairman for the Veterans Employment and Training Committee. The other co-chair was a Vietnam combat veteran named Darron Perkins from East St Louis. Ron took me around the room introducing me to other veterans who, like myself, were committed unequivocally to helping other veterans. There was: Mike Handy (Mayor's Office) from New York; Dave Culmer (therapist) Los Angeles, California Vet Center; Wayne Smith of Vietnam Veterans of America; "Big" Arthur from the "Grunt House" (homeless program) in Washington State; Arthur Barham, Homeless Veterans Reintegration Project in Atlanta, Georgia; "Bro" Powell from the Buffalo Soldiers; Reggie Lawrence, Team Leader in Jacksonville, Florida Vet Center; James Miller, Team Leader in Savannah, Georgia Vet Center, "Sugar Bear" (Rubin) Johnson and Robert Blackwell, two "jungle warriors" from Texas; Lane Knox, Veterans Rep from Chicago; and Tony Hawkins, Director of Minority Affairs for the Secretary of the Department of Veterans Affairs, Jesse Brown. Tony would later become a treasured friend and ally. That afternoon I attended a social function hosted by Congressman John Lewis (D-GA) and while there I met Congressman Sanford Bishop (D-GA), and Congresswoman Cynthia McKinney (D-GA). To my surprise Vice President Al Gore made an appearance at the affair and I was able to meet him and have a photograph taken with him. The next day I met one of my heroes, General Colin Powell.

When I returned to work after my trip to Washington, I noticed that my superiors were uncharacteristically allowing me more latitude in the performance of my duties. I later found out they had seen copies of my Congressional testimony and also saw their names mentioned for not ensuring compliance of services to all veterans seeking our assistance.

I continued to attend my counseling sessions at the Vietnam Vet Center and I made two profound discoveries that drastically altered my life. The first revelation was when I began to understand that in each instance when I had been arrested, gone through a divorce, admitted to the hospital, or faced some great problem in my life it was usually during the months of December and January. Those months represented the most traumatic time in my whole life in 1967-68. During November of 1967, I was at home on leave from the military preparing to go to Vietnam. Daily I watched the war on television as young men my age died in living color. During January of 1968, I was in Vietnam less than a day before the TET Offensive was launched. The TET Offensive was easily one of the bloodiest and deadliest battles to occur during the whole Vietnam War. After surviving those terrifying experiences, I had tried to forget about them and get on with my life, but that fear and terror had been languishing in my sub-conscious for many years waiting to raise their ugly heads. So, every year around December and January those old fears and terrors would awaken and set off alarms in my consciousness creating anxiety and distress within me that I couldn't understand or cope with. At these times I would exhibit aberrant behavior. This psychological phenomenon found in many Vietnam vets was later diagnosed as Post (meaning, later) **Trauma**tic Stress Disorder. PTSD; trauma which manifests itself years later.

The second revelation occurred when I realized that for many years I had been living with the shame and guilt that I had taken someone's life while fighting in the jungles of Vietnam. My childhood introduction to religion had taught me '"Thou shalt not kill." The consequence of my actions in Vietnam caused me a lot of inner turmoil. But, one day while reading my Bible I began to understand that I could ask the Creator for forgiveness of such a sin. And if I truly prayed from my heart to be forgiven, God would judge my heart. Therefore, I had to walk by faith and believe that my sin was forgiven. I came to understand that these two revelations were like keys for me to use to unlock the knowledge that could set me free and allow for the healing of my troubled soul to begin.

After being clean and sober for nine months, I decided to go to Charleston, South Carolina to visit Jim and Lillie Dove, a couple I had met three years before. Lillie was a music teacher in the Charleston school system and she was also director of her church choir. Jim was a retired Navy veteran who worked as a civilian at the Charleston Naval Base. Jim was a quiet, laid-back kind of guy and Lillie was gregarious, talkative, and funny. When I got to their house, it was packed full of people. Lillie explained that they were having a family reunion and they considered me as part of their family, so she took me around and introduced me to all of my newly acquired relatives. We partied late into the night and I had a great time. The next morning as we were having breakfast, Lillie wanted to know how I had overcome my drinking problems. I told her my life story and how God had shown me the way to be free of my vices. Afterwards, she left to go to her Saturday choir practice. When she returned she told me very matter-of-factly that she had talked to the minister while at the church and had gotten him to agree to let me be the guest speaker at church the next day. I was dumbfounded. "What are you talking about?" I stammered. "What am I supposed to be speaking about?"

She responded, "I told him you would give a testimony of how the Lord has changed your life. All you have to do is share the same story with the congregation that you told me about this morning."

I finally agreed to do it. Later that night I sat down and tried to write out a speech, but I couldn't get my thoughts together. So I said a prayer and asked the Lord to work through me and to give me the words to speak. On Sunday morning, I went to the Antioch Baptist Church with the Doves and I was introduced to the minister, Reverend Dees. He welcomed me and motioned for me to follow him to the pulpit where I took a seat next to him. As I looked out at the overflowing crowd, I was comforted by the fact that I saw the familiar faces of many members of Lillie's family reunion. When the service began, a fellow about my age named Greg Bennet, stepped forward and directed the choir as he led them into a rendition of "Amazing Grace" accompanied by Lillie on the organ. When the choir finished singing, Reverend Dees spoke to the congregation for a few minutes and then he told them a little about me, reading from my biography, which I had given him. I was then introduced to the congregation and received a warm welcome. I was very nervous at first but as I began talking, a calming presence came over me and I proceeded to give my testimony starting from my teen years, to college, to Vietnam, to near death and to the present. I tried to not leave anything out as I told about the good and the bad that had touched my life. I told them about the drugs, the alcohol, the killing, and my search for redemption. I told them about the strange "white light" that visited my hospital room and how the nurse, Mrs. Winston, had brought me a Bible. I felt the power of the Lord moving through me as I continued to speak. When I finished, the congregation jumped to their feet and began loudly applauding as comments of "Amen! Amen!" could be heard resonating throughout the church. Everyone finally quieted down as Brother Bennet prepared to lead the choir into another song. Suddenly, he stopped, turned around to face the congregation and there were tears streaming down his face as he said, "Members of the church, I want to thank the Lord for sending Brother Coleman here today to speak to us. You all know that I came here five years ago and you welcomed me into this congregation as your choir leader. But, there was something that I never told any of you. Like Brother Coleman, I too am a Vietnam Veteran and I have been wrestling with many demons for a long time because of that war. But after hearing Brother Coleman talk about his experiences, he has let me know that I'm not the only one going through these things. His words this morning have helped me to start getting free. God bless you, Brother Coleman, and thank the Lord for sending you on this morning." He then turned and led the choir into song as I sat there stunned and thinking to myself, *The spirit of the Lord is truly alive and dwells in each of us.*

That night about twenty of the family reunion members and I went to a private club to party. The manager of the club had prepared an area of the club that could seat all of us together. We were all having a great time when I happened to look toward the door as two women and a man entered together. They were escorted to a table right in front of where we were sitting and I realized that one of the women looked very familiar. I leaned over and said to the woman, "Excuse me, but aren't you from Atlanta?

She turned and smiled saying, "Yes. I sure am. How did you know?"

"You're also a nurse in Atlanta, aren't you?" I asked.

She then regarded me rather cautiously as she replied, "Yes. But, who are you?"

When I told her my name, she momentarily stared, as if in shock. Then she screamed and jumped up from her seat, knocking drinks off of her table, and quickly began backing away from me saying, "You're supposed to be dead!" Everyone around us stood up to see what was going on. The woman calmed down and my friends asked me who this woman was. I told them that this woman was named Mrs. Winston, and she was the nurse I had mentioned in my testimony at church earlier that day. This was the woman that brought me the Bible when I had seen the "white light" in my hospital room. Everyone's mouth was hanging open in disbelief. I asked Mrs. Winston why she was in Charleston, South Carolina. She said that the woman with her was her cousin and the guy was her cousin's husband. She said that she had never been to Charleston before and her cousin had been trying to get her to come to visit for years, so she had decided to come on this weekend. The last time I had seen her was when I left Dr. Morris' care and transferred to another hospital and that had been eleven years ago. I couldn't believe it. The coincidences were phenomenal: she had come to Charleston on the same weekend that I had come; of all the clubs in Charleston she had come to the one where I was; she had been seated right in front of me so that I would be sure to see her; I had told a church full of people about her that same day; and some of those same people were sitting with me to bear witness to the whole event. I thought about what Talley had said years before. 'There are no coincidences. Everything happens by divine order and it's called synchronicity. It's the universe talking to us."

When I returned home I received my long awaited check from the Veterans Administration after clearing up the confusion about my marriage to Karen. I won two of my grievances against my department superiors and all seemed to be going well until my mother told me that she was going to be admitted to the hospital for major surgery. Her doctor had discovered a tumor in her abdomen. My family and I were waiting in the hospital visitor's area when her doctor came out of surgery and gave us the prognosis. He told us that my mother had cancer of the pancreas and its spread was so advanced that all he could do was sew her back up and send her home. I pulled him aside and asked him to tell me how long would she live. He told me, "She has the same type of cancer that President Jimmy Carter's brother Billy had and he lived for one year. So your mother has from right now to one year to live. She will go home and get slightly better; then she will get weaker and slip into a coma and then die." Since I was staying with my parents, I was determined to make her final days as peaceful as possible. Sometimes, as I was caring for my mother, I would notice her looking at me with a twinkle in her eyes. Her look told me that she was at peace, because she could see that the Lord had guided my life back on track. I no longer used drugs or alcohol, and I had found a profession which I loved and which gave me much satisfaction.

CHAPTER NINETEEN

Finding Paula and My Life's Mission

One warm evening in August, I decided to go to the Omega House; a club that offered great music, dancing, and interesting upscale people. I had decided to stop in to have dinner, and as I entered the door, a beautiful woman passed by me on her way out of the door. I realized right away that I knew her and that I hadn't seen her since 1964. More than twenty-seven years! I turned and called out her name, "Paula!" She turned around and immediately knew who I was. We embraced one another and began talking about how long it had been since we had last seen one another. As we talked I became aware of the fact that Paula was more beautiful than I even remembered. Before she got into her car to leave, we exchanged phone numbers and she told me to be sure and call her.

As I sat eating my dinner, my mind began to drift back to the time when I first met Paula. It was our first day of school and I was rather shy as I looked around me and checked out all of my new schoolmates. I saw her across the room as she laughed with her friends and instantly I was smitten by her. She had thick, dark brown hair, which she wore in long plaits. Her brown complexion was flawless, and whenever she laughed one big dimple would appear on her right cheek and her bright eyes were always full of mirth. Whenever the opportunity rose for me to be near Paula, I felt a strange attraction toward her that I had never felt toward anyone before. On the first Valentine's Day that I can remember I knew I wanted Paula to be my Special Valentine. When I tell people the story of how I felt when I first met Paula, they don't believe me, because when it happened we were both two years old! We were just starting nursery school. When we reached the age of six, we were enrolled into different elementary schools. The next time I saw Paula was when we both began the eighth grade at the same high school. When we reached the eleventh grade and I started dating, I wanted to ask her out, but she was so beautiful that I couldn't stand the thought of rejection. Besides, she was a straight A student, a member of the National Honor Society and destined for greatness. And I was just a "jock" on the track team. When we graduated from high school in 1964, she left Atlanta to attend Fisk University in Nashville, Tennessee, and I departed for North Carolina Central University. And that had been the last time that I saw her. But, every now and then, during those twenty-seven years I would think about her and wonder what could have been. For the next few days after seeing Paula I thought about calling her, but like in the past, I couldn't face the possibility of rejection. I rationalized that since she had recently returned home after living in New York City for eighteen years she was just trying to re-establish old friendships and I knew that deep in my heart I wouldn't want just a friendship with Paula. I would want to develop a relationship with her.

One evening after I got home, my mother told me that I had received a phone call from Paula. My mother began to tease me about Paula as she told me how I would come home from nursery school talking on and on about Paula. I didn't return the call and eventually my mother insisted saying, "I told Paula that I would have you to return her call when you got home. Now call her!" I couldn't tell my mother about my insecurity of being rejected by the girl of my dreams, so I called her. Talking with Paula seemed was so comfortable that before I realized it I had asked her to go with me to a dance that I had invitations to. She readily accepted and I told her I would pick her up in a couple of hours. I was a nervous wreck all the way to her house. I rang the doorbell and when she opened the door, she looked exquisite. She was wearing an aqua blue silk dress, which accentuated her very nice figure. As I drove us to the dance we talked and reminisced about our childhood days. The dance was well attended and I saw many old friends and acquaintances. I also saw the looks on their faces, which asked the question, "Where did Rock find that fine, beautiful woman?"

I held Paula in my arms as we danced to a slow song the band was playing. The nearness of her and the subtle fragrance of her perfume was an intoxicating combination. We left the dance about one o'clock in the morning and stopped at restaurant and had breakfast. Afterwards, I took her home. She invited me in and we sat talking and looking through old photo albums and yearbooks. Paula said that she wanted to tell me something and she hoped that I wouldn't take it the wrong way. She said, "You're like an old shoe." She explained that talking with me felt comfortable, like putting on a comfortable old shoe. We laughed our way through the photo albums and high school yearbooks. Then I noticed that the sun was coming up! I was so enthralled by Paula that I had lost all concept of time.

During the next few weeks, Paula and I spent a lot of time together and as we talked we found that we had quite a lot in common. Paula had been working for eighteen years at Harlem Hospital in New York City. Her significant other had been a doctor and my significant other had been a nurse and we had entered these relationships about the same time. After five years in our individual relationships, we both stepped away from them about the same time. Paula had moved back to Atlanta. We also discovered that our birthdays were eighteen days apart and that we were both born under the sign of Aries. It didn't take me very long to discover that Paula was my soul mate and that at last I had found true love. Paula would sit with my mother during her illness and they would have "girl talk." I could tell that my mother was happy that Paula and I had found each other after so many years.

My mother's illness became worse and she was admitted to Our Lady of Perpetual Mercy Hospice. One morning my father woke me up to tell me that the hospital had just called and my mother's condition had worsened. The doctor requested that the family come immediately to the hospice. I jumped up, and as I was about to leave my father told me to wait until my brother arrived and we would all go together. I told my father I couldn't wait and I left. When I entered my mother's room a nun was sitting by her side and when she saw me she quietly left the room. When I approached my mother's bed she was in a coma and she was breathing very heavily. Both of her hands were up to her chest and clutching a large crucifix. I called her name over and over, but she gave no indication that she could hear me or that she even knew that I was there. I leaned over and opened her eyes. She just stared into space, her eyes fixated and clouded over, comatose. I sat down and realized that death was lurking in the room. Suddenly, my mother's breathing became normal and peaceful so I stood next to her bed looking down at her. The crucifix started sliding out of her hands. She then put both hands up to the sides of her face and a frown appeared on her brow as if she was trying to back away from something. Then she stretched out both arms and lifted her hands in surrender. Her frown was replaced by a beatific smile, which spread across her face, but her eyes remained closed. She was still in a coma. I leaned over her again and opened her eyes. Now, her eyes were sparkling, but empty, like looking into the eyes of a store mannequin. I stepped back and looked at her hands, which were still outstretched.

I looked at her fingers and realized that her fingers were touching something or someone in another dimension on the other side. I couldn't see who or what it was, but I knew it was there and I could feel it as it welcomed my mother into the transition. It was LOVE. Her hands ever so slowly touched down on the bed and all was still. All works were done. I stood in the aftermath and fully comprehended all that I had just been blessed to witness. My mother took me as far along on her journey as she could take me and showed me the way. Then she left. And I felt all right.

The curtain surrounding my mother's bed was pulled open and my brother stood there and asked, "How is she?"

I said, "She's gone."

He said, "When?"

I told him that she had died ten seconds before he pulled the curtain back. "Where's dad, and what took you so long getting here?" I asked.

"Every time we got ready to leave the house, the phone would ring or someone came by," my bother replied.

I sat back down and waited for my father to arrive. Then I remembered that the week before I had celebrated my forty-fifth birthday which meant that forty-five years ago my mother and I were in a hospital and she was giving birth to me. She was there with me for my first breath. And now, forty-five years later we were again in a hospital. This time, I was with her for her last breath. My mother loved my father, he was her husband. And she loved my younger brother. But I was the most profound thing to ever happen to my mother. I was her first born and what I witnessed when my mother passed on was meant for no one to witness but me. My mother always told me to "keep my hands in the hands of the man upstairs." When I saw my mother's hands reach out into space, she was placing her hands into God's hands and that act was symbolic of what she had taught me. The whole experience changed my life forever. I then understood what my mission in life was to be. And I knew without a doubt that if I put God first in all that I did no slings and arrows would find their mark against me. My mission: service to my fellow man.

In 1992, Paula and I were married and at this time a new commissioner was elected to head the Department of Labor State Employment Service and his name was David Poythress. Commissioner Poythress was a Vietnam veteran who served in Da Nang, South Vietnam in 1969. He was also a Brigadier General in the Air Force Reserve. He immediately appointed George Langford, a Vietnam veteran (1970) as the Labor Department Director for Veterans Programs. A year later, George, impressed by my advocacy for veterans, hired me on his staff for the position of Assistant Director for the Office of State Veterans Programs. I was appointed by the State Commander of the American Legion to the position of Department Chairman for Veterans Employment and Training. The Atlanta NAACP Branch nominated me to its board as Chairman of the Armed Services and Veterans Affair Committee. I knew what my mission was.

When my life had hit rock bottom, I used to ask the question, "Why me?" I never received an answer, but now I understand the answer to the question. The answer is "Why not me!" I didn't realize it at the time, but the enormous troubles and problems that were plaguing my life were preparing me for my life's work if I could survive them. The pendulum of my life swung three hundred and sixty degrees over a number of years to finally bring me back to the understanding of who I truly am and what I am to do with my life. It was a journey, which took me full circle. I believe that when God forms us he then breathes his spirit into us. After giving us breath, he then hooks us up to a tether line that extends from within heaven, into and through this earthly realm, and out the back door of the earthly realm back into the other side of heaven. Alpha to Omega. Once we're hooked up to the tether line, God propels us into the earthly realm to bring forth his spirit, love, understanding and change. As we draw closer to the earth realm we see massive suffering, sickness, killing, and destruction of mankind. We are being sent with the knowledge and power to change the plight of mankind and this understanding becomes our "Birth Vision." As we slide along the tether line or umbilical cord through the birth canal we enter the earthly realm and are immediately confronted by a very uncomfortable, foreboding, and terrifying feeling perpetuated by the ruler of the earth realm, Satan. This feeling that is so foreign to us is called FEAR and we become so preoccupied by it that we forget our "Birth Vision." As we slide along the tether line we learn many things about the earthly realm as we traverse through it. Eventually, something off to the side catches our attention and in order to examine it more closely we must stop and unhook ourselves from the tether line. As we then walk over into uncharted areas of our understanding to investigate that, which caught our attention, we become so mesmerized by our findings that we venture further and further into the unknown. It may be years as we continue to investigate and partake of these new and unknown discoveries. Then we come face to face with dark forces sent by the ruler of the earthly realm. The dark forces have been issued forth to take our precious souls and the FEAR consumes us. We run for our lives desperately searching for the safety of our tether line so we can hook back up and slide away safely. But, we left the safety of the tether line so long ago that the sight of it is obscured by the growth of the tall thistle, thorns and weeds. The FEAR becomes all pervasive as the baying of the dark forces gets closer and closer. Suddenly, the spirit, the breath within, teaches us how to pray; understanding, not our own, but true understanding from God, opens our eyes. Then, we are able to see that which was hidden from us and we discover the way back to the tether line. Once there, we hook ourselves back up, never to separate our life from it again as we now traverse the line doing good works, sharing our inner spirit and the true knowledge of our creator. We safely move towards the Omega, which eventually will lead us to the reward, which God has promised when our work in this earthly realm is completed. Many who become lost out among the thistle and thorns never respond to the God force within themselves because they give the FEAR dominion over them, and they become the lost souls never to know God. I now understand and realize that FEAR in many instances is no more than (F)alse (E)vidence (A)ppearing (R)eal. The "weird feelings," the recurring dreams of being lost and the "flashbacks," which plagued me for many years, were attempts by my inner voice to help me to remember my Birth Vision which is "service to my fellow man."

I say a prayer of thanksgiving everyday for being given a second chance to know God and for the opportunity of coming full circle and hooking back up to the tether line.

THE END